Current Controversies in Philosophy of Mind

Philosophy of mind is one of the most dynamic fields in philosophy, and one that invites debate around several key questions. There currently exist annotated tomes of primary sources, and a handful of single-authored introductions to the field, but there is no book that captures philosophy of mind's recent dynamic exchanges for a student audience. By asking ten leading philosophers to square off on five central, related debates currently engaging the field, editor Uriah Kriegel has provided such a publication. The five debates are:

- Mind and Body: The Prospects for Russellian Monism
- Mind in Body: The Scope and Nature of Embodied Cognition
- Consciousness: Representationalism and the Phenomenology of Moods
- Mental Representation: The Project of Naturalization
- The Nature of Mind: The Importance of Consciousness.

Preliminary descriptions of each chapter, annotated bibliographies for each controversy, and a supplemental guide to further controversies in philosophy of mind (with bibliographies) help provide clearer and richer views of active controversies for all readers.

Uriah Kriegel is Associate Professor of Philosophy at University of Arizona.

For an off-the-page exploration of the topics discussed by Angela Mendelovici and Amy Kind in Section III. Consciousness: Representationalism and the Phenomenology of Moods, visit PhilosTV.com to watch them debate their viewpoints in an online debate.

Current Controversies in Philosophy

In venerable Socratic fashion, philosophy proceeds best through reasoned conversation. Current Controversies in Philosophy provides short, accessible volumes that cast a spotlight on ongoing central philosophical conversations. In each book, pairs of experts debate four or five key issues of contemporary concern, setting the stage for students, teachers, and researchers to join the discussion. Short chapter descriptions precede each chapter, and an annotated bibliography and suggestions for further reading conclude each controversy. In addition, each volume includes both a general introduction and a supplemental guide to further controversies. Combining timely debates with useful pedagogical aids allows the volumes to serve as clear and detailed snapshots, for all levels of readers, of some the most exciting work happening in philosophy today.

Series Editor:

John Turri
University of Waterloo

Volumes in the Series

Published:

Current Controversies in Philosophy of Mind
Edited by Uriah Kriegel

Forthcoming:

Current Controversies in Epistemology
Edited by Ram Neta

Current Controversies in Experimental Philosophy
Edited by Edouard Machery

Current Controversies in Metaphysics
Edited by Elizabeth Barnes

Current Controversies in Political Philosophy
Edited by Thom Brooks

Current Controversies in Virtue Ethics
Edited by Mark Alfano

Current Controversies in Philosophy of Mind

Edited by
Uriah Kriegel

Routledge
Taylor & Francis Group

NEW YORK AND LONDON

First published 2014
by Routledge
711 Third Avenue, New York, NY 10017

Simultaneously published in the UK
by Routledge
2 Park Square, Milton Park, Abingdon, Oxon OX14 4RN

Routledge is an imprint of the Taylor & Francis Group, an informa business

Library of Congress Cataloging-in-Publication Data

A catalog record has been requested for this book

ISBN: 978-0-415-53086-6 (hbk)
ISBN: 978-0-415-53087-3 (pbk)
ISBN: 978-0-203-11662-3 (ebk)

Typeset in Minion
by Apex CoVantage, LLC

Printed and bound in the United States of America by Sheridan Books, Inc. (a Sheridan Group Company).

Contents

Contributors

Daniel Stoljar is Professor of Philosophy at the Australian National University. He is the author, most recently, of *Physicalism* (2010) and *Ignorance and Imagination: The Epistemic Origin of the Problem of Consciousness* (2006).

Derk Pereboom is Professor of Philosophy at Cornell University. He is the author of *Living Without Free Will* (2001), *Consciousness and the Prospects of Physicalism* (2011), and *Free Will, Agency, and Meaning in Life* (2014).

Lawrence Shapiro is Professor of Philosophy at the University of Wisconsin, Madison. He is the author of *Embodied Cognition* (2011) and *The Mind Incarnate* (2004), and the co-editor, with Brie Gertler, of *Arguing about the Mind*.

Alvin I. Goldman is Board of Governors Professor in the Department of Philosophy at Rutgers. His recent books include *Reliabilism and Contemporary Epistemology* (2012), *Joint Ventures: Mindreading, Empathy, and Embodied Cognition* (2013), and *Social Epistemology: Essential Readings* (2010), co-edited with Dennis Whitcomb.

Amy Kind is Professor of Philosophy at Claremont McKenna College. She has published numerous articles and essays on philosophy of mind, metaphysics, and philosophy and popular culture.

Angela Mendelovici is Assistant Professor of Philosophy at the University of Western Ontario. She has papers and essays forthcoming in several publications and books on philosophy of mind.

Uriah Kriegel is Research Director at the Jean Nicod Institute. He is the author of *Subjective Consciousness: A Self-Representational Theory* (2009) and *The Sources of Intentionality* (2011).

Robert D. Rupert is Professor of Philosophy at the University of Colorado, Boulder. He is the author of *Cognitive Systems and the Extended Mind* (2009).

Charles Siewert is Robert Alan and Kathryn Dunlevie Hayes Professor of Humanities and Professor of Philosophy at Rice University. He is the author of *The Significance of Consciousness* (1998).

Geoffrey Lee is Assistant Professor of Philosophy at the University of California, Berkeley. His research interests include philosophy of mind, foundations of cognitive science and neuroscience, and metaphysics.

The Philosophy of Mind: Current and Perennial Controversies

URIAH KRIEGEL

This volume covers five central controversies in current philosophy of mind. There are many more than five current controversies, but arguably the most interesting are those that play out some of the perennial problems of the philosophy of mind. For through the historical progression of philosophical dialectic, certain ancient philosophical problems have taken very specific shapes and have narrowed in on what is felt to be the core of the original problem. This volume focuses on contemporary controversies that reflect such perennial philosophical problems.

The most perennial and virtually definitive problem of the philosophy of mind is the ancient mind-body problem, concerned with the ultimate relationship between mind and matter. In twentieth-century philosophy, this problem tended to be split into two sub-problems, concerned with the two mental features that proved most resistant to accommodation in a purely materialistic and scientifically friendly worldview. The first is consciousness, the felt subjective quality of experience; the second is representation, or intentionality, the mind's special capacity to direct itself at something other than itself.[1] Attempts to resolve the mind-body problem have consequently required special attention to the nature of consciousness and the nature of mental representation or intentionality. Accordingly, the first controversy covered in this book addresses the mind-body problem, the third addresses the nature of consciousness, and the fourth addresses the nature of representation/intentionality.

In addition to the perplexities of body *and* mind, there are some pertaining to body *in* mind, as an increasing number of philosophers and scientists maintain that our mental life is thoroughly embodied. It is rarely clear what this exactly means, however, and the second controversy in this book concerns precisely that issue. The fifth and final controversy is arguably the most significant but also the most open-ended: it concerns the role of consciousness in our understanding of ourselves and the world around us.

For each of these controversies, we have brought together a pair of prominent authors to expound opposing perspectives. In what follows, I describe in more detail the modern shape these controversies have assumed and the contributions offered here by the two authors on each controversy.

The Mind-Body Problem and "Russellian Monism"

For most of its history, the mind-body problem has been conducted under the shadow of a forced choice between materialism and dualism. According to materialism, ultimately there is nothing in our world but physical matter; any mental features exhibited in our world are necessarily fixed by underlying physical features.[2] According to dualism, by contrast, there is more to our world than physical matter and its physical properties: there are also some mental features that enjoy a certain independence from any underlying physical properties, insofar as in principle the latter could be present and yet the former absent (which means that the mental features are not necessitated by the physical).[3] The problem is that both materialism and dualism face deep and principled difficulties that make them hard to accept.

If materialism is true, and mental facts are necessarily fixed by physical ones, we should expect that complete knowledge of pertinent physical facts about someone would allow us to know also the mental facts about her. If we really knew everything there is to know about this person's brain (and body and environment), and these facts necessitated the facts about her mind, then we should be able to figure out what the facts about her mind are. And yet this does not seem to be the case: we can imagine knowing everything about someone's physical existence without knowing much (or anything) about his or her mental life (or even whether s/he has any). This sense of "explanatory gap" between the physical and the mental is well captured by the nineteenth-century thinker John Tyndall:

> Were our minds and senses so expanded, strengthened, and illuminated as to enable us to see and feel the very molecules of the brain; were we capable of following all their motions, all their groupings, all their electric discharges, if such there be; and were we intimately acquainted with the corresponding states of thought and feeling, we should be as far as ever from the solution to the problem, "How are these physical processes connected with the facts of consciousness?" The chasm between the two classes of phenomena would still remain intellectually impassable.[4]

Thus, even if an oracle informed us that whenever our brain is in physical state P, our mind is necessarily in mental state M, we would be utterly unable to see *why* that should be so. Similar ideas go back at least to Leibniz (1714, §17; italics his):

> It must be confessed, however, that *perception*, and that which depends upon it, *are inexplicable by mechanical causes*, that is to say, by figures and motions. Supposing that there were a machine whose structure produced thought, sensation, and perception, we could conceive of it as increased in size with the same proportions until one was able to enter into its interior, as he would into a mill. Now, on going into it he would find only pieces working upon one another, but never would he find anything to explain perception.

Here Leibniz appears to offer a diagnosis of this explanatory gap: physical facts concern structure and function, but at least some mental facts go beyond structure and function, and therefore cannot be physically (mechanically) explained.

Unfortunately, dualism faces its own difficulties. Science seems to have shown that everything we do is ultimately caused by neural processes in our brain: when we smile, some brain cells in the so-called motor cortex fire an electrical impulse; when we jump up and down, other cells do; when we eat ice cream, yet others; and so on and so forth. At the same time, if you ask me why I smile, I am more liable to answer "because I am happy," or "because I saw something amusing," or some such—not "because my motor cortex caused me to." Now, for a materialist there would be no tension between these two explanations of my smiling (as caused by happiness and as caused by neural processes in the brain). For according to the materialist, happiness *just is* a neural process in the brain: to be happy about something is just to be in a certain brain state. However, for the dualist these are two separate states, one mental and one physical. So the dualist cannot embrace both explanations of smiling. She must choose between the happiness-invoking explanation and the brain-invoking one. Choosing the happiness-invoking explanation is eminently commonsensical but appears to be in tension with science, as it renders my brain irrelevant to my smiling. Embracing the brain-invoking explanation instead restores consistency with science but leads to the horribly counterintuitive result that happiness can never make you smile. That is, it leads to the result that the mind is causally inert, entirely unable to affect the world outside it.[5]

In light of these difficulties, philosophers of mind have recently attempted to find new and creative approaches to the mind-body problem that evade the forced choice between materialism and dualism. The hope is to devise a view that gives rise neither to an explanatory gap between mind and matter (as materialism does) nor to causal inertia of mind vis-à-vis matter (as dualism does). The most successful gambit in this vein, sociologically speaking, appears to be so-called Russellian monism.[6] Very schematically, this is the view that the universe includes some special properties that underlie, and are more basic than, both mental and physical properties. They are, in fact, both proto-mental and proto-physical. Their proto-mental status neutralizes the explanatory gap problem, while their proto-physical status neutralizes the problem of causal inertia.

The issue is how to move from this highly schematic characterization, almost a "wish list," to a more substantive and precise one. In his contribution, Daniel Stoljar (Chapter 1) considers four different ways of working out Russellian monism. The first two he considers to be implausible, and the third to collapse to dualism. The fourth he is most optimistic about. According to it, the scientific theory of the world that humanity will ultimately converge on—at the end of inquiry, as it were—will likely refer to properties of whose nature we are currently entirely ignorant. These properties are nothing like the properties cited in current physics, so we cannot consider them physical (but at most proto-physical), and nothing like the properties cited in current psychology, so we cannot consider them mental (but at most proto-mental). Yet these properties, in virtue of their as-yet-unknown nature, will bridge the explanatory gap between mind and matter and secure the causal efficacy of mind vis-à-vis matter. That such properties exist is at present mere speculation. But the fact that their existence would make intelligible the connection between mind and matter strongly suggests that something like them must indeed exist.

This view still faces the Leibnizian worry that scientific facts concern structure and function but at least some mental facts go beyond structure and function. However, the worry is based on the assumption that nonstructural/nonfunctional facts cannot be grounded in structural/functional facts. According to Stoljar, however, this assumption is false—at least if we interpret "structural/functional" to mean "relational."[7] For some nonrelational, or "intrinsic," facts are based on relational ones. Stoljar offers the following example: "From the fact that a series of points in space are arranged in a particular way, you might derive the fact that that the region constituted by the points has a particular shape." The facts about the points' arrangement are relational facts (they concern the spatial relations among the points), but the fact about a region having some shape is arguably a nonrelational fact (the region does not have the shape it does in virtue of standing in a relation to anything outside it so the shape is an intrinsic property of the region).

According to Derk Pereboom (Chapter 2), however, this does not neutralize the Leibnizian worry. Pereboom distinguishes between intrinsic and *absolutely intrinsic* properties. A property is absolutely intrinsic if something has it not only (i) not in virtue of standing in a relation to anything outside it, but also (ii) not in virtue of any of its parts standing in certain relations to each other. Thus a region's shape is intrinsic, but it is not absolutely intrinsic—precisely because it is grounded in the spatial relations among points that are part of it. But there is reason to think that consciousness *is* an absolutely intrinsic property, according to Pereboom. The reason is that consciousness seems both intrinsic and primitive. It seems epistemically primitive in the sense that its nature is fully revealed by introspection, and it seems metaphysically primitive in the sense that there is no collection of underlying properties that constitute it. Crucially, whenever something has an intrinsic property that is primitive in these senses, that property must be absolutely intrinsic. For, being primitive, the property cannot be constituted by a plurality of underlying properties, including a plurality of relational properties of the thing's parts. The upshot, for Pereboom, is that the best version of Russellian monism would have to advert centrally to absolutely intrinsic properties.

The Embodied Mind Research Program

Although the mind-body problem does not prejudge the exact relationship between body and mind, it does create an initial conceptual separation between the two. It presupposes that each can be grasped independently of the other. This conceptual separation has been sometimes rejected as wrongheaded: upon examination, it is claimed, our mental life is shot through with our physical being, as the mind is inherently embodied. For example, when you have to judge the slant of a hill from its bottom, your judgment will demonstrably change depending on how heavy your backpack is (Bhalla and Proffitt 1999). In this and other cases, we think and process information through our bodies. To some, such cases have suggested that we think *with* our body: it is simply false that the brain does all the thinking in the slant case—the back does some too.

Ideas orbiting this notion have proliferated considerably over the past generation of research, leading to a highly energetic but often conceptually confused "embodied cognition research program." One pervasive confusion in this area pertains to whether the body's role in cognition is *causal* or *constitutive*: whether the body merely enables cognition that is strictly speaking performed by the brain, or on the contrary the body itself does the cognizing. The literature on embodied cognition has tended to be fuzzy on such foundational matters, with the result that there is no clear definition of what "embodied cognition" amounts to among either cognitive scientists or philosophers of mind.

In an important recent piece, Alvin Goldman (2012) attempts to distill the plausible core of the program and offer a workable definition of embodied cognition. The key notion is that of a B-format. When you clench your fist, you can represent your fist clenching visually, by *seeing* it clench, but you can also represent it proprioceptively, by sensing the clenching from the inside as it were. Both representations require some representational format, but only the second one uses a body-related one—a B-format. A B-format is thus a format for representing things in a distinctively bodily manner. The core insight of the embodied mind research program, according to Goldman, is that a B-format is in fact pervasive to our cognition and often gets recruited to represent matters entirely unrelated to our bodies. Thus, in processing information on the slant of a hill we typically recruit B-formatted representations of how hard it would be for our body to climb the hill.

In his contribution, Larry Shapiro (Chapter 3) raises three central difficulties for Goldman's account of embodied cognition. The first is that B-formatted representations may not be necessary for embodied cognition, as some robots seem to engage in the latter but may not have the former. The second is that B-formatted representations may not be sufficient for embodied cognition, as it is quite possible that *all* cognition will turn out to employ B-formats but utterly implausible that all cognition is embodied. The third is that if Goldman's characterization of embodied cognition were correct, it would not represent all that deep a challenge to the conceptual separation of mind and body and would be less radical than many embodied-cognition proponents might wish for. Thus, in the film *The Matrix*, humans are enclosed in vats, immobile and unable to use their bodies; yet their mental life is subjectively indistinguishable from ours, and nothing prevents it from employing B-formatted representations pervasively. By Goldman's lights, then, mental life in the Matrix is just as embodied as outside it—even though the body itself has no role to play in it.

Goldman (Chapter 4) provides new empirical and conceptual background to his approach to embodied cognition, before addressing Shapiro's concerns. Goldman argues that the notion of B-format can be understood in such a way that nonhumans certainly have it, so the necessity threat can be neutralized. He then argues that it is a virtue rather than vice of his definition that it leaves open the conceptual possibility that all cognition might turn out embodied (since this is an empirical possibility), so the sufficiency threat is neutralized as well. Finally, Goldman concedes that his definition casts the embodied-cognition program as less radical than many enthusiasts wish for but denies that his definition is supposed to produce consensus. On the contrary, he takes it to constitute a moderate approach that represents a compromise between those who take the body itself, rather than bodily representation, to be involved in cognition (on the one hand) and those who consider that bodily representation is restricted to body-related cognitive tasks rather than be pervasive in cognition (on the other hand).

Intentionalism about Consciousness and the Phenomenology of Moods

One central thread in mainstream philosophy of mind of the late twentieth century ties together the problems of intentionality, consciousness, and mind-body. In a first stage, it offers a purely materialistic, "naturalistic" account of intentionality in terms of physical connections between parts of a person's brain and parts of her external environment;[8] this is often referred to as the "tracking approach to intentionality." In a second stage, it offers a reductive explanation of the subjective character of conscious experience in terms of this capacity to represent one's environment by tracking parts of it; this is often referred to as the "intentionalist" or "representationalist" theory of consciousness. Finally, it suggests that since both intentionality and consciousness can be accounted for in terms of the causal physical processes underlying this tracking capacity, the mind is nothing but this underlying physical process; this is "materialism." Thus are combined materialism about the mind-body problem, intentionalism about consciousness, and the tracking theory of intentionality.

In early twenty-first-century philosophy of mind, all strands in this package have met with increasing resistance. A central challenge to the tracking theory of intentionality will be discussed in the next section. Perhaps the most important challenge to intentionalism about consciousness is the experiential dimension of moods. Accordingly, our third controversy concerns the prospects for an intentionalist or representationalist account of moods.

Moods appear to present a pronounced challenge to intentionalism because many appear to be entirely undirected. One often feels anxious or melancholic or euphoric without feeling so about anything in particular. The feeling often appears free-floating, unmoored from any particular feature of one's immediate environment. It is thus difficult to see exactly how any representation of one's environment could account for it. Nonetheless, some intentionalists have insisted that moods do represent, but in a distinctly unfocused manner: one may be anxious about *everything*, melancholic about *the world*, or euphoric about *life*. Thus William Seager (1999, 183) writes: "Being depressed is a way of being conscious of things in general: everything seems worthless, or pointless, dull and profitless." This may be taken to resonate with our phenomenology of moods, the way they strike us subjectively. Consider Shakespeare's characteristically acute description of Hamlet's melancholia:

> How weary, stale, flat and unprofitable, seem to me all the uses of this world! (I.ii.133–4) . . . it goes so heavily with my disposition that this goodly frame, the earth, seems to me a sterile promontory; this most excellent canopy, the air, look you, this brave o'erhanging firmament, this majestical roof fretted with golden fire, why, it appears no other thing to me than a foul and pestilent congregation of vapours. (II.ii.297–303)

Hamlet's bleak mood does represent, though what it represents are the most general of things: the world, the earth, and the air (the world's "majestical roof"), all of which are represented as insignificant, unspecial, and charmless.[9]

In their respective contributions, both Amy Kind (Chapter 5) and Angela Mendelovici (Chapter 6) oppose this particular intentionalist treatment of moods. Kind argues that in fact no intentionalist account of mood is workable.

Although some aspects of the experiential character of mood can be accounted for in terms of representation of various features of one's body and environment (including the world as a whole), some aspects of mood's distinctive experiential character go beyond any such representation. For example, even if euphoria tends to correlate with representation of everything as wonderful, the experiential *intensity* of euphoric moods—just how elated one feels—can vary without any corresponding variation in represented degrees of wonderfulness: things are not represented as more or less wonderful depending on the constantly fluctuating intensity of one's mood.

Mendelovici too claims that moods can be experienced even without representing any *thing*, not even the world as a whole or everything in it. However, she suggests that moods are still essentially representational, because although they do not represent any *thing*, they always and necessarily represent certain *features*. Euphoria represents wonderfulness, though not any particular thing's wonderfulness (not even the world's); melancholia represents pointlessness or insignificance, though not any particular thing's; and so on and so forth. Typically our conscious experiences represent features as bound to things that exhibit them (a perceptual experience of a brown table represents brownness as bound to the table). It is a peculiarity of moods, suggests Mendelovici, that they can represent altogether unbound features. This peculiarity explains their undirected feel without compromising the intentionalist notion that all conscious experiences, moods included, are essentially representational.

Intentionality and Its Naturalization

Suppose you meet a person who tells you that she is thinking, but when you ask her what she is thinking of, she replies "Oh nothing, I'm just thinking." You would rightly conclude that this person does not understand what the word *thinking* means. When a person is thinking, there is always an answer to the question "what are you thinking of"? It is impossible to think without thinking about something. This is the intentionality of thought: thinking is always directed; it has aboutness.

In this, thought appears to be categorically different from physical objects and processes. A tree, an elephant, a house—these are not about anything, not directed at anything. They just are what they are; they do not send to something other than themselves. The same holds, of course, of the smallest particles of matter: they are what they are and contain no reference to something outside themselves. But this seems to throw a wrench in the project of scientifically explaining thought processes in terms of the physical particles making up the brain. If no individual particles in a person's brain are directed at anything, it is unclear how the vast collection of these particles could yield the person's thought *about a flower*. The person's directedness outside herself, to the flower, is completely inexplicable in terms of her undirected brute particles.

Tracking approaches to intentionality propose to resolve this tension by identifying some scientifically respectable ("naturalistic") relation that holds between a person's brain and the flower when, and only when, the person thinks about the flower. Various notions from information theory help us make sense of the idea that one physical object can bear a physical relation to another physical object that makes the former carry information about the latter, essentially by tracking its presence. The idea is to apply the same information-theoretic analysis to thought: the mind's capacity for representing objects outside it might be fully explained in terms of one's brain states carrying information about one's physical environment.[10]

In my own contribution (Chapter 7), I develop a challenge to this tracking approach. Typically, what our conscious experiences present to us and what they track in the environment are the same: when I see a lemon, my visual experience presents a lemon to me and also tracks the lemon on the counter. But we can imagine unusual circumstances where these two come apart. People in the Matrix can have lemon experiences even if they no longer come in contact with lemons, indeed even long after lemons have gone extinct. Such experiences present lemons to the subject but do not track any lemons in the environment. Should we say that such experiences represent or are intentionally directed at lemons or not? I argue for a mixed answer. There is one sense in which such experiences do not represent lemons, precisely because they do not track lemons; we may say that such experiences are not *objective* representations of lemon. There is another sense, however, in which such experiences do represent lemons, precisely because lemon is what they present to the subjects whose experiences they are; we may say that such experiences are *subjective* representations of lemon. The problem with tracking approaches to intentionality or representation, then, is that although they account for objective representation, they do not account for subjective representation.

Robert Rupert (Chapter 8) argues, however, that the objective notion of representation is sufficient for accounting for all the data in the area, at least when we take note of the cognitive and/or computational architecture in which representations in the objective sense are embedded. Crucially, people in the Matrix do not in fact have representations of lemons in any sense, though we are tempted to think that they do—and the standard account of representation in terms of architecturally embedded objective tracking relations can explain the temptation. The temptation arises, according to Rupert, from the fact that when we have second-order internal states that track our first-order representations, they can track only the presence of the state doing the representing, not the entity being represented. Accordingly, the second-order representation provides no genuine insight into what is being represented by the first-order representation, hence provides no support for the notion that something like a lemon is represented by it.

The Importance of Consciousness

For much of the modern era, mental life and consciousness were treated as one and the same, both in philosophy and in culture at large. But starting in the nineteenth century, two intellectual forces have pushed for ever-expanding daylight between the mental and the conscious. On the one hand, there has been a growing recognition that much of our emotional life, and much of what moves us to act as we do, is determined by unconscious processes often opaque to us; well before Freud's (1915) "The Unconscious," this theme was thoroughly explored in nineteenth-century literature, from Stendhal's novels in the first half of the century to Strindberg's plays in the second half. At the same time, in their search for perfectly mechanical explanations of mental life, British associationist psychologists began highlighting the role of physiologically driven subpersonal mechanisms in shaping our mental life. Ultimately, this led to the realization that most mental activity occurs below the threshold of consciousness, perhaps most explicitly in Henry Maudsley's (1868) *The Physiology and Pathology of Mind*. By the mid-twentieth century, the educated layperson's standard conception of mind had transformed radically, portraying consciousness as merely the visible tip of the mental iceberg.

In early twenty-first-century philosophy, however, consciousness has enjoyed something of a comeback. The value of consciousness can be appreciated from a number of perspectives. One concerns *moral* value. It is natural to hold that even if much of our mental life is unconscious, consciousness is what makes our life *interesting*, indeed what makes it valuable. If *all* our mental life were unconscious, so that we were effectively zombies, life would be essentially pointless. There seems to be no intrinsic difference between death and complete and irreversible loss of consciousness: in both cases, *we* are gone. Another perspective on the value of consciousness concerns our *epistemic* standing in the world: unconscious zombies, even if their subconscious mental activity is indistinguishable from ours, can claim to know much less about themselves and the world than we do. For they lack a consciousness that would present them directly with the world surrounding them and a self-consciousness that would present them with themselves.

In his contribution, Charles Siewert (Chapter 9) attempts to make a case along these lines for the importance of consciousness. Siewert starts by noting that perceptual knowledge of one's surroundings is often based on how things appear to one, and how things appear to one just is one's phenomenal experience. Furthermore, one's knowledge of oneself is based on introspection of one's phenomenal experience, even if introspection is an intellectual rather than quasi-perceptual relation to oneself. And the epistemic significance of consciousness goes beyond perceptual knowledge and self-knowledge: it pertains also to knowledge of what the words we use mean, thus grounding linguistic understanding. Beyond its epistemic importance, phenomenal consciousness is also ethically significant in various ways. First of all, it grounds a kind of irreplaceable, noninstrumental value that one's own life has to one: there is a strong intuition that being the same person tomorrow is better for me than being someone else just like me—but only insofar as I am not a zombie. Furthermore, the point extends to the irreplaceable value some persons have to other persons—it depends on the former being phenomenally conscious (otherwise a duplicate would do just as well, and one's value would not be genuinely irreplaceable).

Geoff Lee (Chapter 10) is more skeptical about the value of phenomenal consciousness. His contribution focuses on the epistemic significance of consciousness but touches on its moral significance as well. It might be thought that one is more justified in believing that some table is brown if one was conscious of the brown table. But Lee argues that this is an illusion. Imagine a creature whose cognitive architecture is exactly like ours but who has no subjective consciousness; call this creature "pseudo-conscious." Lee argues that although it is true that one is more justified in believing that the table is brown if one is conscious of it than if one has no relation whatsoever to it, it is false that one is more justified in believing that the table is brown if one is conscious of it than if one is pseudo-conscious of it. Assuming materialism, consciousness must be some kind of physical property of the brain, and pseudo-consciousness another physical property. Moreover, the strictly physical difference between consciousness and pseudo-consciousness is liable to be relatively small. It is unclear, under such circumstances, why it should matter to one's table belief's justification whether one was conscious or merely pseudo-conscious of the table. It is unlikely, in particular, that the small physical difference between the two should translate into a major epistemic difference. Thus, claims to the effect that consciousness is particularly important may presuppose a nonphysical conception of consciousness. On this view, it is not really possible to make a strong case for the value of consciousness while staying neutral on the debate over materialism and dualism.

How to Read This Book

The articles in this volume are intended to cater both to professional philosophers and to (post)graduate students (as well as rather advanced undergraduates). But there are two ways of reading the book, one more natural for professional philosophers and one more suitable for a seminar.

For the professional philosopher, it would be natural to read the exchanges in the order in which they appear—horizontally from beginning to end, so to speak. In each exchange, the first of the two articles involves a more theoretically neutral setup, so it is recommended to start with it. It is also possible to skip some exchanges, as these are more or less independent of each other, though the third and fourth can be seen as forming something of a module (as can perhaps the first and second).

This order could also be adhered to in a more pedagogical context, but there is another order that might be more suitable there. This is to read the book vertically and backwards: one would start with Chapter 9 about the significance of consciousness, move to Chapter 7 about a consciousness-based account of mental representation, then move to Chapter 5 about consciousness outstripping representation, and finally arrive at Chapter 1 about the elusive metaphysics of consciousness; before turning around, as it were, and reading Chapter 2 about trying to pin down the metaphysics of consciousness, moving on to Chapter 6 about representation exhausting consciousness, then Chapter 8 about explaining representation without appeal to consciousness, and finally Chapter 10 about the *in*significance of consciousness. This order highlights the centrality of the historical tension in philosophy of mind between first-person consciousness-based approaches to the mind and third-person consciousness-free approaches. Crucially, this order also goes from the most accessible, reader-friendly chapters to the most advanced, professionally sophisticated ones in an almost linear fashion.[11] With this in mind, I am tempted to recommend this order of reading for pedagogical settings.

Notes

1. Note that the term *intentionality* is used in a technical way in this context, which derives from the Latin *intentio*, meaning "to be directed at"; it does not in the first instance have to do with intending to do something or otherwise exercising one's will, as everyday use of the word *intentionality* might suggest.
2. There are three main versions of this. One denies that any mental features are ever exhibited, or instantiated, in our world; this is *eliminative materialism*. Another allows that some mental features are exhibited but insists that those turn out to be nothing but physical features, that is, are identical to physical features; this is *reductive materialism*. A third view is that while mental features are distinct from physical features or properties, the former are nonetheless necessarily determined by them (i.e., the former "metaphysically supervene" upon the latter); this is *nonreductive materialism*.
3. This is intended to be consistent with the mental properties being causally fixed by (hence "nomically supervenient upon") physical properties due to the laws of nature. The crucial point is that since the laws of nature could be different, different physical properties could be causally connected with different mental properties (or none at all)—which demonstrated mental's measure of independence from the physical. We may call the emerging view *naturalistic property dualism*. There are also stronger versions of dualism that deny the causal determination of mental properties by physical properties (call this *nonnaturalistic property dualism*) or insist that regardless of what goes on with mental properties, there is also a kind of immaterial stuff of which minds are "made" (this is *substance dualism*).
4. Quoted from Tennant (2007). Tyndall was a professional mathematician and amateur philosopher, and the passage quoted is from an 1868 presentation he delivered to the Mathematical and Physical Section of the British Association.
5. This line of reasoning has been regimented in modern philosophy of mind by Jaegwon Kim (1989), whose essential argument is that dualism (as well as certain types of materialism) is inconsistent with three independently plausible principles. The first is the principle of the causal efficacy of the mental: sometimes such phenomena as happiness do cause bodily effects such as smiling. The second is the principle of the causal closure of the physical: every physical event

has a physical cause, which means that we *must* invoke the brain in explaining such physical phenomena as smiling. Finally, the third is the causal exclusion principle: events in the world do not systematically have two separate causes, so that we *must* choose between the brain-invoking and happiness-invoking explanations. The only way to respect all three principle, argues Kim, is to suppose—with the materialist—that a mental phenomenon such as happiness is one and the same as some physical phenomenon such as a neural process in the brain.

6. The view's name plays homage to an early proponent of it, Bertrand Russell, who writes this: "So long as the 'subject' was retained there was a 'mental' entity to which there was nothing analogous in the material world, but, if sensations are occurrences which are not essentially relational, there is not the same need to regard mental and physical occurrences as fundamentally different. It becomes possible to regard both a mind and a piece of matter as logical constructions formed out of materials not differing vitally and sometimes actually identical" (1959, 103; but see Russell [1921] for a much earlier statement) The view is also often attributed to Spinoza, whose relevant work antedates Russell's by three and a half centuries.

7. A relational fact is a fact consisting in something having a relational property (or several things having relational properties, or there being a relation holding among several things). A relational property is a property something has in virtue of standing in a relation to something. For example, being a brother is a relational property because anybody who has it has it in virtue of standing in a relation to something else. It is in this sense that the fact that I am a brother is a relational fact.

8. The term *naturalistic* is commonly used in modern philosophy of mind to denote a broadly scientifically inspired theory, or one that attempts to dispense with supernatural entities in its explanations of earthly phenomena.

9. That Hamlet is depressed, or melancholy, is explicitly recognized both from Hamlet's first-person perspective (II.ii.602) and from his archrival Claudius's third-person perspective (III.i.165).

10. The classic on this is Dretske (1981). There is also a running debate, within this general approach, regarding whether the information-theoretic relations in question should be supplemented with a teleological component.

11. Nota bene: this order does not integrate the second exchange in the book (Chapters 3 and 4), which is orthogonal to the central tension between first-person and third-person approaches and where both papers are equally (and relatively highly) accessible.

References

Bhalla, M., and D. Proffitt. 1999. "Visual-Motor Recalibration in Visual Slant Perception." *Journal of Experimental Psychology* 25: 1076–1096.

Dretske, F. I. 1981. *Knowledge and the Flow of Information.* Stanford, CA: CSLI.

Freud, S. 1915. "The Unconscious." Trans. J. Stachey. In *On Metapsychology*, 159–222. London: Penguin, 1984.

Goldman, A. 2012. "A Moderate Approach to Embodied Cognitive Science." *Review of Philosophy and Psychology* 3: 71–88.

Kim, J. 1989. "The Myth of Nonreductive Materialism." *Proceedings and Addresses of the American Philosophical Association* 63: 31–47.

Leibniz, G. W. 1714. *The Monadology.* In *Philosophical Works of Leibnitz*, ed. and trans. G. M. Duncan. Whitefish: Kessinger Publishing, 2003.

Maudsley, H. 1868. *The Physiology and Pathology of Mind.* 2nd ed. London: Macmillan.

Russell, B. 1921. *The Analysis of Mind.* London: Allen & Unwin, 1978.

Russell, B. 1959. *My Philosophical Development.* New York: Simon and Schuster, 1975.

Seager, W. 1999. *Theories of Consciousness.* London: Routledge.

Tennant, N. 2007. "Mind, Mathematics, and the *Ignorabimusstreit*." *British Journal for the History of Philosophy* 15: 745–773.

PART I

Mind and Body
The Prospects for Russellian Monism

CHAPTER 1

Four Kinds of Russellian Monism*

DANIEL STOLJAR

Chapter Overview

'Russellian Monism' is a name given[1] to a family of views in philosophy of mind. The family is exciting because it seems to present an alternative both to materialism and to dualism. After briefly setting out the need for this alternative, I will in what follows distinguish four different kinds of Russellian monism (RM), and assess their pros and cons. My own feeling, as will emerge in the final section of the chapter, is that only the fourth of these represents a viable version of the view. But my main aim is less to state my feelings than to get clear on the different versions of the view and on what is involved in choosing among them.

Motivating RM

It is not hard to motivate the thought that neither materialism nor dualism is very attractive and that it would be better in principle if we could make out some alternative.

The problem for materialism is that it is on the face of it incomplete, for it seems to leave out properties constitutive of consciousness. A good way to bring this out is to operate with the following simple definition:[2]

M1. Materialism is true at a possible world w if and only if for every property G instantiated at w, there is some physical property (or some complex of physical properties) F instantiated at w such that F (metaphysically) necessitates G.

This provides an account of what it is for materialism to be true *at* some possible world or other; philosophers who are materialists believe that materialism is true at one world in particular—namely, the actual world.

Why think that materialism so defined is incomplete? Well, at the moment (let us suppose), I am in some sort of total experiential state that might at least partially be captured in the following way. I am sitting in my office; I have a cup of coffee to my left; some people are talking softly in the corridor outside; I smell slightly of chlorine from the pool earlier; the light is coming in through the wooden venetian blinds; and so on. It is conceivable[3] that there could be someone identical to me in respect of whatever physical properties I instantiate and yet who is not in exactly the same experiential state I am in. Maybe, for example, the taste of his coffee is ever so slightly more bitter than the taste of mine. If what is conceivable is possible, then there could be someone identical to me in respect of all physical properties and yet who does not taste the coffee as I do. But then it follows that this property—tasting the coffee in the precise way that I do—is both instantiated and yet is not necessitated by any physical property. By M1, however, this is inconsistent with materialism; hence, materialism is false.

This argument against materialism—the conceivability argument, as it is usually called—looks simple enough, but in fact it is quite complex. As a consequence, the literature on it has become increasingly involved.[4] But suppose we provisionally agree that the conceivability argument is successful; what are our options then? The standard option is to adopt the kind of dualism according to which most, but not quite all, instantiated properties are necessitated by the physical. The exceptions are properties associated with consciousness such as tasting coffee—'experiential properties', as we can call them. According to the dualist, the relation between experiential and physical properties is not metaphysically necessary but is naturally necessary (i.e., necessary given the way the laws of nature in fact are). More generally, on this picture, there are contingent psychophysical laws that tell us that if such and such a complex physical property is instantiated, then such and such an experiential property is instantiated.

Even if it avoids the conceivability argument, however, dualism is on the face of it inelegant. While the previous definition left this implicit, presumably the physical properties invoked in M1 are governed by a relatively small stock of laws that describe regularities in how these properties are instantiated and how they interact with each other. It is not that the materialist cannot countenance laws among complex nonphysical properties as well, but these hold in virtue of the regularities that obtain among physical properties and the laws that govern them. By contrast, dualism seems to require a quite distinct set of psychophysical laws that connect complex physical properties with experiential properties (assumed now to be fundamental); it requires "nomological danglers," as it is often put (Feigl 1967; Smart 1959). But this, as the phrase 'dangler' suggests, is inelegant.

At this point, a natural line of thought is this. Could there not be a theory of the world that is (a) as elegant as materialism but (b) as comprehensive as dualism? Alternatively, could the world not be such that a theory of this sort is true? It is this that provides one part of the motivation for RM. The Russellian monist, as I understand matters, is someone who agrees that materialism (at least of the usual sort) is defeated by the conceivability argument but holds out the hope for some alternative account that preserves its spirit and structure and so avoids the inelegance of dualism.[5]

The desire for a theory that is at once elegant and comprehensive is part of the motivation for RM. The other part involves a suggestion about where to look when thinking about the shape of such a theory. This suggestion is to focus not on the nature of consciousness but—to borrow a phrase from Leopold Stubenberg (1997)—on the "south-pole" of the mind-body relation (i.e., on the nature of the physical). For, in fact, discussions in philosophy of mind *do* seem to unfairly neglect this side of things. Notice, for example, that in my presentation of M1 and the conceivability argument discussed previously, *I failed completely* to say what physical properties are supposed to be; in doing so, I was being quite faithful to the tradition in which I work. But— Russellian monists quite reasonably insist—this will not do; moreover, when we do attend to the nature of physical properties, we will (they say) be able to formulate a theory that is an alternative to both materialism and dualism.

But how should this suggestion be developed? The next four sections consider four different ways.

RM1

The first version of Russellian monism (RM1) starts off from some ideas from John Locke's *An Essay Concerning Human Understanding* (see Locke 1975). There are two ideas in particular that we need.[6] The first is a list of what Locke famously called the "primary qualities" of physical objects. These properties are: size, shape, position, duration, movability, divisibility, and solidity. The second is an assumption about the limits of human understanding at least as regards physical objects—namely, that the properties of physical objects that we may understand are the primary qualities and perhaps logical combinations thereof.

RM1 Formulated[7]

With these ideas in place, our characterization of the first version of RM proceeds in two stages. The first stage formulates a version of materialism by combining the previous definition (i.e., M1) with a view about physical properties that is suggested by Locke's list of primary qualities; according to this view, physical properties just are primary qualities. We may call the resulting version of materialism 'primary quality materialism' or 'PQ-materialism' for short. PQ-materialism is true at a possible world w just in case for every property G instantiated at w, there is some primary quality (or complex of primary qualities) F instantiated at w such that F metaphysically necessitates G.

The second stage presents RM1 as the conjunction of three claims about PQ-materialism. The first is the following:

> RM1.a. PQ-materialism is false, and false for reasons quite distinct from those involved in the conceivability argument.

The reason for RM1.a begins from a consideration about one primary quality in particular—namely, solidity. To be solid, Locke said, an object must be such as to resist penetration from other objects. But this entails that solidity is a *dispositional* property of an object, where, to a first approximation, a dispositional property is a property that constitutively involves various claims about what things *would* or *might* be like in certain circumstances, rather than merely about what things *are* like. On the face of it, however, when an object has a dispositional property, there must be some further property it has in virtue of which it has the dispositional property in question. For example, when a chair is uncomfortable there must be some *other* property of the chair—its shape, say—in virtue of which it is it uncomfortable. By analogy, if some object is solid, there must be some other property of it in virtue of which it is solid.

Why does this show that PQ-materialism is false? Well suppose some object α is solid. By the considerations just reviewed, α must have some further property—which for the moment we can call 'Stuff'—in virtue of which it is solid. If PQ-materialism were true, Stuff must either be a primary quality or be necessitated by some primary quality (or some complex of primary qualities). But neither appears to be the case. First, Stuff is not identical with any primary quality on Locke's list or any complex of such properties. It is not itself solidity, because it is by assumption distinct from solidity; nor is it size, shape, position, duration, divisibility, or movability—or any complex of these—since these can be properties of empty regions of space (i.e., regions of space that contain no matter and so do not contain α in particular). Second, Stuff is not necessitated by any primary quality on Locke's list. It is not necessitated by solidity—indeed, the opposite is closer to the truth, since things are solid in virtue of instantiating Stuff; nor is it necessitated by size, shape, and so forth—or any combination of size, shape, and so forth—for the reason again that regions of space can have these properties and yet are not solid. Conclusion: Stuff is instantiated and yet is not necessitated by any primary quality. Hence PQ-materialism is false.

The second claim of RM1 is the following:

> RM1.b. While PQ-materialism is false for the reason mentioned in RM1.a, there is a substitute thesis that is not false for that reason and that preserves the spirit and structure of PQ-materialism.

The substitute thesis mentioned here—we may call it 'PQ-materialism+'—is exactly like PQ-materialism but with this difference: where PQ-materialism says that the physical properties are the primary qualities, PQ-materialism+ says that the physical properties are *either* the primary qualities *or* whatever properties objects must have in virtue of having primary qualities. So, for example, while PQ-materialism is refuted if Stuff is instantiated, PQ-materialism+ is not refuted, since Stuff counts as a physical property according to it. Does PQ-materialism+ preserve the spirit and structure of PQ-materialism? It would seem so. First, it may be formulated within the framework provided by M1. Second, it seems reasonable to include Stuff as a physical property since it (or a property like it) will be instantiated even at the most obvious possible worlds at which materialism is true. For example, take a world that contains only one lonely atom located in space. This atom is solid; hence, given our assumptions it will instantiate Stuff. And yet surely materialism is true at this world if it is true anywhere. So the existence and instantiation of Stuff is not anathema to materialism.

The third claim of RM1 is the following:

RM1.c. While PQ-materialism is false for the reason mentioned in RM1.a, it is also false for another reason—namely, the conceivability argument. By contrast, PQ-materialism+ escapes this argument.

In part, RM1.c says that PQ-materialism is defeated by the conceivability argument—we saw the reason for this when motivating RM at the start. But RM1.c also says that PQ-materialism+ is *not* defeated by the conceivability argument. The reason for this concerns the second idea we took from Locke, the idea about human understanding. If sound, the line of reasoning we just considered tells us that α instantiates Stuff. But it does not tell us what Stuff is or whether we can understand what it is. Can we understand it? Not if the second Lockean idea is right. That idea tells us that our understanding of the properties of physical objects is limited to the primary qualities. But Stuff is not a primary quality. Hence, we cannot understand what it is. Of course, we *can* name it, refer to it, (partially) describe it, and so on; we called it 'Stuff' after all, and described is the property in virtue of which α is solid. But from the fact that we can name and describe a property it does not follow that we can understand it. Indeed, that is the position we are in with respect to Stuff if RM1 is right.

But why does this point about Stuff mean that PQ-materialism+ escapes the conceivability argument? Well, that argument began with the idea that it is conceivable that there is someone identical to me in respect of physical properties but who does not taste the coffee in quite the way that I do. But is Stuff included here as a physical property or not? This question poses a destructive dilemma. For suppose that Stuff is included as a physical property. Now the conceivability claim loses its force. For it is now not clear that it is conceivable that there is someone identical to me in respect of Stuff who is different from me experientially. Since I have no idea what Stuff is, to say that this is conceivable is to say something for which I have no rational grounds. On the other hand, suppose Stuff is not included as a physical property. Now the argument may succeed but only in a diminished form, for now it targets not PQ-materialism+, but only PQ-materialism. In sum, the lesson of Stuff is that the conceivability argument may refute PQ-materialism, but it does not refute PQ-materialism+.

The following analogy illustrates the situation for PQ-materialism+. Suppose we have a very large box of fruit, perhaps an infinitely large one. And suppose we have some evidence (never mind why) that the box contains a certain kind of fruit—say citrus fruits. Suppose now someone argues as follows: "It is conceivable, and so possible, that there is a box that is identical to this box in every respect but that contains no apples." Is this persuasive? It is correct to answer "no" with something like this commentary: "You have not conceived what you say you have. You might have conceived a box that contains only citrus fruit but that has no apples, but you have not conceived a box that is identical in all respects to this box but that contains no apples. You are ignorant of the kinds of fruits there are in this box, so you can't have conceived that." Just as the conceivability argument fails in the case of the box and apples, it fails with respect to the physical world and consciousness, according to RM1.c.

RM1 Assessed

There are clearly elements of RM1 that are not for everybody. For example, some philosophers insist that what is dispositional here is the word 'solidity' rather than any property; and others say that while solidity is dispositional there is no philosophical reason to assume that must be a further property that grounds it.[8]

But I don't want to focus on these issues, for there is a simpler and more serious problem with RM1. This is that the epistemological idea that we took from Locke is palpably false; we are not limited in our understanding of physical objects to the primary qualities on Locke's list. On the contrary, if we take scientific knowledge more or less at face value, our knowledge of, and so understanding of, physical objects goes way beyond this. After all, consider all of the remarkable things that science has thrown up over the past few hundred years—the identification of matter and energy, quantum wave-functions states, fields, strings in n-dimensional space, and so on and so forth. It is impossible to say that humans as such do not understand these things (though some humans don't of course). But then the epistemological idea at the heart of RM1 should be rejected.

Of course, that RM1 makes implausible epistemological assumptions is hardly surprising; isn't that just what you get if you formulate a theory by adopting ideas that were au courant circa 1689? So it would seem. But it is also true that ideas very close to RM1 have been formulated and discussed sympathetically by many contemporary philosophers (e.g., those mentioned in note 6, this chapter). How do they react to the point that Locke's epistemological assumptions are out of date? Their reaction (I think) is roughly this: true but not relevant to the substance of the issue, for a position rather like Locke's can be formulated no matter what we assume about our understanding of the world. As Armstrong puts it: "Modern theory . . . [is in a] . . . no better position than . . . the Lockean Theory," for the distinctive postulates of modern theory themselves "dissolve into relations, or dispositions to have relations, that one particular has to another" (1961, 188).[9]

Adapting this to our own discussion, the suggestion is that while RM1 may be wrong for the reason given, there is a version of RM that is not wrong, a version that abstracts away from the particular claims about human understanding that Locke makes. To assess this suggestion, I now turn to a second version of RM, a version that allows us all the knowledge and understanding it would be possible for us to have.[10]

RM2

The second version of Russellian monism (RM2) starts off from some ideas set out in David Lewis's paper "Ramseyan Humility" (see Lewis 2009).[11] There are two ideas we need. The first is that there is what Lewis calls "a final theory," a theory that delivers "a true and complete inventory of those fundamental properties that play an active role in the actual workings of nature" (2009, 205). We may never formulate the theory in question, Lewis says, but it "nevertheless exists . . . in the way never-to-be-written poems do" (219). In order to spell out RM2, we will assume something Lewis does not—namely, that the final theory of the world is a physical theory.

The second idea is that the final theory may be divided into (what Lewis calls) 't-terms' and 'o-terms'. The t-terms name the fundamental properties of the world, properties as Lewis says that are "not at all disjunctive, or determinable, or negative. They render their instances perfectly similar in some respect. They are intrinsic; and all other intrinsic properties supervene on them" (2009, 204). The o-terms are any other terms in the theory. Crucially, Lewis assumes that the t-terms are "implicitly defined by the theory" which means that for any t-term T, there is a true definition of the following form: 'x has T if and only if x has the property that meets the condition . . . O . . .', where the vocabulary used to spell out the condition in question is exclusively the o-vocabulary—that is, a vocabulary consisting entirely of o-terms.[12]

RM2 Formulated

With these ideas in place, our characterization of RM2, like that of RM1, proceeds in two stages. The first formulates a version of materialism by combining

M1 with a view about physical properties that is suggested (but not entailed) by Lewis's discussion. According to this view, a physical property is a property expressed[13] by a predicate of the final theory (on the assumption, noted previously, that the final theory is a physical theory)—for short, physical properties are final-theory properties. We may call the resulting version of materialism 'final theory materialism' or 'FT-materialism' for short. FT-materialism is true at a possible world w just in case for every property G instantiated at w, there is some final theory property (or complex of final theory properties) F instantiated at w such that F metaphysically necessitates G.

The second stage is to present RM2 as making three distinct claims about FT-materialism. The first is the following:

> RM2.a. FT-materialism is false, and false for reasons quite distinct from those involved in the conceivability argument.

The reason for RM2.a begins from some considerations that are prominent in Lewis's paper. Suppose we take the final theory, T, and write it as a single long conjunctive sentence; call this 'the postulate of T'. Suppose now we take the postulate of T and write it so that the t-terms are made explicit. The result would be a sentence of the form 'T (t1, t2, t3 . . .)'. Now suppose we replace all the t-terms in the postulate of T with variables; the result would be an open sentence of this form 'T($x1, x2, x3$ . . .)'. If we existentially quantify this open sentence, we get what Lewis calls 'the Ramsey-sentence of T', the theory that says that there exists $x1, x2, x3$ . . . such that T($x1, x2, x3$ . . .). If a *realization* of T is an n-tuple of properties that satisfy this open sentence, the Ramsey sentence of T says in effect that there is a realization for T.

Now, Lewis argues that there is more than one possible realization of T. Suppose that in fact the properties that realize T are the ordered triple <F, G, H>. There might, in an alternative possible world, be a distinct triple < F*, G*, H*> that realizes it. T will be true relative to this alternative possible world just as it is true at the actual world; it is simply that the realization of the theory is different. Why should we assume that <F*, G*, H*> is distinct from (i.e., nonidentical to) <F, G, H>? After all, they realize the same total theory, and so there is no ordinary feature—no feature that may be captured by our total theory of the world—that distinguishes them. Lewis's answer is that <F, G, H> is numerically different from <F*, G*, H*> even if the properties here are duplicates with respect to qualitative features; he captures this by saying that properties constitutive of the first sequence have different quiddities from those constitutive of the second.[14]

Why do these considerations show that FT-materialism is false? Well suppose again that the actual realization of T is <F, G, H>. These properties are named by terms in T but are not expressed by any predicate of T. The reason is that T could be true at some possible world at which distinct n-tuple of properties realizes it—for example, the world just described at which <F*, G*, H*> realizes it. But now it follows that F, for example, is neither expressed by T nor necessitated by any property expressed by T; ditto for G and H. So F, G, and H are instantiated and yet are not physical properties, and FT-materialism is false.

The second claim of RM2 is the following:

> RM2.b. While FT-mate rialism is false for the reason mentioned in RM2.a, there is a substitute thesis that is not false for that reason and that preserves the spirit and structure of FT-materialism.

The substitute thesis—which we may call 'FT-materialism+'—is exactly like FT-materialism but with this difference: where FT-materialism says that the physical properties are those expressed by predicates of the final theory, FT-materialism+ says that the physical properties are *either* those expressed by such predicates or those denoted by expressions of the final theory. So, for example, while FT-materialism is false at the world at which <F*, G*, H*> realizes T, FT-materialism+ is not false, since F*, for example, is named there by T. Does FT-materialism+ preserve the spirit and structure of FT-materialism? For reasons analogous to those reviewed earlier, it certainly seems so.

The third claim is the following:

> RM2.c. While FT materialism is false for the reason mentioned in RM2.a, it is also false for another reason—namely, the conceivability argument. By contrast, the substitute thesis mentioned in RM2.b does not face this argument.

The argument for RM2.c parallels the argument given for RM1.c. The first premise of the conceivability argument says that it is conceivable that there be someone identical to me in all physical respects but different from me in respect of some physical property. Do we include the properties that constitute the actual realization of T as physical properties or not? Suppose they are included. Then the conceivability claim loses its force—for how am I supposed to conceive of a situation I do not understand? Suppose they are not included. Then the argument loses its force against FT-materialism+ even if it remains successful against FT-materialism. Either way, therefore, the conceivability fails as an argument against FT-materialism+.

RM2 Assessed

Once again there are elements of RM2 that are not for everybody. Some philosophers will reject either Lewis's suggestion that t-terms are implicitly defined by o-terms or his quidditism. Others will reject our assumption (which was not Lewis's) that the final theory is a piece of physics.

But again, I don't want to focus on these points, for there is a much simpler problem with RM2. This is that the sort of ignorance that a proponent of RM2 is committed to is (mere) quiddistic ignorance—that is, ignorance of the numerical identity of the properties in question, and about nothing else. It is not (what we might call) qualitative ignorance (i.e., ignorance of what goes beyond the mere numerical identity of the property in question). To put it vividly, with the exception of its numerical identity, any feature at all that F has at the actual world is also a feature that F* has in the alternative world we imagined. If F causes the heat death of the universe, so too does F*. If F is implicated in our suffering, so too is F*. If F is intrinsic or nonrelational or higher order, so too is F*. Indeed, the only difference between F and F* is that they are numerically distinct; equivalently, the only property that F has that F* does not is the property of being F.

Why does its commitment to mere quiddistic ignorance undermine RM2? Well, consider RM2.c as discussed previously. This says that while the conceivability argument defeats FT-materialism, it does not defeat FT-materialism+. Now this could only be true if the difference between them is relevant to the nature of consciousness. But it is hard to see how this could be so. The qualitative information contained in FT-materialism is identical to the qualitative information contained in FT-materialism+. The difference between them is that the former but not the latter leaves open the numerical identity of the realization of the final theory: FT-materialism+ names the actual realizers; FT-materialism does not. But the facts about consciousness are presumably qualitative if anything is. Hence, the difference between FT-materialism and FT-materialism+, while real enough, cannot be relevant to the nature of consciousness.

One might point out that this objection is generated by the assumption that the quiddity of a property is its numerical identity; could one not operate with a thicker notion[15] of a quiddity according to which F is distinct from F* not simply numerically but in some further way as well? Perhaps one could, but this makes no difference to RM2. For suppose F has some thick quiddity that distinguishes it from F*. It is hard to see why this fact about F, whatever it is, would not be included in the final theory of the world the existence of which RM2 presupposes. After all, the only thing we are assuming about that theory is that it is, as we saw before, "a true and complete inventory of those fundamental properties that play an active role in the actual workings of nature." Such an inventory would presumably have the resources to say what the thick quiddities of fundamental properties are, assuming they have them.[16]

So it would seem that the situation we are in at this point is this. RM1 makes an assumption about our epistemic situation that is implausible. RM2 avoids that problem by making assumptions that are defensible, even if philosophically controversial. But the problem is that we cannot use these assumptions in philosophy of mind; hence, RM2.c is false.

Is there a version of RM that unlike RM1 is empirically adequate but that unlike RM2 leaves us with a usable form of ignorance? Well, a striking feature of the discussion so far is that, contrary to expectations, it has had nothing to do with either Russell or monism! Since Russellian monism must have something to do with Russell or monism, weaving those elements into the formulation of the doctrine will (or so one might think) yield something that is an improvement on what we have considered so far.

Now, in the present context, referring to 'monism' is merely a way of marking the fact that RM is, as noted at the outset, not intended to be a traditional kind of dualism. So little of value may be wrung from the 'monistic' part of Russellian monism. But it *is* possible to inject a bigger element of his lordship into proceedings than we have done so far. The result of doing so is the next version of RM that I will consider.

RM3

The third version of Russellian monism (RM3) starts off from a famous idea from Russell's *The Analysis of Matter*—namely, that "the aim of physics, consciously or unconsciously, has always been to discover what we may call the causal skeleton of the world" (1927, 391).[17] To say this is not to deny that the world contains things apart from its causal skeleton; the beast of nature may have flesh as well as bones. Rather it is to say that physics has no business talking about the flesh.

RM3 Formulated

With this in place, our characterization of RM3 proceeds as before in two stages. The first combines M1 with a theory about what it to be a physical property. The theory is that a physical property is a property expressed by a term of the physical theory in Russell's sense—for short, a physical property is a causal skeletal property. The resulting version of materialism—causal skeletal materialism or CS-materialism—is true at a possible world w if and only if for every property G instantiated at w, there is some causal skeletal property (or complex of causal skeletal properties) F instantiated at w such that F necessitates G.

The second stage is to present RM3 as making three claims. The first is as follows:

RM3.a. CS-materialism is false, and false for reasons quite distinct from those involved in the conceivability argument.

The reason for RM3.a is closely analogous to the one given for RM1.a. Suppose the true physical theory, whatever it is, tells us about some sequence of events causally related to each other. As we noted, it certainly does not follow that the events do not have further properties. Moreover, for reasons closely related to the previous discussion of RM1.a, one might think it very plausible that they do have such properties; that is, one might think that if one event causes another, there must be some property of that event in virtue of which it does. However, if we agree with this, it would seem that CS-materialism is false. For on the face of it, these further properties neither are nor are necessitated by further causal structural properties.

The second claim is the following:

RM3.b. While CS-materialism is false for the reason mentioned in RM3.a, there is a substitute thesis that is not false for that reason and that preserves the spirit and structure of CS-materialism.

The substitute thesis—which we may call 'CS-materialism+'—is exactly like CS-materialism but with this difference: where CS-materialism says that the physical properties are causal skeletal properties, CS-materialism+ says that the physical properties are *either* causal skeletal properties or whatever properties events have in virtue of having causal skeletal properties. For reasons analogous to those we have reviewed earlier, CS-materialism+ preserves the structure and spirit of CS-materialism.

The third claim is the following:

RM3.c. While CS materialism is false for the reason mentioned in RM3.a, it is also false for another reason—namely, the conceivability argument. By contrast, CS-materialism+ does not face this argument.

The argument for RM3.c parallels the argument given for RM1.c. The first premise of the conceivability argument says that it is conceivable that there be someone identical to me in all physical respects but different from me in respect of some physical property. Do we include the properties in virtue of which causal skeletal properties obtain or not? Either way, therefore, the conceivability fails as an argument against CS-materialism+.

RM3 Assessed

Once again, there are elements here that are not for everybody. Some philosophers, for example, will question the assumption that if one event causes another, there must be some further property of the event in virtue of which it does.

But I don't want to focus on this, for there is a more serious problem with RM3. The problem concerns why physics is limited to describing the causal skeleton of the world in the first place. Russell's claim here is not empirical.[18] It is not that physics *as a matter of fact* only describes the causal skeleton, or that it only does so *currently*. Instead, what is lying behind Russell's view is a theory about what empirical knowledge as such consists in.

Russell sets out this theory—sometimes called 'representative realism'—in the middle section of *The Analysis of Matter*. The first part of this theory says that in the first instance we have knowledge of the instantiation of particular properties and relations—qualities, as Russell called them—to which we bear a direct perceptual or quasi-perceptual relation. The qualities include colors, shapes, experiential properties mentioned earlier, and logical and mathematical properties. The second part of the picture concerns how we might draw inferences about the external world from knowledge of the instantiation of these qualities. Russell's idea is that this sort of inference preserves mathematical structure but nothing else: "wherever we infer from perceptions, it is only structure that we can validly infer; and structure is what can be expressed by mathematical logic" (1927, 254). So for Russell the reason that *physics* aims at describing structure is that *any* inquiry about the external world at all is based on a structural similarity between the qualities we know directly and items in the world.[19]

Now, to the extent that RM3 is connected to representative realism, it is fair to say it is unattractive, though for reasons of space I will simply mention the relevant points here rather than work them through. First, many contemporary philosophers reject representative realism outright; they hold against Russell that we can and do have noninferential knowledge of the external world. Second, even if the first part of Russell's representative realism is true, it is not clear why the second part is: why are we limited to hypotheses about structure, as opposed to hypotheses of other sort? Third, even if both parts of it are right, Russell's picture is plausibly committed to dualism anyway, which drains it of interest as far as Russellian monism is concerned, since, as we saw at the start, RM is supposed to be a view that gets away from dualism. If representative realism is true, if one instantiates an experiential property, one knows what it is in what Lewis much later called 'an uncommonly demanding sense'. But notoriously, if one knows what it is in that sense, it is hard to see how anything short of dualism could be true.[20]

So RM3 is implausible if it is given the background Russell gave it. Can one detach it from that background? I take David Chalmers to be suggesting this when he says that "physical descriptions of the world characterize the world in terms of structure and dynamics" (2010, 120) and goes on to explain that "in formal terms, a structural-dynamic description is one that is equivalent to a Ramsey sentence whose O-terms include at most spatiotemporal expressions, nomic expressions, and logical and mathematical expressions" (2010, 120). Here, the reference to 'Ramsey-sentences and 'O-terms' should be understood in the way we saw that Lewis does, and so Chalmers may be read as combining elements of Lewis and Russell, as follows. Like Russell, for Chalmers a causal-structural property is one expressed by a predicate of physics; unlike Russell, however, for Chalmers physics is understood not in the light of representative realism, but rather as a proper part of Lewis's final theory (i.e., the part in which the o-terms are restricted in the way indicated).

This version of RM3 certainly improves on the original. Moreover, while this version of RM3 uses ideas from Lewis, it avoids the problem we noted for RM2. The underlying reason is that the Ramsey sentence of the final theory is different in the case of RM2 and RM3. In the case of RM2, one arrives at the Ramsey sentence of the final theory by replacing with variables all the terms in it for fundamental properties; every other term is an o-term. But in the case of RM3, one arrives at the Ramsey sentence by replacing with variables all the terms in it that are not spatiotemporal, logical, mathematical or nomic. Both Ramsey sentences permit more than one realization. But where for RM2 these distinct realizations are qualitatively identical though numerically distinct, for RM3 these realizations might be qualitatively distinct too, so long as they are identical from the point of view of spatiotemporal, nomic, and mathematical properties.

However, while this version of RM3 is attractive, a serious problem for it emerges when we ask what 'spatiotemporal expressions' are. In another part of his work, Chalmers argues that spatial expressions "function to pick out that manifold of properties that serves as the normal causal basis of a corresponding manifold of properties in our spatial experience" (2012, 335). But, if we assume that this applies to spatiotemporal expressions generally, the result is that physics for Chalmers is somewhat open ended. This by itself is no objection; open-endedness is appropriate for many purposes. But it is no good if one is out to defend RM3. For we now lose our reason to believe RM3.a, the claim that CS-materialism is false for a reason distinct from the conceivability argument. Suppose physics tells us about some sequence of causally related events, and that we agree (never mind why) that the events in the sequence have some further properties in virtue of which they stand in these causal relations. Why should these further properties not count as physical by Chalmers's lights? They too, after all, serve as the normal causal basis for the manifold of spatial, and spatiotemporal, experiences.

It might be replied that this objection neglects an important distinction—namely, between first- and second-order properties.[21] To illustrate the distinction, consider again the point mentioned in the course of discussing RM1, that when a chair is uncomfortable there must be some property of it in virtue of which it is uncomfortable. In this example, first-order property of the chair is its shape (i.e., the property that causes discomfort), while the second-order property is the property of having some property that causes discomfort. Now suppose again that physics tells us about some sequence of causally related events, and that these events must have some further properties in virtue of which is so. I argued that these further properties are physical on the ground that they are the normal causal basis for spatiotemporal experiences. But one might think (a) that the events in question have two sets of properties (i.e., both first- and second-order properties), and (b) that CS-materialism as intended by Chalmers is committed only to the second-order properties being physical. If so, we retain our reason to believe RM3.a, for the first-order properties of the events will be instantiated and yet not be physical.

It is true that if this line of argument is correct, we retain our reason to believe RM3.a. But by the same token, we lose our reason to believe RM3.c, the claim that CS-materialism+ does not face the conceivability argument. Unlike CS-materialism, CS-materialism+ will treat both the first- and second-order properties as physical, and it will evade the conceivability argument only if physical theory does not tell us about the first-order properties. But that does not seem right. It might be that physics is limited in various ways; there might be first-order (and indeed second-order) properties *of some kind* that physics does not tell us about. But to say that physics cannot tell us about the first-order properties *that cause our spatiotemporal experiences* is to say that physics cannot tell us about the causes of those experiences. But whatever else it does, surely physics can tell us about the causes of our experiences![22]

So it would seem that the situation we are in at this point is this. RM1 assumes a view about our access to the physical world that is empirically inadequate. RM2 makes no such assumption but has no application to philosophy of mind. RM3 in the form suggested by Russell is associated with an implausible epistemology and in the form suggested by Chalmers is either too open ended or has the consequence that physics does not tell us about the causes of our experiences.

How to move forward? The only possibility I see starts from two general observations about the versions of RM we have examined so far. First, all of them respond to the conceivability argument in a particular sort of way; that is, they try to make plausible the hypothesis that we are ignorant in a certain sort of way about the physical and then exploit that hypothesis to undermine the conceivability argument. Second, all of them try to make that hypothesis plausible in what might be called an a priori sort of way (i.e., by a priori reflection on physical science, and related matters).

Can we develop RM by separating the first observation here from the second; in other words, instead of trying to argue that we are ignorant of the nature of the physical a priori, can we start by assuming this as an empirical (but not implausible) starting point? It is that sort of perspective that motivates the final version of Russellian monism that I will consider.

RM4

The final version (RM4) starts off from some ideas set out in Thomas Nagel's *The View from Nowhere*, particularly in passages such as the following:

> The difference between the mental and the physical is far greater than the difference between the electrical and the mechanical. We need entirely new intellectual tools, and it is precisely by reflection on what appears

impossible—like the generation of mind out of the recombination of matter—that we will be forced to create such tools. It may be that the eventual result of such exploration will be a new unity that is not reductionist. We and all other creatures with minds seem to be composed of the same materials as everything else in the universe. So any fundamental discoveries we make about how it is that we have mind and what they actually are, will reveal something fundamental about the constituents of the universe as a whole. (1986, 52–53)

There are three ideas to take from this passage.[23] First, the sort of scientific theories that we have currently are incomplete in a fairly strong sense, particularly as regards consciousness. Second, while this is so, we might hold out the hope that in the limit of inquiry (a limit that we will perhaps never reach) a complete theory will be arrived at, a theory according to which the relation of consciousness to matter will be in some respects at least like the relation of the electrical to the mechanical. Third, we can take this sort of picture as implying that we are currently ignorant about theoretically important aspects of matter (or of what we call 'matter'); hence, we find in Nagel a focus on the south pole (as we called it earlier) of the mind-body relation.

RM4 Formulated

With these ideas in place, our characterization of RM4 proceeds in two stages. The first combines M1 with a view about physical properties that is suggested by (but not entailed by) Nagel's discussion. According to this account, a physical property is a property expressed by a predicate of our total current scientific theory—for short, physical properties are current-theory properties. We may call the resulting version of materialism 'current theory materialism' or 'CT-materialism' for short. CT-materialism is true at a possible world w just in case for every property G instantiated at w, there is some current theory property (or complex of current theory properties) F instantiated at w such that F metaphysically necessitates G.

The second stage is to present RM4 as making three distinctive claims about CT-materialism. The first claim of RM4 is the following:

> RM4.a. CT-materialism is false, and false for reasons quite distinct from those involved in the conceivability argument.

The reason for RM4.a is simply the sort of perspective suggested by Nagel's passage. If we think of ourselves as inquirers within a world, then it is difficult to deny that the picture of the world that we have developed to this point is incomplete in various ways—not for a priori reasons but for empirical though abstract reasons.

The second claim is the following:

RM4.b. While CT-materialism is false for the reason mentioned in RM4.a, there is a substitute thesis that is not false for that reason and that preserves the spirit and structure of CT-materialism.

The substitute thesis—which we may call 'CT-materialism+'—is exactly like CT-materialism but with this difference: where CT-materialism says that the physical properties are those expressed by predicates of the current theory, CT-materialism+ says that the physical properties are *either* those expressed by such predicates or those expressed by the final theory, the theory that exists, as Lewis put it, in the way that yet-to-be-written poems do. Does CT-materialism+ preserve the spirit and structure of CT-materialism? As before, it certainly seems so.[24]

The third claim of RM.4 is the following:

RM4.c. While CT materialism is false for the reason mentioned in RM4.a, it is also false for another reason—namely, the conceivability argument. By contrast, the substitute thesis mentioned in RM4.b does not face this argument.

The idea behind RM4.c is the same as that behind the counterpart theses in the other versions of Russellian monism. The conceivability argument says that it is conceivable that there be someone identical to me in physical respects but for whom the coffee is less bitter. Are future physical properties included as physical? For reasons analogous to those we have seen already, either answer to this question leaves the conceivability argument unpersuasive.

RM4 Assessed

Once again there are elements here that are not for everyone. Lewis, for example, famously holds that current physics is very nearly complete—that is, that every type of physical truth was known or nearly so, and that every contingent truth follows a priori from physical truths (see, e.g., Lewis 2009, 219n5).

I find optimism of this sort incredible, but I don't want to focus on it here. For there is a more serious problem for RM4, sometimes called the 'structure and dynamics objection'. In Chalmers's canonical formulation, it goes as follows:

First, physical descriptions of the world characterize the world in terms of structure and dynamics. Second, from truths about structure and dynamics, one can deduce only further truths about structure and dynamics. Third, truths about consciousness are not truths about structure and dynamics. (2010, 120)

If these premises are true, CT-materialism+ is no better off with respect to the conceivability argument than CT-materialism. The reason is that both theories will tell us that truths about consciousness are necessitated by truths about structure and dynamics; hence, while we may well for other reasons find CT-materialism+ more plausible than CT-materialism, doing so leaves the issues surrounding the conceivability argument unaffected. Hence, RM4.c, and RM4 itself, should be rejected.

If the structure and dynamics objection is sound, the overall situation looks bleak. The Russellian monist hoped for a theory that is (a) as elegant as materialism but (b) as comprehensive as dualism. But if what I have been saying so far is right, that hope is baseless. In particular, there are four versions of Russellian monism, but all of them are implausible.

As against this, however, if we look harder we will see that the structure and dynamics objection ('SDO', henceforth) is more complicated, and much less plausible, than it appears. Explaining why this is so is the topic of my final section.

Structure and Dynamics Again[25]

Looking over the intellectual achievements of the twentieth century, references to structure are very common. We have (of course) *The Analysis of Matter*, the *Aufbau*, *Syntactic Structures*, *The Structure of Scientific Revolutions*, Lévi-Strauss, and so on. In this century too, references to structure aren't hard to find: structuralism in philosophy of science, Sider on structure and fundamentality, and so forth.[26]

I mention this not to poo-poo structure; that would be silly. But the fact that references to it are ubiquitous should remind us that if a philosopher mentions 'structure' in the course of developing an argument or objection, the first thing we should do is ask what precisely is meant.

What then does 'structure'[27] mean in SDO? One suggestion is in Russell: by 'structure' is meant (mere) *mathematical* structure. But this renders the first premise of SDO quite implausible. Physics does not characterize the world in terms of mere mathematical structure, because characterizations of that sort are mathematical rather than empirical.[28]

Another suggestion is that structure means *metaphysical* structure—that is, a system (any system) of relations (i.e., n-place properties, where $n > 1$). But on this interpretation, the SDO is subject to a number of objections, which I have set out in detail elsewhere (Stoljar 2006, 2009a). First, on this interpretation, the first premise says that physics tells us only about relational truths. But that is implausible at least if it is a thesis about physics as such—surely physics can and does tell about the one-place properties of the systems it studies? Second, it is false that from truths about relations you can only derive more truths about relations. For example, from the fact that a series of points in space are arranged in a particular way, you might derive the fact that that the region constituted by the points has a particular shape. Third, it is false that no truth about consciousness is a truth about relations, for some truths about consciousness are themselves relational.

Derk Pereboom (2011, 102, 112; see also Alter and Nagasawa 2012) has responded to these points by describing the notion of an absolutely intrinsic property, which is (roughly) a property that is (a) nonrelational and (b) is not (a priori) derivable from any relational set of facts. In particular, Pereboom says, truths about absolutely intrinsic properties are not derivable from truths about relations, and so the second premise of the SDO is true if it is read as saying that from truths about relations you may derive only truths that do not concern absolutely intrinsic or nonrelational properties.

I agree that if you understand the premise that way, it is true; indeed, on this interpretation it is analytic as Pereboom points out (2011, 113). But the key question is whether this helps the polemic purposes of a proponent of the SDO. And it is clear that it does not. For the only way in which this could help the argument is if the third premise were interpreted now as saying that the truths about consciousness are or include truths about absolutely intrinsic properties. But this is highly questionable. There is certainly some intuitive basis to the idea that truths about consciousness concern nonrelational or intrinsic properties, but whether they concern absolutely nonrelational or intrinsic properties seems to me something that is left open by anything we know or believe about consciousness, either as a matter of theory or as a matter of introspection.

David Chalmers has responded to these criticisms by accepting them so far as they go but suggesting that they miss their target (2010, 210n18). What he has in mind by 'structure' is neither mathematical nor metaphysical structure, but rather spatiotemporal and nomic structure: "formally, a structural-dynamic description is one that is equivalent to a Ramsey sentence whose O-terms are limited to spatiotemporal expressions, nomic expressions, and mathematical and logical expressions." Of course, we have looked at this idea already, during the examination of RM3. We criticized it in that context for being either too open ended or as entailing objectionably that physics does not tell us about the causes of our experiences—at least given Chalmers's suggestion that spatiotemporal expressions pick out whatever properties are the causal basis of the manifold of spatiotemporal experiences. Something similar is true when we consider it in the context of SDO. In particular, if we interpret this view as entailing that the properties that cause our experiences are physical, a proponent of RM4 will deny the third premise of the SDO: "we don't know currently what those properties are," he will say, "so we are in no position to assert that no truth about consciousness is a truth about them." On the other hand, if we interpret this view as supposing that physics tells us only about the properties of having some properties that cause experiences, the proponent of RM4 will deny the first premise of SDO: "surely physics can tell us about the causes of our experience," he will say, "so physics does not characterize the world merely in terms structure and dynamics in the relevant sense."

In sum, if by 'structure' one means either mathematical, metaphysical, or nomic and spatiotemporal structure, SDO is unpersuasive, and RM4 emerges as the most promising version of Russellian monism. Still, one might wonder in closing whether there is a slightly different objection lying behind these animadversions about structure. This objection is that RM4 is not a genuine sort of Russellian monism, not because of structure and dynamics, but because it does not use key metaphysical ideas that each of RM1–3 uses. In particular, RM4 makes no theoretical use of the dispositional/nondispositional distinction of RM1, the role/realizer distinction of RM2, and the structural/nonstructural distinction of RM3.[29]

Actually, I have some sympathies with this. RM4 *is* different in this way from the other versions; and in other places, I have treated Russellian monism as a specific version of RM4, rather than the other way around (see Stoljar 2006).[30] Nevertheless, there are two points to make. First, in view of the elusiveness of terms like 'structure' and so forth, it is unclear that one can use them to mark any natural division between RM1–3, on the one hand, and RM4 on the other. Second, even supposing there is a difference in this respect between RM4 and RM1–3, there remains an important similarity—namely, their common strategy for answering the conceivability argument. So perhaps our conclusion should be this: RM4 might not (*might not*) be a version of Russellian monism, but it remains the closest thing that is plausible.

Notes

* I am very much indebted to the following for their help: Torin Alter, David Chalmers, Uriah Kriegel, Leon Leontyev, Derk Pereboom, and Jon Simon.

1. As far as I can make out, the first explicit occurrence of the name 'Russellian Monism' is in Chalmers (1999). It is now used widely (see, e.g., Chalmers 2010; Pereboom 2011; Alter and Nagasawa 2012, forthcoming) and has its own entry on PhilPapers: http://philpapers.org/browse/russellian-monism. Similar names names include (at least) "The Russellian Identity Theory" (Lockwood 1989, chap. 10), "the Russellian View" (Chalmers 1996), "The Russellian theory of Mind" (Holman 2008), "Russellian Physicalism" (Montero 2010), and the considerably more prosaic "o-physicalism" (Stoljar 2001) and "the Russellian version of the epistemic view" (Stoljar 2006).

2. For statements of materialism (aka physicalism) of this sort, see Stoljar (2010). The definition used in the text is a simple one; for example, it takes for granted exactly what metaphysical necessitation is. I will set aside such complications here.

3. There is a very big literature on what 'conceivability' means; we will not go into the details here. (You will not go too far wrong if you read 'it is conceivable that' as 'it seems possible that'.) For some recent discussion, see Chalmers (2010) and Pereboom (2011).

4. See, for example, Chalmers (2010) and Pereboom (2011).

5. Of course there is no a priori guarantee that the world is such that a theory of this sort is true, or that we can formulate the theory even if it is. The hope rather is that there is no philosophical objection to there being such a theory, where a 'philosophical objection' in this context is, roughly, an objection to the existence of such a theory that can be made in advance of formulating it.

6. Since Locke's essay was published in 1689, the historical issues are difficult, and I won't address them here. The point is to take from Locke (and to take from those who take from Locke) ideas that can then be used to formulate a version of RM. Among those who take from Locke, I have in mind mainly Armstrong (1961, esp. chap. 15) here, but see also Armstrong (1968), Foster (1982), and Blackburn (1990). Langton (1998) describes a somewhat similar position in the course of defending an interpretation of Kant.

7. Nota bene: in this section my aim is to provide an *exposition* of RM1 and the arguments for it (ditto for parallel sections about RM2–4). Assessment will come later.

8. See, for example, the papers in Handfield (2009).

9. In the passage quoted, Armstrong apparently treats the possibility of relations and dispositions in the same way. I think to the contrary they are very different, since relations are properties that are instantiated by more than one thing, while dispositions are a particular sort of property or relation (i.e., ones that involve modality in a very distinctive way). But I will set this issue aside here.

10. I will assume in the text that the natural response to the empirical inadequacy of RM1 is to adopt one of RM2–4. But it is worth mentioning another idea that sometimes comes up at this point—namely, that one's knowledge of physical objects at the end of the day depends on our causal interaction with them, and that in consequence one cannot know the intrinsic nature of these objects. For ideas along these lines, see Jackson (1998) and Langton (1998). I will not try to assess that idea here, beyond mentioning three points: first, these suggestions are subject to the prima facie difficulty that a causal explanation for our knowledge of physical objects does not by itself tell us much about the content or limits of that knowledge; second, it is plausible that suggestions along these lines will resolve themselves into a position akin to RM2–4 (indeed, I read Lewis's comments at the beginning of "Ramseyan Humility" as suggesting that that paper represents the best way to make sense of the causal argument); and third, I am in any case sympathetic with the existing critical discussion of this idea in the literature—I have in mind in particular Van Cleve (2002) and Pereboom (2011).

11. Lewis himself did not defend Russellian monism, it is rather that the materials he describes can be used to formulate a version of that view.

12. The definitions here are intended by Lewis as reductive definitions along the lines of 'x is a bachelor if and only if x is an adult unmarried male' (assuming that *is* a reductive definition of course).

13. Why are physical properties those *expressed* by a predicate of the final theory rather than those *named* by a term of that theory? The answer is that only then will knowledge of the theory tell us exactly what the properties are—indeed, this point is prominent in the reasoning from Lewis that I am about to set out.

14. For discussion of Lewis on quidditism and related matters, see D. Locke (2009, forthcoming, and the references therein).

15. For a discussion to the thicker notion of quiddity, see Chalmers (2012, 350), who introduced the phrase 'thick quiddity'.

16. As Chalmers pointed out to me in discussion, one might argue here that the thick quiddity here is part of Lewis's final theory but is not part of physics. This is a possibility, but in the framework of this chapter, the suggestion moves us away from RM2 and toward RM3. For one thing, as a matter of stipulation, RM2 requires, while RM3 does not, identification of the final theory and physics. Moreover, to implement the suggestion there must be some way to discriminate physics from the final theory; RM3 (as we will see) has such a way, while RM2 does not.

17. As in the case of Locke, there are serious issues of interpretation here, but I will mostly ignore them. For discussion of Russell, see Demopoulos and Freidman (1985) and, more recently, Chalmers (2012).

18. That Russell's claim here is not empirical is consistent with what I take to be an obvious fact—namely, that *The Analysis of Matter* is motivated by developments within physics.

19. One might wonder why for Russell the hypotheses of physics are causal, in addition to structural. The answer comes in passages like this, in which it is clear that for him to say that a hypothesis is causal says something about the way it is used rather than about its subject

matter: "There is a causal relation whenever two events, or two groups of events . . . are related by a law which allows something to be inferred about the one from the other" (1927, 369).

20. This sort of argument is in Lewis (1995); for discussion, see Stoljar (2009b).
21. I am very much indebted to a discussion with David Chalmers here. It should be noted that my discussion in the text greatly simplifies the account of spatial expressions presented in Chalmers (2012); in particular, it does not discuss the distinction between concepts and properties. I will not try to deal with this issue here, however.
22. Since Chalmers explains spatiotemporal expressions in terms of experiential expressions, there is the further worry that his version of RM3, like Russell's, is committed to dualism anyway. I will not try to press that concern here.
23. This passage is quoted in Pereboom's (2011, 116) recent discussion of Russellian monism; indeed, it was reading Pereboom that brought this passage to my attention. For a reason I mention in the last two paragraphs of the chapter, is not quite clear to me that Nagel is endorsing Russellian monism here, but there is no doubt he is endorsing something similar. Nagel (2000) expresses some sympathy for a Russellian view.
24. Is CT-materialism+ the same thesis as either FT-materialism or FT-materialism+? If the proponent of RM4 accepts the presuppositions of the proponent of RM2, the answer would appear to be 'yes', though I will not assume here that these presuppositions are shared.
25. 'Again' because I have discussed this objection twice before; see Stoljar (2006, 2009a).
26. I will leave it as an exercise for the reader to chase down the references mentioned in this paragraph.
27. The concept of dynamics is simply the concept of something changing its structure over time, so what we say will apply here pari passu.
28. This point is very closely related to a famous objection to Russell made in Newman (1928) according to which (very roughly) he confuses physics and mathematics. See Demopolous and Friedman (1985) and Chalmers (2012).
29. This point is reflected in an influential taxonomy of positions set out in Chalmers (2010). Chalmers would, I think, classify RM4 as a version of materialism—type-C materialism, in particular—and would set it aside from genuine Russellian monism, which would be classified as type-F monism.
30. In his contribution to this volume, Derk Pereboom suggests a different way to respond to this objection—that is, to advance a version of RM4 that requires that the properties of which are ignorant are absolutely intrinsic. I have no objection to the idea that this *might* be true (the version of RM4 I discuss in the text permits it), but I am unconvinced by Pereboom's suggestion that it *must* be. For one thing, Pereboom's argument for this point apparently relies on the idea sometimes called 'revelation'—and this is an idea I have been critical of elsewhere (see Stoljar 2009a). But more generally, consider again Nagel's suggestion that the relation of consciousness to the physical might be like the relation of the mechanical to the electrical. It is very doubtful that the notion of an absolutely intrinsic property played a crucial role in the complicated empirical process that resulted in the unification of the mechanical and the electrical—why then suppose that it must play a role in an analogous process (as yet not undergone) that concerns consciousness?

References

Alter, T., and Y. Nagasawa. 2012. "What Is Russellian Monism?" *Journal of Consciousness Studies* 19 (9–10): 67–95.

Alter, T., and Y. Nagasawa, eds. Forthcoming. *Russellian Monism.* New York; Oxford University Press.

Armstrong, D. M. 1961. *Perception and the Physical World.* London: Routledge.

Armstrong, D. M. 1968. *A Materialist Theory of Mind.* London: Routledge.

Blackburn, S. 1990. "Filling in Space." *Analysis* 50: 62–65.

Chalmers, D. 1996. *The Conscious Mind.* New York: Oxford University Press.

Chalmers, D. 1999 "Précis of *The Conscious Mind*." *Philosophy and Phenomenological Research* 59 (2): 435–438.

Chalmers, D. 2010. *The Character of Consciousness.* New York: Oxford University Press.

Chalmers, D. 2012. *Constructing the World.* Oxford: Oxford University Press.

Demopoulos, W., and M. Friedman. 1985. "Critical Notice: Bertrand Russell's *The Analysis of Matter*: Its Historical Context and Contemporary Interest." *Philosophy of Science* 52: 621–639.

Feigl, H. 1967. *The "Mental" and the "Physical."* Minneapolis: University of Minnesota Press. (Original publication 1956.)

Foster, J. 1982. *The Case for Idealism.* London: Routledge.

Jackson, F. 1998. *From Metaphysics to Ethics: A Defense of Conceptual Analysis* Oxford: Oxford University Press

Handfield, T., ed. 2009. *Dispositions and Causes.* Oxford: Clarendon Press.

Holman, E. 2008. "Panpsychism, Physicalism, Neutral Monism and the Russellian Theory of Mind." *Journal of Consciousness Studies* 15 (5): 48–67.

Langton, R. 1998. *Kantian Humility.* Oxford: Oxford University Press.

Lewis, D. 1995. "Should a Materialist Believe in Qualia?" *Australasian Journal of Philosophy* 73: 140–144.

Lewis, D. 2009. "Ramseyan Humility." In *Conceptual Analysis and Philosophical Naturalism*, ed. David Braddon-Mitchell and Robert Nola, 203–222. Cambridge, MA: MIT Press.

Locke, D. 2009. "A Partial Defense of Ramseyan Humility." In *Conceptual Analysis and Philosophical Naturalism*, ed. David Braddon-Mitchell and Robert Nola, 223–241. Cambridge, MA: MIT Press.

Locke, D. Forthcoming. "Quidditism without Quiddities." *Philosophical Studies.* Available at: http://www.cmc.edu/pages/faculty/dlocke/Quidditism%20without%20Quiddities.pdf

Locke, J. 1975. *An Essay Concerning Human Understanding*, ed. P. H. Nidditch. Oxford: Oxford University Press.

Lockwood, M. 1989. *Mind, Brain and the Quantum.* Oxford: Blackwell.

Montero, B. 2010. "A Russellian Response to the Structural Argument against Physicalism." *Journal of Consciousness Studies* 17 (3–4): 70–83.

Nagel, T. 1986. *The View from Nowhere.* New York: Oxford University Press.

Nagel, T. 2000. "The Psychophysical Nexus." In *New Essays on the A Priori*, ed. Paul Boghossian and Christopher Peacocke, 432–471. Oxford: Clarendon Press.

Newman, M. H. A. 1928. "Mr Russell's Causal Theory of Perception." *Mind* 37: 137–148.

Pereboom, D. 2011. *Consciousness and the Prospects of Physicalism.* New York: Oxford University Press.

Russell, B. 1927. *The Analysis of Matter.* London: Kegan Paul.

Smart, J. J. C. 1959. "Sensations and Brain Processes." *Philosophical Review* 68: 141–156.

Stoljar, D. 2001. "Two Conceptions of the Physical." *Philosophy and Phenomenological Research* 62 (2): 253–281.

Stoljar, D. 2006. *Ignorance and Imagination: The Epistemic Origin of the Problem of Consciousness* New York: Oxford University Press.

Stoljar, D. 2009a. "The Argument from Revelation." In *Conceptual Analysis and Philosophical Naturalism*, ed. David Braddon-Mitchell and Robert Nola, 113–138. Cambridge, MA: MIT Press.

Stoljar, D. 2009b. "Reply to Alter and Bennett." *Philosophy and Phenomenological Research* 79 (3): 775–784.

Stoljar, D. 2010. *Physicalism.* London: Routledge.

Stubenberg, L. 1997. "Austria versus Australia: Two Versions of the Identity Theory." In *Austrian Philosophy Past and Present: Essays in Honour of Rudolf Haller*, ed. K. Lehrer and J. Mare, 125–146. Dordrecht: Kluwer.

Van Cleve, J. 2002. "Receptivity and Our Knowledge of Intrinsic Properties." *Philosophy and Phenomenological Research* 65: 218–237.

CHAPTER 2

Russellian Monism and Absolutely Intrinsic Properties

DERK PEREBOOM

Chapter Overview

According to Russellian monism, both consciousness and the microphysical properties encountered in current physics are grounded in underlying fundamental features of a single kind. We currently lack knowledge of such fundamental features. On some versions of the view, these yet undiscovered properties are mental, while on others they are close enough in kind to our paradigmatic physical properties to count as physical. I set out a Russellian monism of the second sort. What distinguishes my formulation from others is that in mine these currently unknown properties are not only categorical but also intrinsic in a certain demanding sense: they are not reducible to or constituted by purely extrinsic properties. Following Kant, I call them *absolutely intrinsic properties*. Here I also defend this view against objections raised by Daniel Stoljar in the previous chapter.

Russellian Monism

It's at least initially reasonable to conjecture that consciousness is not a fundamental phenomenon, and that there are more fundamental features of reality that underlie and explain it. Current physics encourages the hypothesis that the fundamental features of reality are physical; candidates include particles, forces, and quantum fields. But there are serious considerations, such as the conceivability argument (explained subsequently) that count against the view that anything physical of the sort we now understand can account for consciousness. This situation gives rise to the thought that the account must consist at least in part in presently unknown fundamental features of reality.

Add to this that the history of philosophy has witnessed a strong predilection for ontological monism—that is, for thinking that the world has fundamental features only of a single sort (materialism and idealism are cases in point). These motivations give rise to a proposal in which not only consciousness but also the kinds of physical features encountered in current physics are grounded in fundamental features of a single sort. This view is known as Russellian monism, named for one of its proponents, Bertrand Russell.[1]

One specific Russellian monist proposal involves the notions of dispositional and categorical properties. Dispositional properties are essentially tendencies to produce certain effects, and while categorical properties may have powers to produce effects, they are not essentially tendencies to produce them. Fragility and flammability are clear examples of dispositional properties; shape and size are often cited as paradigmatic categorical properties. Many find it intuitive that categorical properties are required to account for dispositional properties; for instance, a ball's disposition to roll requires an explanation, and it is explained by its categorical properties of spherical shape and rigidity.[2] The more specific Russellian monist proposal then is this: the most basic properties current physics reveals are all dispositional, while it leaves us ignorant of the categorical properties needed to explain them, and these unknown categorical properties account for consciousness. An electron's negative charge, for instance, is one of those basic physical properties, and it is a disposition to repel other particles with negative charge and to attract particles with positive charge. This dispositional property must have a categorical basis, and it, the Russellian monist hypothesizes, is the kind of property that can also account for consciousness. Russellian monists have proposed a range of such more fundamental but yet undiscovered properties—from conscious properties, of, for instance, microphysical particles, to properties similar enough to paradigmatic physical properties to qualify as physical themselves, to properties unlike any we've encountered, but capable of explaining consciousness.[3]

The version of Russellian monism that I set out in *Consciousness and the Prospects of Physicalism*[4] is subtype of Daniel Stoljar's (this volume, Chapter 1) RM4, according to which the yet-to-be discovered properties crucial to explaining consciousness are of the second sort, close enough in kind to our paradigmatic physical properties to count as physical. What distinguishes my version of RM4 from the one Stoljar favors is that these currently unknown properties are not only categorical but also intrinsic—that is, nonrelational—in a certain demanding sense. In what follows, I explain my proposal and defend it against the objections Stoljar raises.[5]

Stoljar on Russellian Monism

On Stoljar's account, RM4 is inspired by the following thoughts. First of all, it's highly plausible that our current scientific theories are significantly incomplete, in particular in accounting for consciousness. At the same time, we may reasonably hold out the hope that there is available a theory according to which the relation of consciousness to matter is relevantly analogous to the relation between temperature in a gas and the kinetic energy of the gas molecules. That is, just as the kinetic energy of these molecules provides a good scientific explanation of what temperature in a gas is, so properties of matter will eventually yield a satisfying explanation of what consciousness is. Stoljar's formulation of RM4 proper begins with a notion of a physical property as one expressed by a predicate of our total current scientific theory, such as 'electron' and 'gravitational force.' The resulting version of materialism is 'current-theory materialism' or 'CT-materialism' for short. CT-materialism is true at a possible world w just in case for every property G instantiated at w, there is some current-theory property (or complex of current-theory properties) F instantiated at w such that F metaphysically necessitates G. RM4 then features three distinctive claims about CT-materialism. First, because it's difficult to deny that our current materialist theory is incomplete,

> RM4a. CT-materialism is false, and false for reasons quite distinct from those involved in the conceivability argument.

But there is a more complete descendent of CT-materialism:

> RM4b. While CT-materialism is false for the reason mentioned in RM4a, there is a substitute thesis that is not false for that reason and that preserves the spirit and structure of CT-materialism.

The substitute thesis—'CT-materialism+'—is exactly like CT-materialism, except that while in CT-materialism the physical properties are those expressed by predicates of the current theory, in CT-materialism+ the physical properties are either those expressed by such predicates or those expressed by the final theory. Unlike CT-materialism, CT-materialism+ explains consciousness:

> RM4c. While CT materialism is false for the reason mentioned in RM1a, it is also false for another reason—namely, the conceivability argument. By contrast, the substitute thesis mentioned in RM1b does not face this argument.

The core idea of RM4 is that as a proposal for a complete theory, CT-materialism+ is not undercut by the conceivability argument and can account for consciousness.

Russellian Monism and Chalmers's Conceivability Argument

What reason do we have to believe that the kinds of physical properties revealed by current physical theory cannot account for consciousness? Historically, the most prominent justification for antiphysicalist views of this sort is provided conceivability arguments against physicalism. Conceivability arguments, advanced by René Descartes and more recently by Saul Kripke and David Chalmers, propose first that certain mental truths can be conceived absent relevant physical truths or that the relevant physical truths can be conceived without certain mental truths, then derive from this that such situations are metaphysically possible, and conclude that physicalism is false.[6] The argument assumes that if physicalism is true, the complete physical truth will metaphysically necessitate all the mental truths, and this assumption is generally accepted by all parties. Thus, if the conceived situations are indeed shown to be metaphysically possible, it will be generally accepted that physicalism is false.

Chalmers's influential version is sometimes called the zombie argument. It focuses on the phenomenal aspect of consciousness, the paradigm case of which is a subject's being in a sensory state, such as sensing red, where there is something it is like for that subject to be in that state.[7] In short, Chalmers's argument hinges on the claim that it is conceivable, in an appropriately sophisticated way, that a world that is (nothing but) an exact physical duplicate of the actual world features no phenomenal consciousness—in other words, that a zombie world is conceivable. From this premise, the argument reasons to the conclusion that the complete physical truth does not necessitate the complete phenomenal truth, or even any phenomenal truth, and that therefore physicalism is false. But a notable feature of Chalmers's version of the argument is that it allows for Russellian monism as a potential escape from its antiphysicalist conclusion, and consequently, this version is especially pertinent to our discussion.

A factor that gives rise to complexity in Chalmers's argument is that not all conceivable scenarios are metaphysically possible. Sometimes a subject can conceive a scenario only because he is deficient in reasoning, as when someone conceives of a right triangle the square of whose hypotenuse is not equal to the sum of the squares of each of the two sides.[8] Conceiving is then less than ideal. Or else, as Saul Kripke contended, at times what is really being conceived is mischaracterized—for instance, when someone reports that she is conceiving of water that is not H_2O but is really conceiving of something that merely appears to be water or only has the evident causal role water has in our world. Chalmers's aim is to ensure that none of the available ways of explaining how deficiency in conceivability fails to establish metaphysical possibility applies to the conceivability of a physical duplicate of the actual world absent phenomenal consciousness, and that it therefore sustains valid reasoning to the conclusion that a zombie world is metaphysically possible or Russelian monism is true.

Chalmers's argument employs the following elements: (i) 'P,' the complete physical truth. (ii) 'P' is supplemented with 'T,' a 'that's all' provision, so that 'PT' enumerates all the physical truths about the actual world with the specification that there are no further truths—that is, other than those entailed by those physical truths.[9] (iii) 'Q' is an actual phenomenal truth—we might imagine that it is *Mary senses red at time t*. The argument begins with the premise that 'PT' conjoined with the negation of 'Q' is conceivable in a very strong sense—it is ideally, positively, primarily conceivable. Chalmers distinguishes several dimensions of conceivability: prima facie versus *ideal, positive* versus *negative*, and *primary* versus *secondary*.[10] First, a statement or proposition S is prima facie conceivable when S is conceivable on first appearance, and it is ideally conceivable when it is conceivable on ideal rational reflection. To spell out 'conceivable on ideal rational reflection,' Chalmers suggests: "S is ideally conceivable when there is a possible subject for whom S is prima facie conceivable, with justification that is undefeatable by better reasoning."[11] Next, S is negatively conceivable when one cannot rule S out. Thus, S is ideally negatively conceivable when one cannot prima facie rule S out, but with justification that is undefeatable by means of possible better reasoning.[12] Positive conceivability is hard to characterize, but a core variety involves being able to form, by imagination, a mental picture of a situation in which S is true.[13]

Primary and secondary conceivability are less familiar notions. In Chalmers's view, one way to think about a possible world is as a kind of epistemic possibility—that is, as the way the world might actually turn out to be, given what we can know a priori. When we do this, we consider that possible world as actual. So then, S is possible in this sense just in case S is true in a world considered as actual.[14] For example, when one considers as actual a world in which all the 'water' samples are not H_2O but XYZ instead, then 'water = XYZ' is true in that world, and consequently, 'water $\neq H_2O$' is primarily possible. The term *considering as actual* is linked to Chalmers's idea that to determine whether a statement S is primarily possible, one can evaluate indicative conditionals of the form 'If possible world W *is* actual, then S.' In the case of the XYZ world, the indicative conditional 'if the XYZ world is actual, then water $\neq H_2O$' comes out true, and thus the 'water $\neq H_2O$' is primarily possible.

One might by contrast *consider a world W as counterfactual*. One then holds the nature of the actual world fixed and thinks of W as a way things might have been. If one thinks of the XYZ world in this way, then at the XYZ world 'water = XYZ' and 'water $\neq H_2O$' turn out to be false. In Chalmers's framework, S is *secondarily possible* just in case S is true in some world considered as counterfactual. Accordingly, 'water $\neq H_2O$' is primarily possible, but not secondarily possible. Secondary possibility is what is more commonly known as metaphysical possibility. The term *considering as counterfactual* derives from Chalmers's proposal that to determine whether a statement S is possible in this sense, one can evaluate subjunctive conditionals of the form 'if possible world W *were* actual, then S.' One might resist the idea that conditionals of this sort can have an important role in determining this kind of possibility and claim instead that the salient test involves holding an appropriate aspect of S fixed—perhaps what is expressed by S in the actual world, or the proposition expressed by S in the actual world—and then to evaluate whether there is some W in which this is true.[15]

These two notions of possibility yield characterizations of primary and secondary conceivability. Retaining Chalmers's preferred ways of construing these notions, S is primarily conceivable just in case S can be conceived as true in some world considered as actual, and S is secondarily conceivable just in case S can be conceived as true in some world considered as counterfactual.

Chalmers then sets out his argument as follows:

(1) 'PT and ~ Q' is ideally, positively, primarily conceivable.
(2) If 'PT and ~ Q' is ideally, positively, primarily conceivable, then 'PT and ~ Q' is primarily possible.
(3) If 'PT and ~ Q' is primarily possible, then 'PT and ~ Q' is secondarily possible or Russellian monism is true.
(4) If 'PT and ~ Q' is secondarily possible, materialism is false.
(5) Materialism is false or Russellian monism is true.[16]

(From here on, I'll often, like Chalmers, assume the 'that's all there is' condition 'T' while not explicitly indicating it.) In premise (1), Chalmers specifies that 'P and ~ Q' is ideally, primarily, and not only negatively but also positively conceivable. If one's initial thought is that 'P and ~ Q' can be ruled out a priori, one's justification for this can be defeated by better reasoning, reasoning that in this context must be a priori, because primary conceivability is at issue; and what's more, one can form a positive conception of a scenario in which 'P and ~ Q' is true. Exactly what information is included in 'P'? Chalmers favors a microphysical option, 'P' features complete microphysical information, including information about microphysical laws, but nothing more. Significantly, the microphysical information is about the kinds of entities featured in current physics—this will be relevant for the Russellian monist escape route.

Rejecting premise (1), in Chalmers's conception, involves claiming that an ideal reasoner could derive a priori the arbitrarily selected actual phenomenal truth 'Q' from 'P,' supposing she has the minimal information required to ensure adequate possession of the phenomenal concepts involved in representing 'Q.' He argues that it is strongly intuitive that this claim is false. By contrast, in his view a truth like 'water exists' can be derived a priori from 'P,' and thus 'P and there is no water' will not be ideally, positively, primarily conceivable. Indeed, given the complete microphysical conception of the actual world, together with the minimum phenomenal conceptual information, the falsity of 'Q' would not appear to be ruled out, no matter how much better one's reasoning about that conception became—by contrast with the falsity 'there is no water.'

Chalmers then defends Premise (2): if 'P and ~ Q' is ideally, positively, and primarily conceivable, then 'P and ~ Q' is primarily possible; that is, it is true in a world considered as actual—there is a metaphysically possible world W, such that if W is actual, then 'P and ~ Q' is true. Denying Premise 2 is tantamount to endorsing what he calls a *strong necessity*: "a statement that is falsified by some positively conceivable situation (considered as actual), but which is nevertheless true in all possible worlds (considered as actual)."[17] Chalmers contends that it is advantageous to affirm the entailment from ideal, positive, primary conceivability to primary possibility, because on the hypothesis that there are instances where this entailment fails, there would in these cases be no explanation of why primary conceivability does not entail primary possibility. If a statement were ideally, positively, primarily conceivably false and yet true in all worlds considered as actual, there would be no way to explain the resulting mismatch between conceivability and possibility. Chalmers argues that there are also no convincing counterexamples to the thesis that ideal, positive, primary conceivability entails primary possibility—that there are no convincing examples of strong necessities.[18]

The next step in this argument is as follows:

> Premise (3): If 'PT and ~ Q' is primarily possible, then either 'PT and ~ Q' is secondarily possible or Russellian monism is true.

For Chalmers, this claim is equivalent to the following:

> If 'P and ~ Q' is true in a world considered as actual, then either 'P and ~ Q' is true in a world considered as counterfactual or Russellian monism is true.

To understand this premise, it helps to see, as Chalmers indicates, that his conceivability argument formalizes certain features of Kripke's antiphysicalist argument in *Naming and Necessity*.[19] Kripke contends that identity claims involving natural kind terms, such as 'water = H_2O,' are necessarily true if true, with the consequence that showing that such a claim is contingent is enough to establish that it is false. But it appears conceivable, or seems possible, that water not be H_2O, which suggests that 'water = H_2O' is in fact contingent and therefore false. However, in Kripke's account, this does not pose a successful challenge to the claim that water = H_2O, because in this case the claim's apparent contingency can be explained away. What one is really conceiving is a liquid that is not H_2O, but whose appearance is like water's, or the ordinary, nonscientific qualitative evidence for whose nature is the same as our ordinary qualitative evidence for the nature of water, and this is compatible with water nevertheless being identical to H_2O.

In Chalmers's theoretical framework, the failure of this type of challenge to the claim that water = H_2O is accounted for by the fact that the statement 'water $\neq H_2O$' is ideally primarily conceivable and primarily possible but not ideally secondarily conceivable or secondarily possible. 'Water ≠ H_2O' is conceivable as true, and is in fact true, in a possible world considered as actual—in the XYZ world, for example. But at no possible world considered as counterfactual is this claim true; there is no possible world in which it is compatible with both the a priori and the a posteriori truths in that world. Even though there is a world considered as actual in which 'water = H_2O' is false—and this fact ultimately explains our intuition that this statement is contingent—at no world considered as counterfactual is it false, and this explains why the contingency is merely apparent.

Kripke argued that, by contrast, the apparent contingency of 'pain = C-fiber firing' cannot similarly be explained away, because any state that seems to be pain is in fact pain. Making a similar point about consciousness more generally, Chalmers contends that if 'there is consciousness' is true in world W considered as actual, then in W considered as counterfactual 'there is consciousness' is true, and vice versa; if 'there is consciousness' is true in W considered as actual, then "it contains something that at least *feels* conscious, and if something *feels* conscious, then it *is* conscious."[20] But Chalmers does not want to rest his case solely on the relationship between how things seem or feel and how things are. In his discussion of what he labels *pure phenomenal concepts*, he makes a claim crucial to the way he prefers to develop his conceivability argument. A pure phenomenal concept "characterizes the phenomenal quality as the phenomenal quality it is."[21] Such a concept will be *epistemically rigid*:

> It picks out the same referent in every epistemically possible scenario (considered as actual). By contrast, ordinary rigid concepts are merely subjunctively rigid, picking out the same referent in every possible scenario (considered as counterfactual).[22]

The related semantic notion is the following:

> Concept C is *primarily rigid* just in case C has the same referent in every possible world considered as actual.[23]

Chalmers affirms that unlike the concept 'water,' a pure phenomenal concept refers to the same entity, in this case to the same phenomenal property, in every scenario not ruled out a priori. By contrast, the concept 'water' is not primarily rigid, because there are correct applications of the term *water* in scenarios not ruled out a priori in which it does not refer to H_2O—for instance, in the XYZ world. For this reason there will be worlds considered as actual in which 'water' fails to refer to H_2O. By extension, statements and propositions can be primarily rigid by having the same truth value in every world considered as actual. It would follow from the primary rigidity of phenomenal concepts that they are also secondarily rigid; that is, they pick out the same property in every world considered as counterfactual.

Setting aside its Russellian monist component for just a moment, Premise (3) states that if 'P and ~ Q' is primarily possible, it is also secondarily possible. Crucial to the argument for this premise is the claim that 'Q'—and for now we are assuming 'P'—is primarily rigid. Then, in any world considered as actual in which 'P and ~ Q' is true, it will also be true in that world considered as counterfactual, which is to say that it would be secondarily possible.[24] Premise (3) would thus be true as a matter of the logic of primary rigidity. If (3) is in fact false, it would have to be because primary rigidity is incorrectly attributed to some relevant concept or statement.

The Russellian Monist Escape

Now suppose we agree with Chalmers that Russellian monism provides a potential escape from the argument's antiphysicalist conclusion. In this spirit, Stoljar's RM4 affirms that if the specification of 'P' is limited by the resources of CT, 'P and ~ Q' will be conceivable in the relevant strong sense, but this does not show that materialism is false. If 'P' were replaced with a 'P*,' embellished by the new resources of CT+, the resulting 'P* and ~ Q' would no longer be ideally, positively, primarily conceivable. The idea is that the failure of the ideal, positive, primary conceivability of 'P* and it is not the case that Mary senses red at time t' (we're assuming that Mary does in fact sense red at time t) would be on a par with the failure of the ideal, positive, primary conceivability of 'P and there is no water.'

The main objection to RM4 that Stoljar vets is this: because the new theory is still a form of materialism, it yields no advantage over CT-materialism in answering the conceivability argument and in accounting for consciousness. The main support for this objection is the argument that all physical truths are *structural* truths, which are plausibly construed as truths about relational or extrinsic properties. By contrast, the core truths about phenomenal properties are nonstructural, for, intuitively, phenomenal properties are intrinsic and nonrelational properties of experiences. Because from structural truths only structural truths are derivable, the nonstructural truths about consciousness will not be derivable even from the enhanced physical base. The proposal that all physical truths are truths about relational properties is connected with the claim that all fundamental physical truths are truths about dispositional properties. Dispositional properties can plausibly be construed as relations to effects. For an electron to have the dispositional property of being negatively charged is for it to stand in potential attraction and repulsion relations to other particles. On this hypothesis, if the most fundamental physical properties are dispositional, they will also be relational. And if all the most basic physical properties are relational, then it would seem that in some sense all physical properties are relational, or, equivalently, structural.

I agree with several of the points Stoljar makes in reply: current physics does not tell us just about relational truths—the size and shape of molecules are intrinsic to them, and physics tells us about such properties; from truths about relations one can derive truths about intrinsic properties—for example, from truth relations among points in space, one can derive that the region constituted by the points has a particular shape; and some truths about consciousness are truths about relations—for instance, some pains are more intense than other pains. But a worry about Stoljar's version of RM4 is that it proposes that the discovery of properties not especially different in metaphysical kind from the properties of current physics will yield the requisite account of consciousness. Thus, an objection to Stoljar's version is that it appears not to address the concern that motivates Russellian monism in the first place.

This concern is not initially a clear one, but it can be expressed as follows. Current physics does tell us about intrinsic properties, but it does not reveal properties that are intrinsic in a relevantly more demanding sense. While truths about intrinsic properties can indeed be derived from truths about relational properties, truths about properties that are intrinsic in the more demanding sense cannot be derived solely from truths about properties that are completely relational. I will explain and defend these claims in the next section. Crucially, phenomenal consciousness features intrinsic properties of this more demanding sort, and they will resist any account restricted to current physics. Stoljar thinks that the claim that consciousness features intrinsic properties in this more demanding sense can reasonably be doubted, and I agree. But this claim's being subject to reasonable doubt is compatible with its nevertheless being highly plausible and, more importantly, with its giving rise to the nonphysicalist intuition about consciousness. This is what I will subsequently argue. Finally, I will canvas various proposals for what these intrinsic properties might be like and evaluate them in accord with Russellian monist standards for success.

Absolutely Intrinsic Properties

Let me now outline the version of Russellian monism I develop in *Consciousness and the Prospects of Physicalism*. It's a historical story that begins with Leibniz and features the contrast between intrinsic/nonrelational and extrinsic/relational properties.[25] Leibniz contends that a conception of the physical world that does not include intrinsic properties of a certain fundamental sort is in an important sense incomplete.[26] In his view, an examination of Descartes's theory of matter, on which the essence of matter is just extension in three spatial dimensions, reveals why this is so.[27] Leibniz argues that this theory is unsatisfying for the reason that extension is in an important sense an extrinsic property, and that any real thing cannot feature only properties that are extrinsic in this way, but must possess intrinsic properties as well: "there is no denomination so extrinsic that it does not have an intrinsic denomination at its basis. This is itself one of my important doctrines."[28]

Leibniz's criticism suggests first of all that in his view properties can be more and less extrinsic. To spell this out, note that it's plausible that extrinsic properties can have intrinsic components. For example, *being wise* is an extrinsic property of Sophie because it involves a relation to a comparison class: she is wiser than Bill, Jane, and so on. But *being wise* also includes an intrinsic component—having a certain type and level of intelligence. Thus *being wise* is a complex property that has at least one extrinsic and one intrinsic component. It is therefore not a *purely* extrinsic property, which might be defined in this way:

> P is a *purely extrinsic property* of X just in case P is an extrinsic property of X and P has no intrinsic components.

Being one among many is a credible purely extrinsic property of a point in space, for instance.

To Leibniz's charge against Descartes, one might reply that properties like *having such-and-such an extension* and *being spherical* are paradigmatically intrinsic properties of things. But Leibniz has in mind that a Cartesian sphere's extension is not intrinsic to it in a more demanding sense, for there remains a respect in which the extension of a thing is extrinsic:[29]

> Nor do I think that extension can be conceived in itself, but I consider it an analyzable and relative concept, for it can be resolved into plurality, continuity, and coexistence or the existence of parts at one and the same time.[30]

Leibniz contends that the extension of the Cartesian sphere can be analyzed as, or reduces to, the plurality, continuity, and coexistence of parts of the sphere. Properties of each of these three sorts are purely extrinsic properties of these parts. Being one of a collection of more than one thing, being spatially continuous with other things, and coexisting temporally with other things are all purely extrinsic properties of their bearers. So it may be that P is an intrinsic property of X, while P is not in a sense fundamentally intrinsic to X, or, as James van Cleve points out, in Kant's terminology, *absolutely* intrinsic to X.[31] This is the case when X's having P can be analyzed as, or reduces to, X's parts having properties Q, R, S . . . , and these properties are purely extrinsic properties of these parts. Correlatively, when P *can* be analyzed as or reduces to purely extrinsic properties of these parts, it is instead, in Kant's terminology, merely comparatively or relatively intrinsic. However, it's best to avoid the notions of analysis and reduction in characterizing these properties. As Chase Wrenn points out, even if for general reasons supporting antireductionism, properties of the whole fail to be analyzable in terms of or to reduce to properties of the parts, an intrinsic property of the whole could still be merely comparatively intrinsic.[32] We can instead appeal to the notion of necessitation:

P is an *absolutely intrinsic* property of X just in case P is an intrinsic property of X, and this instance of P is not necessitated by purely extrinsic property instances of parts of X.

By contrast,

P is a *comparatively intrinsic* property of X just in case P is an intrinsic property of X, and this instance of P is necessitated by purely extrinsic property instances of parts of X.[33]

Thus, the extension of a Cartesian sphere, if Leibniz is right about the property of extension, turns out to be a comparatively intrinsic property of it. One might object that a Cartesian sphere's extension is not necessitated by the purely extrinsic properties of the parts of the sphere, for the reason that the parts have an intrinsic property that serves as the foundation for the extrinsic properties. But in the Cartesian theory of matter, the parts consist just in extension, and the extension of each of these parts is subject to the same metaphysical treatment of the extension of the whole: the extension of each of these parts will be necessitated by the plurality, continuity, and coexistence of their parts. The same holds for the extension of the parts of these parts, on to infinity.

However, Leibniz thinks that it is not credible that substances have only purely extrinsic properties:

But it would appear from this that something must always be assumed which is continuous or diffused, such as the white in milk, the color, ductility, and weight in gold, and resistance in matter. For by itself, continuity (for extension is nothing but simultaneous continuity) no more constitutes substance than does multitude or number, where something is necessary to be numbered, repeated, and continued.[34]

The idea is that there must be some absolutely intrinsic property that confers substantive character on any substantial entity—one might call a property of this sort a *substantival absolutely intrinsic property*—for this substantive character cannot be accounted for by purely extrinsic and merely comparatively intrinsic properties alone. To get a sense of what Leibniz is after, it's intuitive that a mind-independently real substantive thing can't consist just in properties such as being next to, existing at the same time as, and being one of several—that such relational properties would need to be accompanied by some absolutely intrinsic property.

In this passage, Leibniz specifies the absolutely intrinsic property as that which has extension, in the sense that it is that which is continuous. But what are the candidates for the absolutely intrinsic properties of physical things?

Medieval Aristotelians proposed prime materiality, the fundamental subject of inherence of positive features, which is in itself just the pure potentiality for inherence of such features. This proposal is rejected by all the major modern philosophers, typically on the grounds of unintelligibility. Locke suggested solidity, the categorical basis of impenetrability, as the absolutely intrinsic physical property.[35] Leibniz's positive proposal is to ascribe force to matter as the missing property.[36] But is force adequate for this role? Consider gravitational force. The gravitational force exerted by a sphere on another body is a function of the gravitational force exerted by its parts, but the sphere's force is not obviously necessitated by purely extrinsic properties of its parts. So one possibility is that there are properties of type T that are in some sense intrinsic to material thing X, and while X has P by virtue of its parts having certain properties, X has P by virtue of its parts having properties precisely of type T itself, and these properties are intrinsic to these parts. Furthermore, these parts have these properties by virtue of *their* parts having intrinsic properties of type T, ad infinitum. If force meets this condition, then material things' having force will be an absolutely intrinsic property of them.

It is important to note that, as the previous reasoning shows, force can be an absolutely intrinsic property even if there is no fundamental level, and thus no fundamental entity has force.[37] This result is accommodated by this notion as it is defined previously. This is a welcome result, for the Leibnizian principle at issue, which I will provisionally formulate as follows:

> (Intrinsicness Principle, first pass) Any substantial entity must have at least one substantival absolutely intrinsic property,

does not depend for its truth or plausibility on there being a fundamental level of reality—although Leibniz did believe for other reasons that there must be one.[38]

Significantly, Leibniz maintains that physical force is not an absolutely intrinsic property of a material substance. He calls physical force *derivative*, and he suggests that it is the phenomenal appearance of *primitive* force, which is an intrinsic mental property of a nonphysical soul or monad. Primitive force is a law-governed tendency of a monad to pass from one perception to another.[39] For Leibniz, the underlying ground of primitive force is found in the representational states of souls or monads, and it is these nonphysical representational states that provide the missing absolutely intrinsic properties. This account features no absolutely intrinsic *physical* properties. For Leibniz, this is part of the explanation for why physical things are not substantial or real in the fundamental sense and instead merely well-founded phenomena (*phenomena bene fundata*). The fact that derivative force has an appropriate foundation in absolutely intrinsic properties of a monad nevertheless allows physical things to be substantial in the lower-grade sense in which they are real, as well-founded phenomena. This story is of particular interest given our topic, for this is the first time we see an explicit formulation of the view that the absolutely intrinsic properties of the mind-independently real world are mental.

Kant's reaction to these claims of Leibniz's is first of all to deny that we have knowledge or cognition of any absolutely intrinsic properties of material things:

> All that we cognize in matter is nothing but relations. What we call the intrinsic determinations of it are intrinsic only in a comparative sense, but among these relations some are self-subsistent and permanent, and through these we are given a determinate object.[40]

In material things such as trees and houses, we discover comparatively intrinsic properties, but never any absolutely intrinsic properties. This is not merely an epistemic claim, but also a metaphysical one. For Kant contends that all properties of matter, *substantia phaenomenon*, even its apparently intrinsic properties, are ultimately purely extrinsic: "It is quite otherwise with a *substantia phaenomenon* in space; its intrinsic determinations are nothing but mere relations, and it itself is entirely made up of mere relations."[41] He then specifies force as a feature of matter: "We are acquainted with substance in space only through forces which are active in this and that space, either bringing objects to it (attraction), or preventing them penetrating into it (repulsion and impenetrability)"—so for him force is also ultimately a purely extrinsic property of material things.[42] In particular, in Kant's conception forces are relations between points: attractive forces are by definition causes by which two points approach one another, and repulsive forces are causes by which two points recede from another.[43] (Alternatively, Kant might be interpreted here as claiming that force is dispositional, and relational for that reason.)

Kant admits that it is initially unintuitive that all of the properties of matter are ultimately purely extrinsic: "It is certainly startling to hear that a thing is to be taken as consisting wholly of relations."[44] But this sense of implausibility can be explained away: "Such a thing is, however, mere appearance, and cannot be thought through pure categories: what it itself consists in is the mere relation of something in general to the senses."[45] Because matter is only appearance, for Kant it need not have any physical absolutely intrinsic properties. If matter were not merely appearance, but a thing in itself, then it would possess such absolutely intrinsic properties. In making these claims, Kant indicates that he accepts a version of the Leibnizian doctrine that intrinsic properties must ground extrinsic properties: that the extrinsic properties of mind-independently real substantial entities—things in themselves—must be grounded in absolutely intrinsic properties, although in his view we are irremediably ignorant of such properties. This suggests the following formulation of the intuition underlying the demand for absolutely intrinsic properties:

(Intrinsicness Principle) Any mind-independently real substantial entity
must have at least one substantival absolutely intrinsic property,

which I think best captures the intuition at play in the views of Leibniz and
Kant. In the next section, I show how this principle is crucial to a viable version
of Russellian monism. It is the one I favor, and we may label it RM4-AI ('AI'
for absolutely intrinsic).

Ignorance of Absolutely Intrinsic Properties

An assumption made by the various Russellian monist proposals is that we are
currently ignorant of the fundamental properties that underlie and explain
consciousness. Like Stoljar, I think it's implausible to ground this ignorance in
our lack of acquaintance with such properties.[46] The H_2O-structural property
is an intrinsic property of water, and we arguably understand the complete
nature of this property and that it's the essence of water. We have this knowledge despite lacking acquaintance with this property. Our knowledge in this
case is instead grounded in best explanation—we know the complete nature of
the H_2O-structural property as the essence of water because we've conceived
a model of the unobserved basis of water dispositions that turned out to be a
component of a best explanation. In principle, could we not do the same for
absolutely intrinsic properties? We might imagine: physics provides a model
for the fundamental particles in which their absolutely intrinsic property is
medieval Aristotelian prime materiality or Lockean categorical solidity.[47] The
model turns out to be so explanatorily impressive that it yields knowledge that
categorical solidity is an instantiated absolutely intrinsic property.

But given this abductive model, it remains credible that we are now ignorant
of which absolutely intrinsic properties are instantiated. Several distinct candidates for such properties have been conceived that are not abductively ruled
out, and it is open that we have not yet conceived all of the candidates. This will
be so on David Lewis's quidditism, according to which different fundamental
properties can have had the same causal role; he calls properties of that satisfy
this description 'quiddities'.[48] This is also the case if, following Shoemaker, quiddities are rejected in favor of a causal structuralist view of properties, according
to which the causal role of a property constitutes its individual essence, so that if
P1 and P2 have the same complete causal role, they are ipso facto the same property.[49] Shoemaker's causal structuralism does not preclude distinct absolutely
intrinsic properties with causal profiles that we are unable to distinguish, either
because the distinguishing elements of these causal profiles are uninstantiated[50]
or because we lack the ability to discern them. Even if we could individuate
the instantiated absolutely intrinsic properties by a causal-role specification, we
might yet be significantly ignorant of them because a causal role specification
provides us with only limited knowledge of a property's nature.[51]

Which candidates for absolutely intrinsic properties have we heretofore conceived? Prime materiality and categorical solidity have already been mentioned, as has Leibniz's model in which the absolute intrinsic properties are mental properties of immaterial entities. In Leibniz's conception, every entity has such mental properties, and thus his view is a variety of *panpsychism*. On Galen Strawson's view, the absolutely intrinsic properties are mental properties of certain microphysical entities; he calls his position *micropsychism*.[52] Robert Adams defends a theistic variant on this exclusively mentalistic proposal on which the divine volitions constitute the absolutely intrinsic properties.[53] Chalmers specifies a *protophenomenal* alternative according to which the absolutely intrinsic properties are neither conscious properties nor paradigmatically physical properties, but nonetheless ground both consciousness and the properties current physical reveals.[54] David Armstrong at one time proposed primitive color as the intrinsic physical property missing from the scientific story, and one might embellish this proposal to include primitive versions of the other secondary qualities.[55] One might want to say that a number of these proposals can be ruled out as too wild to be in play. However, reflection on the strength of the conceivability argument against physicalism suggests that possibilities that initially seem wild remain salient after all. Moreover, it seems far from certain that any proposed candidate that we understand is actually instantiated, and so it may well be that there are possibilities for such properties that we do not comprehend that are also salient alternatives.

In summary, our reason for claiming ignorance about which absolutely intrinsic properties are actually instantiated is that that there is a plurality of candidates for such properties, and some of which we're aware are not currently understood. More than one of these candidates is in the running for yielding the best explanation of the relevant phenomena. But as things now stand, none of them convincingly meets this standard. The conclusion to this argument is not inevitable and permanent ignorance, but rather a sort that is potentially remediable. It is thus congenial to Chalmers's protophenomenalist proposal, which leaves it open that we will come to understand the nature of the relevant intrinsic properties.

How might we assess the various proposals for currently unknown absolutely intrinsic properties as ways of filling out Russellian monism? If we supplemented 'P' just with putative truths about Aristotelian prime materiality or Lockean categorical solidity, the sense that the physical is conceivable without the phenomenal is undiminished. Imagine instead, inspired by David Armstrong's suggestion, that we embellished 'P' just with putative truths about primitive colors or primitive versions of other secondary qualities. Aristotle conceived of such properties as physical, so maybe the result could be a variety of physicalism. But the idea that these are the missing absolute intrinsic properties does not seem especially plausible, since they have dismissed from our scientific picture of reality since the seventeenth century. At this point, we seem to have run out of candidates for the missing absolutely intrinsic physical properties that have been conceived.

What remains are the mental candidates such as panpsychism and micro-psychism, proposed by Leibniz and Strawson, and, as Thomas Nagel, David Chalmers, and Colin McGinn suggest, possible candidates that we have not conceived.[56] The most favorable prospect for a resolutely physicalist Russellian monism would appear to lie in properties whose nature is currently unconceived. Chalmers's protophenomenalism allows for a view of this sort. The kind of ignorance about the properties at issue that would be in place, together with the fact that the tradition in physics allows for properties not hitherto countenanced as physical (such as quantum fields) to count as physical, would seem to make protophenomenalism the physicalist Russellian monist's best hope. If there are currently unconceived possibilities for physical and protophenomenal absolutely intrinsic properties, they might remain unconceived. More optimistically, as physics develops, we may come to conceive them. Or as Chalmers suggests, phenomenology together with physics might arrive at such a conception.[57]

Stoljar's Challenge to RM4-AI

Chalmers argues that that what underwrites the conceivability argument is the following structure-and-dynamics thesis:

> (SDT) There are experiential [or phenomenal] truths that cannot be deduced from truths solely about structure and dynamics.[58]

Structural and dynamic properties contrast with intrinsic properties; as Stoljar plausibly suggests, structural properties are relational properties, and dynamic properties are changes in structural properties over time. Chalmers's idea is that since the properties that current physics specifies are exclusively structural and dynamic, and phenomenal properties are intrinsic properties of experiences, one can conclude that experiential truths about phenomenal properties cannot be deduced from current physics, or from any descendent that specifies only structural and dynamic properties.59 But Stoljar contends that SDT is mistaken, and that it may be that these experiential truths are derivable from structural and dynamic physical truth after all.

As Torin Alter explains it, SDT is based on three claims:

(1) There are experiential truths;
(2) *The from-structure-only-structure thesis*, that is, from truths solely about structure and dynamics, one can deduce only truths solely about structure and dynamics; and
(3) *The experience-isn't-just-structure thesis*, that is, experiential truths are not solely about structure and dynamics.[60]

In his critical discussion of Chalmers's view in *Ignorance and Imagination*, Stoljar rejects (2) and raises issues for (3). In criticism of (2), he remarks:

> The simplest way to see that the from-structure-only-structure thesis is false is to note that one can derive the instantiation of an intrinsic property from a relational one just by shifting what thing you are talking about. For example, being a husband is a relational property of Jack Spratt, and being a wife is a relational property of his wife. But *being married* is an intrinsic property of the pair (or the sum) of Jack Spratt and his wife. To take a different example, it seems plausible to say that I have the property of having a hand intrinsically, but my having this property obviously follows from a relation between my hand and the rest of my body, and that the truth concerning this is a relational truth.[61]

Alter agrees that Stoljar has a point: if objects x and y compose object z, then it is possible to derive intrinsic properties of z from relational properties of x and y. But he thinks that this observation undercuts the from-structure-only-structure thesis only if nonstructural/nondynamic properties are identified with intrinsic properties, and in his view that identification is mistaken, for "the property *being married* is purely structural/dynamic despite being intrinsic to the Spratts. Any structural/dynamic duplicate of the actual world contains a corresponding married pair."[62] (A caveat: Being married is plausibly extrinsic, since it builds in a relation to civic institutions. Arguably, *being a dancing pair* avoids this problem.) Alter contends that such examples show not that we should reject the from-structure-only-structure thesis, but rather that we should resist identifying nonstructural/nondynamic properties with intrinsic properties.

The distinction between comparatively and absolutely intrinsic properties yields a way to vindicate Alter's claim. While the property of *being a married pair* is intrinsic to the Spratts, at the same time it can be derived from, and is necessitated by, Jack's purely extrinsic property of *being married to Jill* and Jill's purely extrinsic property of *being married to Jack*. *Being a married pair* is thus merely a comparatively intrinsic property and not an absolutely intrinsic property of the Spratts. One might now propose that all nonstructural/ nondynamic properties will be absolutely intrinsic properties (and all nonstructural/nondynamic components of properties will be absolutely intrinsic components of properties). Stoljar's counterexample would then fail against the from-structure-only-structure thesis. With this in mind, we can reformulate the from-structure-only-structure thesis in this way:

(2*) Truths about absolutely intrinsic properties (and absolutely intrinsic components of properties) are not necessitated by and cannot be derived just from truths about purely extrinsic properties.

The SDT can be restated along the same lines:

> (SDT*) There are experiential truths that are not necessitated by and cannot be derived just from truths about purely extrinsic properties.

Stoljar (this volume, Chapter 1) expresses a doubt about whether characterizing the new properties proposed by Russellian monism as absolutely intrinsic is effective. He agrees that (2*) is true, but objects that this "does not help with the polemic purpose of an advocate of the structure-and-dynamics argument":

> For the only way in which this could help the argument is if the third premise were interpreted now as saying that the truths about consciousness are or include truths about absolutely intrinsic properties. But this is highly questionable. There is certainly some intuitive basis to the idea that truths about consciousness concern nonrelational or intrinsic properties, but whether they concern *absolutely* nonrelational or intrinsic properties seems to me something that is left open by anything we know or believe about consciousness, either as a matter of theory or as a matter of introspection.

Now I agree with Stoljar that whether truths about consciousness concern absolutely intrinsic properties is left open by introspection and by reasoning about the nature of consciousness. In fact, in the first part of *Consciousness and the Prospects of Physicalism*, I propose that the reason we have a tendency to think that the nature of consciousness is not straightforwardly physical is that in introspection we systematically misrepresent phenomenal properties as having qualitative natures that they actually lack.[63] According to this proposal, which I argue is an open possibility, but which rejects the intuitive claim that introspection accurately represents those natures, phenomenal properties could be relational despite how they appear to introspection. So I agree that it's questionable that truths about consciousness concern absolutely intrinsic properties.

But my subsequent discussion of Russellian monism there was predicated on the assumption that introspection does accurately represent the qualitative nature of phenomenal properties. This is also a serious open possibility (but it's a claim to which I'm not committed). And if we let PRP be any epistemically possible description of the world that features only purely relational properties, the intuition that 'PRP and ~ Q' is ideally, primarily, and positively conceivable will be very strong. If from this we can conclude that the phenomenal truths are not necessitated by or derivable from the purely relational truths, we can also conclude that the phenomenal truths are not truths exclusively about purely relational and merely comparatively intrinsic properties. And this in turn would entail that the phenomenal truths are at least partly about absolutely intrinsic properties and/or absolutely intrinsic aspects of properties.

Moreover, there is good reason to think that antiphysicalist intuitions about consciousness are fueled by a belief that phenomenal properties are primitive, and supposing that they are represented as intrinsic properties of experience, they would then also have to be absolutely intrinsic properties. In the sense at issue, a primitive property is (i) one whose entire qualitative nature or essence is revealed in our sensory or introspective representation of it, and thus is not identical to a property with a qualitative nature distinct from what is revealed by the representation, and (ii) one that is metaphysically simple and thus not constituted by a plurality of other properties. Properties can also be *represented as primitive*. For the redness of a sunset to be represented as primitive requires that it be represented as having that familiar simple qualitative nature revealed in visual experience of red things under normal conditions and as not identical with any property, such as *being spectral reflectance profile S* or *being molecular basis M of spectral reflectance profile S*, whose qualitative nature is not revealed in that sensory experience.[64] It's plausible, I think, that either introspection represents phenomenal qualities as primitive or that how we introspect them generates a strong tendency to believe that they are primitive.[65] But if phenomenal properties are primitive, and if they are intrinsic properties of experience, they will also be absolutely intrinsic properties of experience. This is because their being primitive precludes their being constituted by properties not revealed in introspection, and no purely extrinsic constitution base is so revealed.[66]

Thus, I agree with Stoljar that whether truths about consciousness concern absolutely intrinsic properties is left open by introspection and by reasoning about the nature of consciousness. But suppose, as is often simply assumed, that introspection accurately represents the qualitative nature of phenomenal properties, and how we introspect them generates a strong tendency to believe that they are primitive. Then we would have good reason to believe that phenomenal properties are indeed absolutely intrinsic properties of experiential states.

The Prospects of RM4-AI

Chalmers's Russellian monist thought is that one can ideally, positively, primarily conceive 'P and ~ Q' (that is, conceive it as true in some world considered as actual) only because one is conceiving just structural properties on the physical side. We can now suggest that if 'P' were replaced with an embellished 'P*' that includes concepts that allow for representation of the natures of the currently unknown nonstructural, absolutely intrinsic properties, the resulting 'P* and ~ Q' would not be ideally, positively, primarily conceivable. For although 'Q'—that is, 'Mary senses red at time *t*'—is not a priori derivable from 'P,' this claim about Mary's phenomenal experience would be a priori derivable from 'P*.'[67] The Russellian monism that ensues has versions on which the natures of the absolutely intrinsic properties are phenomenal, as in Strawson's micropsychism, or else protophenomenal, as Chalmers advocates. On the phenomenal-micropsychist option, the absolutely intrinsic properties that account for phenomenal consciousness are themselves phenomenal and irreducibly so, while on the protophenomenalist alternative, they are not phenomenal but nonetheless account for phenomenal consciousness.[68]

Imagine first that 'P*' supplements 'P' by adding in the proposed micropsychist truths, statements or propositions about phenomenal absolutely intrinsic properties of fundamental physical entities that specify the natures of those properties. Suppose 'Q' is the phenomenal truth about Mary's experience of red. Would 'P* and ~ Q' be ideally, positively, and primarily conceivable? We might ask whether there is any less reason to think 'P* and ~ Q' is ideally, positively, and primarily conceivable than there is to believe that 'P and ~ Q' is. Imagine that every fundamental particle has some absolutely intrinsic phenomenal property or other, and that ordinary introspectible phenomenal entities are composed of many fundamental particles of this sort. It may appear as easy to conceive of any such array of fundamental particles without Mary's phenomenal redness as it is to conceive of any arrangement of conventionally characterized fundamental physical particles without it.

But in support of the micropsychist, we can invoke a misrepresentation thesis of a Leibnizian sort, on which introspection merely fails to represent experience as having features it in fact has.[69] While Mary's experience of red is represented introspectively to feature only phenomenal redness, and this occasions the belief that the phenomenal redness is primitive, it is in fact composed of an introspectively unrepresented complex microphenomenal array. Here phenomenal micropsychism might have an advantage over an uncontroversially physicalist proposal for the absolutely intrinsic properties, since it is arguably more plausible that Mary's phenomenal redness is composed of an unrepresented complex microphenomenal array than that it is uncontroversially physically constituted. Micropsychism requires only that introspection mistakenly represents phenomenal redness as lacking a complex phenomenal composition. An uncontroversially physicalist alternative would seem to require in addition that the phenomenal redness of Mary's experience does not have any qualitative phenomenal nature of the general type that introspection represents it as having at all.[70]

Note that micropsychism would claim that there are laws governing how truths about microphenomenal properties yield truths about macrophenomenal properties such as Mary's experience's phenomenal redness. These laws would have to be derivable from 'P*' alone (P* adds in the micropsychist truths), for 'Q' must be derivable from 'P*' alone. This general proposal might be rendered credible by the analogy of the derivability of certain macrophenomenal properties from their known components, such as phenomenal tastes from the components of sweet, sour, salty, bitter, and umami.[71] Introspectible phenomenal properties would be analogously derivable from currently unknown microphenomenal absolutely intrinsic properties together with the rest of the base described by 'P*,' and the relevant laws would then be similarly derivable from, and necessitated by, this base. Despite our tendency to believe that phenomenal tastes are primitive properties, and thus simple, the discovery that phenomenal tastes are structured by these components convinces us that this belief is mistaken. But it does not also undermine the claim that phenomenal tastes are absolutely intrinsic properties, since the base for derivation does not consist in purely relational properties. This lesson can be applied to the micropsychist proposal more generally.

At the same time, there is reason to be skeptical about the prospects of micropsychism. Building on a point made by Karen Bennett, the envisioned sort of phenomenal micropsychism would need to posit fundamental or brute laws linking the micropsychist absolutely intrinsic properties with the microphysical properties that they underlie, without which the truths about the microphysical properties cannot be derived from the micropsychist truths.[72] This is a reason to think that phenomenal micropsychism cannot provide a deeply illuminating explanation of the properties specified by current microphysics—any such explanation would rely crucially on brute laws. And it would be theoretically advantageous if the absolutely intrinsic properties provided such explanations for both phenomenal properties and the properties specified by current microphysics.

Chalmers's protophenomenalist proposal appears better equipped for this twofold task. It is much less specific about the nature of the absolutely intrinsic properties, and partly for this reason, it leaves open the possibility that these properties would count as physical. But then it would also be open that the protophenomenal properties yield explanations for the microphysical properties they underlie without fundamental laws linking the protophenomenal properties with the microphysical properties. This situation issues in a potential advantage over phenomenal micropsychism. Now imagine that 'P*' supplements 'P' by adding the truths about protophenomenal absolutely intrinsic properties of fundamental physical entities by way of concepts that allowed for the representation of the natures of such properties. Would the resulting 'P* and ~ Q' be ideally, positively, primarily conceivable? It seems epistemically open that there are protophenomenal properties such that the phenomenal truths are derivable a priori from truths about them, together with the rest of what is included in 'P*,' and this would undercut the ideal, positive, and primary conceivability of 'P* and ~ Q.' The resulting all-inclusive potential explanatory advantage of protophenomenalism over phenomenal micropsychism is offset by the liability that it proposes properties of which we currently have at best only a minimal conception.

Might we ever possess concepts that allow us to represent the natures of protophenomenal properties? Chalmers is cautiously optimistic. In a slightly different context, McGinn is skeptical. That there exist protophenomenal properties is consistent with McGinn's claims, but he would deny that concepts that would represent their natures are available to us. For him, to solve the mind-body problem, we would need to acquire concepts that would bridge the gap between conscious properties as revealed by introspective acquaintance concepts and neural and physical properties broadly construed. By contrast with acquiring concepts that facilitated past major theoretical shifts in science, such as the advance to relativity theory, this we cannot achieve; "what we need is a perspective shift, not just a paradigm shift—a shift not merely of world view, but of ways of apprehending the world. We need to become another type of cognitive being altogether."[73] But Nagel and Chalmers think it is open that our cognitive and imaginative capacities are up to forming this sort of concept.[74]

What plausibly explains McGinn's reluctance to take this route is that for him any concepts available to us will be closely tied to acquaintance. This limitation stands to foreclose the possibility of our acquiring concepts of the bridging sort specified. For Nagel and Chalmers, by contrast, it's open that our imagination is capable of venturing beyond these limits to form the kinds of concepts at issue. McGinn could be right to argue that the sorts of concepts in question cannot result from acquaintance, empirical or otherwise. What could be required is an impressively creative power to fashion concepts that transcends the ability McGinn accepts. Whether we have such a power is in contention. If we do have it, what we can currently think and understand would not preclude that we eventually acquire concepts of protophenomenal absolutely intrinsic properties, whereupon we, through further investigation, might also come to know whether such properties are actually instantiated.

Final Words

According to the Russellian monist option for physicalism that I've set out, the currently unknown properties that explain both fundamental physical dispositions and phenomenal consciousness are absolutely intrinsic properties, intrinsic properties whose instances are not necessitated by instances of purely relational properties. These properties, by contrast with those endorsed by other Russellian monisms, are nonmental and sufficiently similar to paradigmatic properties of current physics to count as physical, while they nonetheless have a crucial role in grounding phenomenal properties. An important advantage of this proposal is that it can accept the attractive accuracy claim about phenomenal representation, that introspection represents phenomenal properties as having qualitative natures that they in fact possess. It is this accuracy claim that provides the conceivability argument against physicalism with much of its characteristic force, and so any physicalism that can endorse it is in an advantageous dialectical position.[75] Absolutely intrinsic properties of this kind are currently at best only minimally conceived, and therein lies the fragility of the proposal. But for anyone with physicalist sympathies, and who at the same time wishes to preserve the accuracy claim, this version of Russellian monism should be a live and attractive option.[76]

Notes

1. Bertrand Russell, *The Analysis of Matter* (London: Kegan Paul, 1927); the classic passage is on p. 384.
2. Michael Fara, "Dispositions," *The Stanford Encyclopedia of Philosophy*, Summer 2009 Edition, Edward N. Zalta (ed.), http://plato.stanford.edu/entries/dispositions/.
3. From here on, I will generally use 'consciousness' to refer to the 'macro' sort of which we can be ordinarily aware, by contrast with, for example, the 'micro' consciousness had by elementary particles according to some panpsychists. Russellian monists aim to explain macroconsciousness, and some propose that it can be explained by microconsciousness, and hold that microconsciousness is fundamental.
4. Derk Pereboom, *Consciousness and the Prospects of Physicalism* (New York: Oxford University Press, 2011).
5. I generally agree with Stoljar's criticisms of RM1–3.
6. René Descartes, *Meditations on First Philosophy*, in *The Philosophical Writings of Descartes*, vol. 2, p. 54 (AT VII 78); "Fourth Replies," in *The Philosophical Writings of Descartes*, vol. 2, pp. 154–62 (AT VII 219–31); Saul Kripke, *Naming and Necessity* (Cambridge, MA: Harvard University Press, 1980), pp. 144–53; George Bealer, "Modal Epistemology and the Rationalist Renaissance," in *Conceivability and Possibility*, ed. Tamar Szabó Gendler and John Hawthorne, (Oxford: Oxford University Press, 2002), pp. 77–125. For an exposition of Descartes's argument, see Margaret Wilson, *Descartes* (London: Routledge, 1978); Stephen Yablo, "The Real Distinction between Mind and Body," *Canadian Journal of Philosophy* 16 (1991), pp. 149–201; Marleen Rozemond, *Descartes's Dualism* (Cambridge, MA: Harvard University Press, 1998); Joseph Almog, *What Am I? Descartes and the Mind-Body Problem* (New York: Oxford University Press, 2002).
7. Thomas Nagel, "What Is It Like to Be a Bat," *Philosophical Review* 83 (1974), pp. 435–50.
8. This is the example Antoine Arnauld directs at Descartes's conceivability argument for dualism; "Fourth Objections," in *The Philosophical Writings of Descartes*, vol. 2, p. 142 (AT VII 202).
9. About 'PT' Chalmers and Jackson say:

   Intuitively, this statement says that our world contains what is implied by P, and *only* what is implied by P. More formally, we can say that world W1 outstrips world W2 if W1 contains a qualitative duplicate of W2 as a proper part and the reverse is not the case. Then a minimal P-world is a P-world that outstrips no other P-world. (David Chalmers and Frank Jackson, "Conceptual Analysis and Reductive Explanation," *Philosophical Review* 110 (2001), pp. 315–61, at p. 317)

10. David Chalmers, "Consciousness and Its Place in Nature," in *Blackwell Guide to the Philosophy of Mind* (Oxford: Blackwell, 2002); reprinted in *Philosophy of Mind: Classical and Contemporary Readings*, ed. David Chalmers (New York: Oxford University Press, 2002), pp. 247–72, at pp. 255–56. Chalmers's formalization is controversial and has given rise to criticism; see, for example, Bealer, "Modal Epistemology and the Rationalist Renaissance," pp. 87–99; Stephen Yablo, "Shoulda, Woulda, Coulda," in *Conceivability and Possibility*, ed. Tamar Gendler and John Hawthorne (Oxford: Oxford University Press, 2002), pp. 441–92.
11. David Chalmers, "Does Conceivability Entail Possibility?" in *Conceivability and Possibility*, ed. Tamar Gendler and John Hawthorne (Oxford: Oxford University Press, 2002), pp. 145–200, at p. 148.

12. Chalmers, "Does Conceivability Entail Possibility?" p. 147.
13. Chalmers, "Does Conceivability Entail Possibility?" pp. 148–49.
14. Chalmers's scheme is similar to Jackson's with a difference in terms; Frank Jackson, *From Metaphysics to Ethics* (Oxford: Oxford University Press, 1998), pp. 46–52.
15. Yablo discusses such a view in "Shoulda, Woulda, Coulda," p. 446.
16. Chalmers, "Does Conceivability Entail Possibility?" p. 198, with equivalent terminology sometimes substituted; cf. "Consciousness and Its Place in Nature," pp. 256–57.
17. Chalmers, "Does Conceivability Entail Possibility?" p. 189.
18. Chalmers, "Does Conceivability Entail Possibility?" pp. 189–94.
19. Kripke, *Naming and Necessity*, pp. 144–53.
20. David Chalmers, "The Content and Epistemology of Phenomenal Belief," in *Consciousness: New Philosophical Perspectives*, ed. Q. Smith and A. Jokic (Oxford: Oxford University Press, 2003), pp. 220–72..
21. By Chalmers's characterization, a pure phenomenal concept is difficult to express in language. The term *phenomenal red* might seem to express the relational concept 'the phenomenal quality typically caused in normal subjects within my community by paradigmatic red things,' but a pure phenomenal concept is not relational. The term *phenomenal red* might appear to express the demonstrative concept 'this property of my experience' in appropriate circumstances, but a pure phenomenal concept is not demonstrative; see Chalmers, "The Content and Epistemology of Phenomenal Belief."
22. Chalmers, "The Content and Epistemology of Phenomenal Belief."
23. For a statement to be primarily necessary is for it to be a priori true; for a concept to be primarily rigid is for its reference to be a priori fixed.
24. Chalmers, "Does Conceivability Entail Possibility?" p. 197.
25. There is voluminous literature on how to characterize intrinsic and extrinsic properties more exactly. For comprehensive discussions, see Lloyd Humberstone, "Intrinsic/Extrinsic," *Synthese* 105 (1996), pp. 205–67, and Brian Weatherson and Dan Marshall, "Intrinsic vs. Extrinsic Properties," *The Stanford Encyclopedia of Philosophy* (Spring 2013 Edition), Edward N. Zalta, ed. Retrieved from http://plato.stanford.edu/archives/spr2013/entries/intrinsic-extrinsic/>.
26. The material in this section is a revision of the account I set out in Derk Pereboom, "Is Kant's Transcendental Philosophy Inconsistent?" *History of Philosophy Quarterly* 8 (1991), pp. 357–71; and in "Kant's Amphiboly," *Archiv für Geschichte der Philosophie*, 73 (1991), pp. 50–70.
27. René Descartes, *Principles of Philosophy*, Part II, 1–22, in *The Philosophical Writings of Descartes*, pp. 223–32 (AT VIII, 40–52).
28. Leibniz to deVolder, April 1702, in G.W. Leibniz, *Philosophical Papers and Letters*, ed. L.E. Loemker (Dordrecht, the Netherlands: D. Reidel, 1969) (hereafter: Loemker), pp. 526–27; Gottfried Wilhelm Leibniz, *G. W. Leibniz, Die philosophischen Schriften*, ed. C.I. Gerhard, 7 vols. (Hildesheim, Germany: Olms, 1965) (hereafter: Gerhardt II), p. 240.
29. Alyssa Ney makes this point in "Physicalism and Our Knowledge of Intrinsic Properties," *Australasian Journal of Philosophy* 85 (2007), pp. 41–60, at p. 50. She also suggests that the next move to make is to define a more fundamental notion of intrinsic property.
30. Leibniz to De Volder, April 1699, Loemker, p. 516 = Gerhardt II, pp. 169–70.
31. Immanuel Kant, *Critique of Pure Reason*, A277/B333, translations by Norman Kemp Smith (London: Macmillan, 1929) and by Paul Guyer and Allen Wood (Cambridge: Cambridge University Press, 1987). James van Cleve, "Inner States and Outer Relations: Kant and the Case for Monadism," in *Doing Philosophy Historically*, ed. Peter H. Hare (Buffalo, NY: Prometheus, 1988), pp. 231–47.
32. Wrenn made this point in discussion. Thanks also to Torin Alter and Ralf Bader for correspondence about this issue.
33. The notions of absolutely and comparatively intrinsic properties might also be expressed in terms of a priori derivability, although since these notions are metaphysical, such epistemic characterizations will be less fundamental:

P is an *absolutely intrinsic* property of X just in case P is an intrinsic property of X, and the proposition that X has P is not a priori derivable from R, a proposition that details all the purely extrinsic properties of X's parts.

P is a *comparatively intrinsic* property of X just in case P is an intrinsic property of X, and the proposition that X has P is a priori derivable from R.

James van Cleve, in his "Inner States and Outer Relations: Kant and the Case for Monadism," p. 235, proposes alternative definitions of the notions of comparatively and absolutely intrinsic properties:

P is a *monadic* property of X = df it is possible for something *x* to have P even if no individual *distinct* from *x* [i.e., not identical with *x*] exists;

and,

P is *nonrelational* = df it is possible for something *x* to have P even if no individual *discrete* from *x* [i.e., having no part in common with *x*] exists.

He then characterizes absolutely intrinsic properties as nonrelational and monadic, and comparatively intrinsic properties as nonrelational but not monadic. Absolutely intrinsic properties of X are the intrinsic properties of X that X could have if it had no parts, or if the parts it does have did not exist, while the comparatively intrinsic properties of X are the other intrinsic properties of X.

34. Leibniz to De Volder, April 1699, Loemker, p. 516 = Gerhardt II, p. 170; cf. G.W. Leibniz, *Specimen Dynamicum*, Loemker, pp. 435–52 = G.W. Leibniz, *Mathemathische Schriften*, ed. C.I. Gerhardt (Berlin and Halle: Asher et Comp, 1849–1856), VI, pp. 234–54.
35. John Locke, An Essay Concerning Human Understanding, ed. P.H. Nidditch (Oxford: Oxford University Press, 1975), II, iv.
36. Cf. Leibniz, *Specimen Dynamicum*, Loemker, p. 445 = Leibniz, *Mathematische Schriften*, VI, p. 246.
37. Jonathan Schaffer, "Is There a Fundamental Level?" *Noûs* 37 (2003), pp. 498–517.
38. G.W. Leibniz, "On Nature Itself," Loemker, pp. 498–508 = Gerhardt IV, pp. 504–16; Schaffer, "Is There a Fundamental Level?" pp. 498–517. For reasons to be skeptical about this principle, see Jennifer McKitrick "The Bare Metaphysical Possibility of Bare Dispositions," *Philosophy and Phenomenological Research* 66 (2003), pp. 349–69; James Ladyman, and Don Ross, with David Spurrett and John Collier, *Every Thing Must Go* (Oxford: Oxford University Press, 2007).
39. Leibniz, Gerhardt II, p. 275.
40. Immanuel Kant, *Critique of Pure Reason*, A285/B341. In a similar vein, David Armstrong writes: "If we look at the properties of physical objects that physicists are prepared to allow them such as mass, electric charge, or momentum, these show a distressing tendency to dissolve into relations that one object has to another"; see *A Materialist Theory of Mind* (London: Routledge, 1968), pp. 74–75.
41. Immanuel Kant, *Critique of Pure Reason*, A265/B321; cf. *Metaphysical Foundations of Natural Science*, tr. Michael Friedman (Cambridge: Cambridge University Press, 2004), Ak IV, p. 543. See Thomas Holden's exposition of Kant's position, and also of Roger Boscovich's similar theory, in *The Architecture of Matter* (Oxford: Oxford University Press, 2004), pp. 236–63.
42. Immanuel Kant, *Critique of Pure Reason*, A265/B321.
43. Immanuel Kant, *Metaphysical Foundations of Natural Science*, Ak IV, pp. 498–91.
44. Immanuel Kant, *Critique of Pure Reason*, A285/B341; this passage conflicts with Thomas Holden's claim (*The Architecture of Matter*, p. 261) that Kant was unmoved by the idea that matter must fill space by virtue of an intrinsic property.

45. Immanuel Kant, *Critique of Pure Reason*, A285/B34l.

46. Kant is arguably the first to claim that we lack knowledge of absolutely intrinsic properties, and he argues that for us this ignorance is irremediable. For expositions of the nature of this ignorance, see van Cleve, "Inner States and Outer Relations: Kant and the Case for Monadism"; Pereboom, "Is Kant's Transcendental Philosophy Inconsistent?" "Kant's Amphiboly," and *Consciousness and the Prospects of Physicalism* (chap. 6); Rae Langton, *Kantian Humility: Our Ignorance of Things in Themselves* (Oxford, Oxford University Press, 1998).

47. Locke, *An Essay Concerning Human Understanding*, book II, chap. IV.

48. David Lewis, "Ramseyan Humility," in *Conceptual Analysis and Philosophical Naturalism*, ed. David Braddon-Mitchell and Robert Nola (Cambridge, MA: MIT Press, 2009), pp. 203–22; Dustin Locke, "A Partial Defense of Ramseyan Humility," in *Conceptual Analysis and Philosophical Naturalism*, pp. 223–41; Jonathan Schaffer, "Quiddistic Knowledge," in *Lewisian Themes*, ed. Frank Jackson and Graham Priest (Oxford: Oxford University Press, 2004), pp. 210–30.

49. Sydney Shoemaker, "Causality and Properties," in *Time and Change*, ed. P. van Inwagen (Dordrecht, the Netherlands: D. Reidel, 1980), pp. 109–35; reprinted in Sydney Shoemaker, *Identity, Cause, and Mind*, 1st ed. (Cambridge: Cambridge University Press, 1984), pp. 206–33, and in the expanded 2nd ed. (Oxford: Oxford University Press, 2003), pp. 206–33.

50. John Hawthorne makes this point in "Causal Structuralism," *Philosophical Perspectives* 15 (2001), pp. 361–78.

51. One might think that on Shoemaker's conception all there is to a property is its causal role, but he assures me that this is not so. In his view, properties typically also feature intrinsic aptnesses for the causal roles that individuate them.

52. Galen Strawson, "Realistic Monism," in his *Real Materialism and Other Essays* (Oxford: Oxford University Press, 2008), pp. 54–74; cf. Galen Strawson, "Real Materialism," in his *Real Materialism and Other Essays,* pp. 19–51.

53. Robert Adams, "Idealism Vindicated," in *Persons, Human and Divine*, ed. Peter van Inwagen and Dean Zimmerman (Oxford: Oxford University Press, 2007), pp. 35–54.

54. Chalmers, "Consciousness and its Place in Nature," and "Does Conceivability Entail Possibility."

55. David Armstrong, *Perception and the Physical World* (London: Routledge, 1961); Armstrong rejects this proposal in *A Materialist Theory of Mind* (London: Routledge, 1968).

56. Thomas Nagel, *The View from Nowhere*, New York: Oxford University Press, 1986; Chalmers, "Does Conceivability Entail Possibility?"; Colin McGinn, "What Constitutes the Mind-Body Problem," in his *Consciousness and Its Objects* (Oxford: Oxford University Press, 2004).

57. In his presentation on structuralism in physics at the Australian National University, November 2005.

58. This formulation is from Torin Alter, "Does the Ignorance Hypothesis Undermine the Conceivability and Knowledge Arguments?" *Philosophy and Phenomenological Research* 79 (2009), pp. 756–65, at p. 760.

59. David Chalmers, "Does Conceivability Entail Possibility?" p. 197.

60. Alter, "Does the Ignorance Hypothesis Undermine the Conceivability and Knowledge Arguments?" pp. 761–63; cf. Daniel Stoljar, *Ignorance and Imagination: The Epistemic Origin of the Problem of Consciousness* (New York: Oxford University Press, 2006), pp. 147–53.

61. Stoljar, *Ignorance and Imagination*, p. 152.

62. Alter adds: "I assume instantiating *being married* in no way consists in having experiences. Otherwise instantiating the corresponding relational properties would also consist at least partly in having experiences, in which case those properties might not be purely structural/dynamic"; see Alter, "Does the Ignorance Hypothesis Undermine the Conceivability and Knowledge Arguments?" p. 763, note 8.

63. Pereboom, *Consciousness and the Prospects of Physicalism*, chap. 1; cf. Derk Pereboom, "Bats, Brain Scientists, and the Limitations of Introspection," *Philosophy and Phenomenological Research* 54 (1994), pp. 315–29.

64. Alex Byrne and David Hilbert, "Color Primitivism," *Erkenntnis* 66 (2007), pp. 73–105; David Chalmers, "Perception and the Fall from Eden," in *Perceptual Experience*, ed. Tamar Szabó and John Hawthorne (Oxford: Oxford University Press, 2006), pp. 49–125.
65. There is a reason to think that this belief-occasioning alternative is more credible than the first option. One might question whether the specific content at issue could be represented introspectively. In particular, the thought that introspection could represent the qualitative nature of a phenomenal property *as exhausted by* what the experience reveals seems less plausible to me than the corresponding claim about belief.
66. A property is absolutely intrinsic so long as it's intrinsic and its instances are not necessitated just by purely relational property instances. This allows a property that's not primitive to be absolutely intrinsic—for example, it's possible that a property be absolutely intrinsic and its nature not be revealed in any experience, and to be absolutely intrinsic and not be metaphysically simple.
67. The idea is that the a priori derivability of 'Mary senses red at time t' from 'P*' will be on a par with the a priori derivability of 'there is water' from 'P.' As a result, just as 'P and there is no water' is not ideally, positively, primarily conceivable, 'P* and Mary does not sense red at t' will not be ideally, positively, primarily conceivable.
68. See Strawson, "Realistic Monism"; there Strawson also defends the stronger view, panpsychism; see also Thomas Nagel, "Panpsychism," in his *Mortal Questions* (Oxford: Oxford University Press, 1979).
69. Thanks to Nico Silins for this characterization.
70. See my *Consciousness and the Prospects of Physicalism*, chap. 1.
71. Thanks to Louis deRosset for this suggestion.
72. Karen Bennett, "Why I Am Not a Dualist," ms.
73. McGinn, "What Constitutes the Mind-Body Problem," p. 24.
74. Nagel, *The View from Nowhere*, pp. 52–53.
75. I argue for this view in the first four chapters of *Consciousness and the Prospects of Physicalism*.
76. Thanks to Torin Alter, Ralf Bader, Karen Bennett, David Chalmers, Andrew Chignell, Louis deRosset, Tyler Doggett, Uriah Kriegel, Andrew McGonigal, Alyssa Ney, Sydney Shoemaker, Nico Silins, and Daniel Stoljar for valuable comments and discussion.

References

Adams, Robert. "Idealism Vindicated." In *Persons, Human and Divine*, ed. Peter van Inwagen and Dean Zimmerman, 35–54. Oxford: Oxford University Press, 2007.

Almog, Joseph. *What Am I? Descartes and the Mind-Body Problem.* New York: Oxford University Press, 2002.

Alter, Torin. "Does the Ignorance Hypothesis Undermine the Conceivability and Knowledge Arguments?" *Philosophy and Phenomenological Research* 79 (2009): 756–65.

Armstrong, David. *Perception and the Physical World.* London: Routledge, 1961.

Armstrong, David. *A Materialist Theory of Mind.* London: Routledge, 1968.

Arnauld, Antoine. "Fourth Set of Objections (to René Descartes's *Meditations on First Philosophy*)." In *The Philosophical Writings of Descartes*, vol. 2, trans. and ed. John Cottingham, Robert Stoothoff, and Dugald Murdoch. Cambridge: Cambridge University Press, 1984.

Bealer, George. "Modal Epistemology and the Rationalist Renaissance." In *Conceivability and Possibility*, ed. Tamar Szabó Gendler and John Hawthorne, 77–125. Oxford: Oxford University Press, 2002.

Berkeley, George. *Three Dialogues between Hylas and Philonous*, ed. Jonathan Dancy. Oxford: Oxford University Press, 1998.

Berkeley, George. *A Treatise Concerning the Principles of Human Knowledge*, ed. Jonathan Dancy. Oxford: Oxford University Press, 1998.

Byrne, Alex, and David Hilbert. "Color Primitivism." *Erkenntnis* 66 (2007): 73–105.

Chalmers, David. *The Conscious Mind*. Oxford: Oxford University Press, 1996.

Chalmers, David. "Materialism and the Metaphysics of Modality." *Philosophy and Phenomenological Research* 59 (1999): 473–96.

Chalmers, David. "Consciousness and Its Place in Nature." In the *Blackwell Guide to the Philosophy of Mind*. Oxford: Blackwell, 2002. Reprinted in *Philosophy of Mind: Classical and Contemporary Readings*, ed. David Chalmers, 247–72. New York: Oxford University Press, 2002.

Chalmers, David. "Does Conceivability Entail Possibility?" In *Conceivability and Possibility*, ed. Tamar Gendler and John Hawthorne, 145–200. Oxford: Oxford University Press, 2002.

Chalmers, David. "The Content and Epistemology of Phenomenal Belief." In *Consciousness: New Philosophical Perspectives*, ed. Q. Smith and A. Jokic. Oxford: Oxford University Press, 2003, pp. 220-72.

Chalmers, David. "Perception and the Fall from Eden," in *Perceptual Experience*, ed. Tamar Szabó and John Hawthorne. Oxford: Oxford University Press, 2006, pp. 49–125.

Chalmers, David. "The Two-Dimensional Argument against Materialism." In *The Character of Consciousness*. New York: Oxford University Press, 2012.

Chalmers, David, and Frank Jackson. "Conceptual Analysis and Reductive Explanation." *Philosophical Review* 110 (2001): 315–61.

Descartes, René. *Oeuvres de Descartes*, 11 vols., ed. Charles Adam and Paul Tannery. Paris: J. Vrin, 1964–1976. (Abbreviated as "AT.")

Descartes, René. *The Philosophical Writings of Descartes*, 3 vols., trans. and ed. John Cottingham, Robert Stoothoff, and Dugald Murdoch. Cambridge: Cambridge University Press, 1984.

Fara, Michael. "Dispositions." *The Stanford Encyclopedia of Philosophy* (Summer 2009 Edition), Edward N. Zalta (ed.). Retrieved from http://plato.stanford.edu/archives/sum2009/entries/dispositions/

Hawthorne, John. "Causal Structuralism." *Philosophical Perspectives* 15 (2001): 361–78.

Holden, Thomas. *The Architecture of Matter*. Oxford: Oxford University Press, 2004.

Humberstone, Lloyd. "Intrinsic/Extrinsic." *Synthese* 105 (1996): 205–67.

Jackson, Frank. *From Metaphysics to Ethics*. Oxford: Oxford University Press, 1998.

Kant, Immanuel. *Kants gesammelte Schriften*, 29 vols., ed. Koniglichen Preussischen Akademie der Wissenschaften. Berlin: Walter de Gruyter, 1902–1980. (Abbreviated as "Ak.")

Kant, Immanuel. *Critique of Pure Reason*, trans. Paul Guyer and Allen Wood. Cambridge: Cambridge University Press, 1987.

Kant, Immanuel. *Metaphysical Foundations of Natural Science*, trans. Michael Friedman. Cambridge: Cambridge University Press, 2004.

Kripke, Saul. *Naming and Necessity*. Cambridge, MA: Harvard University Press, 1980.

Ladyman, James, and Don Ross, with David Spurrett and John Collier. *Every Thing Must Go*. Oxford: Oxford University Press, 2007.

Langton, Rae. *Kantian Humility: Our Ignorance of Things in Themselves*. Oxford, UK: Oxford University Press, 1998.

Langton, Rae. "Elusive Knowledge of Things in Themselves." *Australasian Journal of Philosophy* 82 (2004): 129–36.

Langton, Rae, and David Lewis. "Defining 'Intrinsic.'" *Philosophy and Phenomenological Research* 58 (1998): 333–45.

Leibniz, Gottfried Wilhelm. *G. W. Leibniz, Mathemathische Schriften*, 7 vols., ed. C. I. Gerhardt. Berlin and Halle: Asher et Comp, 1849–1856.

Leibniz, Gottfried Wilhelm. *G. W. Leibniz, Die philosophischen Schriften*, 7 vols., ed. C. I. Gerhard. Hildesheim, Germany: Olms, 1965.

Leibniz, Gottfried Wilhelm. *Philosophical Papers and Letters*, trans. and ed. L. E. Loemker. Dordrecht, the Netherlands: D. Reidel, 1969.

Lewis, David. "Ramseyan Humility." In *Conceptual Analysis and Philosophical Naturalism*, ed. David Braddon-Mitchell and Robert Nola, 203–22. Cambridge, MA: MIT Press, 2009.

Locke, Dustin. "A Partial Defense of Ramseyan Humility." In *Conceptual Analysis and Philosophical Naturalism*, ed. David Braddon-Mitchell and Robert Nola, 223–41. Cambridge, MA: MIT Press, 2009.

Locke, John. *An Essay Concerning Human Understanding*, ed. P. H. Nidditch. Oxford: Oxford University Press, 1975.

McGinn, Colin. "How Not to Solve the Mind-Body Problem." In *Physicalism and Its Discontents*, ed. Carl Gillett and Barry Loewer. Cambridge: Cambridge University Press, 2001.

McGinn, Colin. "What Constitutes the Mind-Body Problem." In *Consciousness and Its Objects*. Oxford: Oxford University Press, 2004.

McKitrick, Jennifer. "The Bare Metaphysical Possibility of Bare Dispositions." *Philosophy and Phenomenological Research* 66 (2003): 349–69.

Nagel, Thomas. "What Is It Like to Be a Bat?" *Philosophical Review* 83 (1974): 435–50.

Nagel, Thomas. "Panpsychism." In *Mortal Questions*. Oxford: Oxford University Press, 1979.

Nagel, Thomas. *The View from Nowhere*. New York: Oxford University Press, 1986.

Ney, Alyssa. "Physicalism and Our Knowledge of Intrinsic Properties." *Australasian Journal of Philosophy* 85 (2007): 41–60.

Pereboom, Derk. "Is Kant's Transcendental Philosophy Inconsistent?" *History of Philosophy Quarterly* 8 (1991): 357–71.

Pereboom, Derk. "Kant's Amphiboly." *Archiv für Geschichte der Philosophie* 73 (1991): 50–70.

Pereboom, Derk. "Bats, Brain Scientists, and the Limitations of Introspection." *Philosophy and Phenomenological Research* 54 (1994): 315–29.

Pereboom, Derk. *Consciousness and the Prospects of Physicalism*. New York: Oxford University Press, 2011.

Rozemond, Marleen. *Descartes's Dualism*. Cambridge, MA: Harvard University Press, 1998.

Russell, Bertrand. *The Analysis of Matter*. London: Kegan Paul, 1927.

Schaffer, Jonathan. "Is There a Fundamental Level?" *Noûs* 37 (2003): 498–517.

Schaffer, Jonathan. "Quiddistic Knowledge." In *Lewisian Themes*, ed. Frank Jackson and Graham Priest, 210–30. Oxford: Oxford University Press, 2004.

Shoemaker, Sydney. "Causality and Properties." In *Time and Change*, ed. P. van Inwagen, 109–35. Dordrecht, the Netherlands: D. Reidel, 1980. Reprinted in Sydney Shoemaker, *Identity, Cause, and Mind*, 1st ed., Cambridge: Cambridge University Press, 1984, 206–33; and in the expanded 2nd ed., Oxford: Oxford University Press, 2003, 206–33.

Shoemaker, Sydney. "Causal and Metaphysical Necessity." *Pacific Philosophical Quarterly* 79 (1998): 59–77.

Stoljar, Daniel. *Ignorance and Imagination: The Epistemic Origin of the Problem of Consciousness*. New York: Oxford University Press, 2006.

Strawson, Galen. "Real Materialism." In *Real Materialism and Other Essays*, 19–51. Oxford: Oxford University Press, 2008. (An earlier version appeared in *Chomsky and His Critics*, ed. L. Antony and N. Hornstein. Oxford: Blackwell, 2003.)

Strawson, Galen. "Realistic Monism." In *Real Materialism and Other Essays*, 54–74. Oxford: Oxford University Press, 2008. First published in *Consciousness and Its Place in Nature*, ed. A. Freeman, 3–31. Thorverston, England: Imprint Academic, 2006.

van Cleve, James. "Inner States and Outer Relations: Kant and the Case for Monadism." In *Doing Philosophy Historically*, ed. Peter H. Hare, 231–47. Buffalo, NY: Prometheus, 1988.

van Cleve, James. "Receptivity and Our Knowledge of Intrinsic Properties." *Philosophy and Phenomenological Research* 65 (2002): 218–37.

Weatherson, Brian and Marshall, Dan, "Intrinsic vs. Extrinsic Properties." The Stanford Encyclopedia of Philosophy (Spring 2013 Edition), Edward N. Zalta (ed.). Retrieved from plato.stanford.edu/archives/spr2013/entries/intrinsic-extrinsic/.

Wilson, Margaret. *Descartes*. London: Routledge, 1978.

Yablo, Stephen. "The Real Distinction between Mind and Body." *Canadian Journal of Philosophy* 16 (1991): 149–201.

Yablo, Stephen. "Shoulda, Woulda, Coulda." In *Conceivability and Possibility*, ed. Tamar Gendler and John Hawthorne, 441–92. Oxford: Oxford University Press, 2002.

Suggestions for Further Reading

Chalmers, David. 2002. "Consciousness and Its Place in Nature." In *Philosophy of Mind: Classical and Contemporary Readings*, ed. D. J. Chalmers, 247-272. Oxford: Oxford University Press.
This article provides a now-authoritative organization of the modern logical space of positions on the mind-body problem, with particular emphasis on what the author calls "Type-F monism," which is effectively Russellian monism.

Lockwood, Michael. 1981. "What *Was* Russell's Neutral Monism?" *Midwest Studies in Philosophy* 6: 143–158.
This is a seminal text for the more recent revival of Russellian monism as an original option in the landscape of positions on the mind-body problem; it emphasizes the (epistemic) possibility of "qualitative continuity" between the mental and the physical.

Russell, Bertrand. 1927. *The Analysis of Matter*. London: Kegan Paul.
This is the main original text in which Russell develops and defends his brand of "neutral monism"; its main claim is that physics tells us only about the interrelations among properties, not about these properties' intrinsic natures, which therefore may well be neither physical nor mental.

Stoljar, Daniel. 2001. "Two Conceptions of the Physical." *Philosophy and Phenomenological Research* 62: 253–281.
In the eyes of many, this paper offers the most worked out version of Russellian monism, distinguishing two kinds of physicalism and arguing that one of them may accommodate the traditional motivation for dualist views.

PART II

Mind in Body

The Scope and Nature of
Embodied Cognition

CHAPTER 3

When Is Cognition Embodied?

LAWRENCE SHAPIRO

Chapter Overview

Alvin Goldman has the right idea. The idea: to offer "a philosophical, or conceptual, proposal, namely, an interpretation of the notion of embodied cognition, a proposed definition of the phrase" (forthcoming: 1). The rightness: Embodied Cognition (the field)[1] seems to need just such a philosophical, or conceptual, interpretation of embodied cognition (the subject). I begin this chapter explaining in more detail the rightness of Goldman's idea, why his endeavor is an important one. I then turn to the idea itself—the definition of embodiment that Goldman proposes. Evaluation of the idea reveals some significant problems, but attaining the perspective from which these problems become visible sheds useful light on the nature of Embodied Cognition.

The Whats, Whichs, and Whys of a Science

Ask a bunch of chemists what they study, which concepts are important for understanding their subject matter, and why modern chemistry was necessary in the first place, and you're likely to receive answers that, while perhaps not exactly uniform, are nevertheless pretty similar. "We study atoms, molecules, compounds and reactions," they're likely to say. And to understand these things, they'll continue, you need concepts like atomic number, charge, chemical bond, and phase. Historically inclined chemists might go on to note that modern chemistry differs significantly from its alchemical predecessors, which took as a main goal the transmutation of common metals into gold and, more generally, sought to bring metals (and human beings too) closer to their states of perfection.

That chemists can agree on these three topics—namely, *what* they study, *which* concepts are necessary for studying it, and *why* chemistry is necessary in the first place—is a good thing, for reasons we'll soon come to, but it's also hardly surprising. A rough consensus about the subject matter, central concepts, and departures from preceding ideas can be readily found also among biologists. Biologists study living organisms, and concepts like the cell, evolution, mutation, and sex are fundamental to understanding the properties and diversity of living things. Modern biology replaced earlier, inadequate, theories that ran aground on entelechies, life forces, and the heritability of acquired traits.

One last example, and the only one with which I can claim to speak with any semblance of expertise: cognitive science, at least from its inception in the mid-twentieth century until today, has as its subject matter capacities like memory, perception, attention, language processing, and reasoning. The concepts that cognitive scientists take to be essential for understanding their domain include information, representations, and algorithms (where I remain neutral on whether these things are to be implemented in more traditional computational architectures or connectionist networks). Finally, cognitive science grew in prominence as its behaviorist predecessors, committed as they were to a sparse explanatory apparatus of stimulus, response, and reinforcement, failed to deliver the goods.

I mention chemistry, biology, and cognitive science to make a simple point. Scientists typically know what they're talking about when they're talking about their science.[2] They can say with a fair amount of precision what's in their domain of investigation and what is not, which concepts are necessary for understanding their subject matter and which are not, and why older concepts failed and newer ones were introduced to take their place. Consensuses are good for a number of reasons. Because scientists know what they're talking about when they're talking about their science, courses like Introduction to Chemistry (or Biology, or Cognitive Science) are possible, where students learn "the basics" and the next generation of scientists is born. Articles can be submitted to journals and judged with respect to their significance, quality, and general interest. Teams of researchers in different laboratories in different countries can tackle the same problems and share their discoveries and insights. When recalcitrant data appear, scientists can puzzle over which fundamental assumptions might be at fault and whether they should be abandoned. The tree of knowledge blossoms, bearing fruit which ripen and fall to the ground, creating new trees.

The stage is now set to appreciate the value in Goldman's effort to look for a consensus within Embodied Cognition. The whats of Embodied Cognition appear to be unmanageably diverse. Consider the variety in the following list of topics:

1) The development of stepping behavior in infants (Thelen and Ulrich 1991).
2) Robots that navigate through busy environments collecting soda cans (Brooks 1991).

3) The action-sentence compatibility effect, which is taken as evidence that the motor system plays a role in sentence comprehension (Glenberg and Kaschak 2002).
4) The use of "deictic codes," involving the fixation of ocular focus on objects in the environment, in the completion of matching tasks (Ballard, Hayhoe, Pook, and Rao 1997).
5) Categorical perception in a simulated agent (Beer 2003).
6) Coordination dynamics, as in the shift from out-of-phase finger wagging to in-phase (Kelso 1995).
7) An organism's capacity to create its own world via its unique sensory-action systems (Varela, Thompson, and Rosch 1991).
8) The role of metaphor in concept acquisition (Lakoff and Johnson 1999).
9) The placement of ears to facilitate song recognition and phonotaxis in a robot cricket (Lund, Webb, and Hallam 1998).
10) The dependence of perceptual experience on the particularities of sensorimotor systems (O'Regan and Nöe 2001).

Anyone who has read introductory guides to Embodied Cognition (e.g., Clark 1997, 2008; Shapiro 2007, 2011, 2012; Wilson 2002; Wilson and Foglia 2011) will recognize most or all of the examples listed previously. They comprise the standards that presumably define the field. Yet, saying why these ten items should be *explananda* of a single science is achingly difficult. It is hardly clear what unifies these items. Items (1), (2), and (6), for instance, seem primarily concerned with the explanation of gross behavior and might indeed be objects of investigation in a behaviorist's laboratory. The authors emphasize the role of interactions between muscles or bodies, with each other or with the environment. They minimize or reject altogether the need for representation as an explanatory tool. On the other hand, (8), (9), and (10) investigate phenomena more closely associated with traditional cognitive psychology. In each case, the role of the body is thought to play something like a constitutive role in processing, either by determining the content of an agent's concepts, serving a function usually assigned to neural circuitry, or fixing the content of perceptual experience. The real content of (7) is far from clear but suggests ideas from ecological psychology. Item (5) also sounds like a capacity that a classically trained cognitive scientist might study, and yet in this case the investigator sides with the antirepresentationalism that pervades (1) and (2). Item (3) buys into some of the Gibsonian ideas that motivate (7) but also resembles (8) and (10) in its suggestion that the body somehow informs cognition. Item (4) is somewhat akin to (9), (10), and (2) in emphasizing the body's (in this case, the eyes') capacity to do a job traditionally attributed to psychological processes.

In a number of illuminating efforts to pull together the apparently disparate subject matters of Embodied Cognition, theoretically inclined researchers have offered tentative characterizations of the field (Clark 1997, 1999, 2008;

Wilson 2002; Anderson 2003; Ziemke 2003; Shapiro 2007, 2011, 2012; Wilson and Foglia 2011). These are the "whichs" of Embodied Cognition—the lists of concepts necessary to explain the phenomena. Although these efforts do not square precisely, a family resemblance in their proposals is undeniable.

Consider, for instance, Clark's (2008) description of crucial explanatory concepts. Clark lists a number of ideas as being particularly important for understanding embodied cognition, of which I'll mention just three:

(1) *Nontrivial Causal Spread*: In a shift from trying to explain an agent's behavior as the exclusive product of internal workings, as, say, the behavior of a grandfather clock might be, research in Embodied Cognition assumes that agents might make do with far less internal processing by exploiting relationships between their bodies and the environment. Thus, bipedal robots, instead of relying on sophisticated programming and fancy in order to walk, might exploit instead the mechanical properties of their legs and physical properties of the surfaces on which they walk. Collins et al. (2005: 1083) describe one of the "passive-dynamic walkers" they have created as marking a contrast to traditional robots, "which actively control every joint angle at all times." Collins et al.'s robots are not programmed or equipped to control any joint angles, but rather take advantage of external forces like gravity and friction.

(2) *Open Channel Perception*: Rather than analyzing perception as a process in which images of the environment are collected, processed, and interpreted for purposes of action, perception should be viewed as "the opening of a channel" (Clark 2008: 16) between an agent and its environment. The agent is in close and intimate contact with its environment at all times, as a blind person might be when using a cane to navigate through a shopping mall. The continuous interactions between the cane and the environment make unnecessary the construction of a map or model for purposes of navigation.

(3) *Information Self-Structuring*: Agents are not passive recipients of the information they require to solve cognitive tasks but act on the world in ways that cause it to release valuable information. For instance, robots and humans alike can acquire knowledge about their worlds by pushing, pulling, touching, tapping, and slapping. These actions reveal information about object size, object boundaries, object surfaces, and object distances. Thus, through manipulations of its body, an agent gathers more information than it could if simply waiting for the information to come on its own, thereby changing and simplifying the processing tasks of the brain.

How do these ideas make contact with the ten areas of investigation I listed previously? Very well, perhaps raising hope that they are not so disunified as I earlier intimated. But I shall now argue that this hope must be forsaken. First, let's agree that Clark's concepts succeed in describing explanatory ideas that bring results in most of the ten areas. To argue this in detail would be tedious, so let the following suffice. Most of the ten research areas emphasize one or more of nontrivial causal spread (1, 2, 4, 5, 6, 7, 9, and 10), open channel perception (2, 4, 5, 7, and 9), and information self-structuring (2, 5, 7, 9, and 10). Problematic cases are (3) and (8), which appear concerned with explaining phenomena that depend less on body-world interaction than on body-mind interaction. For instance, Glenberg's research suggests that sentence comprehension, a psychological capacity, might depend on activity in motor centers in the brain that typically correlates with bodily movement; Lakoff and Johnson believe that properties of the body constrain the kinds of concepts we are capable of acquiring.

But even granting that Clark's explanatory principles figure importantly in eight of the ten items on the list, I think they do not actually unify the list. The problem can be put like this: we can accept that *if* each of the remaining eight phenomena are instances of cognition, then the ideas of nontrivial causal spread, open channel perception, and information self-structuring turn out to be important for their investigation. Thus, we could go so far as to suggest that cognition of these eight sorts is embodied. However, Clark's principles don't tell us about the nature of *cognition*, only about the nature of *embodiment*. Hence, they are mute as far as providing a guide to embodied *cognition*. The passive-dynamic walkers mentioned previously make this point clearly—their capacity to walk is embodied yet clearly involves no more cognition than does a Slinky's descent down a staircase.

Considering (1), (2), (5), and (6) brings this point into clearer relief. Thelen's work on infant stepping behavior, Brooks's work on robot navigation, Kelso's on finger wagging, and Beer's on categorical perception in a simulated agent might all be rejected as genuinely cognitive abilities despite the fact that they serve well as illustrations of nontrivial causal spread, open channel perception, and information self-structuring. Indeed, we might harbor reservations that these phenomena are genuinely cognitive for precisely the reasons their investigators take them to be embodied—their explanations attribute so much to body-world dynamics that there's very little need for cognition proper. It's no wonder that the authors of these studies demur when asked whether representational states—a hallmark of cognition—figure into their explanatory frameworks.[3]

On the other hand, (4), (9), and (10) also illustrate Clark's concepts but do so without repudiating the standard conception of cognition as involving information processing and representation. In the first case, Ballard essentially attributes to the world the role of memory storage that cognitive scientists traditionally ascribe to internal representational states. In the second, Lund et al.'s study of a cricket robot reveals the importance of the physical location and connections of the cricket's auditory sensors (on its legs and upper body) in song recognition and localization but never denies the significance of information processing. In the last, O'Regan and Nöe attribute sensorimotor activities a more prominent role in perceptual experience than typically supposed and reject the necessity of internal representations, but nevertheless insist that the "outside world serves as its own, external, representation" (2001: 939). Ballard et al., Lund et al., and O'Regan and Nöe thus prove that ideas of embodiment can coexist with the standard conception of cognition as involving representation.

So, my tentative conclusion is that Clark may be of help to those who wish to understand how *embodied* cognition differs from *nonembodied* cognition, but he can't satisfy those who wish to understand how embodied *cognition* differs from embodied *noncognition*. His concepts of embodiment cross-classify the cognitive and noncognitive domains. Indeed, researchers who favor dynamic approaches to "cognition" seem to recognize that they have adopted a nonstandard view of cognition, as when, for instance, Chemero writes "cognitive scientists ought to try to understand cognition as intelligent behavior and to model intelligent behavior using a particular sort of mathematics, most often sets of differential equations" (2009: 25). "Intelligent behavior" is a neutral label, not entailing anything about the mechanisms that produce behavior, be they cognitive in the traditional "rules and represention" sense, or not, as in the case of Brooks's robots or passive-dynamic walkers.

Granting my claim that attempts like Clark's to articulate the basic ideas of Embodied Cognition fail to unify its subject matter, disagreement over the relationship between embodied cognitive science and what I have been calling traditional, or classical, cognitive science is hardly surprising. This takes us to the "why" of Embodied Cognition. What justifies a shift from traditional cognitive science? Some in the Embodied community take world-agent relationships to obviate the need for representational capacities that are the usual explanatory targets of traditional cognitive scientists. As noted, this attitude is most conspicuous in laboratories that pursue dynamic approaches to cognition. If correct, then rejection of traditional cognitive science may well be warranted. However, we might wonder whether the "new" science of embodied cognition tracks the same *explananda* of the old, or whether, as I just suggested, alongside the dynamic approaches is an entirely different conception of cognition. Also worth noting is that plenty of dynamicists remain convinced of the importance of traditional ideas like representation, and show no real enthusiasm for tossing out the "old" (e.g., Spivey 2007). Others (e.g., Lakoff 2003; Glenberg 1997) believe that attention to the body's role in cognition marks a significant departure from traditional cognitive science, but whether this constitutes an actual break or merely a shift in emphasis is open to question (Shapiro 2011, 2012; Wilson and Foglia 2011). In part, the answer depends on a precise characterization of the role that the body plays—Is it a causal influence on cognition? An actual constituent of a cognitive process? A cognitive process itself?—that to date remains elusive.

Much more can and should be said about the subject matter and explanatory concepts of Embodied Cognition, as well as the relationship between Embodied Cognition and traditional cognitive science (see Shapiro [2011] for some efforts in these directions). However, because the previous remarks are mainly intended to underscore the interest of Goldman's project, they suffice. Embodied Cognition lacks the uniformity that other sciences boast. The borders of its subject matter are nebulous and disagreements persist over whether it replaces, extends, or complements standard cognitive science. A "philosophical, or conceptual, proposal" regarding how we are to interpret the phrase "embodied cognition" would be most welcome indeed.

Goldman's Idea: Neural Reuse

One way to arrive at the whats, whichs, and whys of Embodied Cognition would be to *define*, in the traditional sense of offering necessary and sufficient conditions, precisely when cognition is embodied. Such a strategy invites a hunt for counterexamples, but it also makes for a tidy package. Goldman opts for tidy: "Cognition C is a specimen of embodied cognition if and only if C uses some member of a special class of *codes* or *formats* for representing and/or processing its content, viz., a *body-related* code or format (*B-code* or *B-format*)" (forthcoming: 3).

The idea of a code (or format) for representing is uncontroversial, reflecting nothing more than a familiar distinction between the formal and semantic properties of a language. Comprising the formal properties of a particular expression in, for example, English, are the shapes of the individual components of the expression in virtue of which they stand as tokens of particular letter types, in combinations that make them tokens of particular word types, with grammatical markers that tie them together in ways that make them tokens of particular sentence types. The semantic or representational properties of an English expression are said to "mirror" the formal ones, so that the meaning of the expression depends on how letters are strung into words are composed into sentences. Exactly how collections of symbols come to have meaning—secrete a semantics—is a matter of ongoing debate, but that they do is rarely questioned.

Most neuroscientists believe that the brain contains codes of its own. Whereas the English code consists of characters of various shapes and rules of grammar for their composition, and American Sign Language code consists of other kinds of shapes (produced by hands in motion) and a grammar for *their* composition, so too the brain employs codes in a neural syntax for the purpose of representing a variety of states of affairs. Moreover, distinct codes might be used for representing different kinds of facts. For instance, some neurons might encode some features of a stimulus (e.g., light intensity) in terms of rate of firing, but rate of firing might be a poor way to encode other features of a stimulus. Spatial location too might play an important coding role, as it seems to in various topographic maps of sensory surfaces.

We can think of neural codes as differing along two dimensions. The first dimension concerns their formal features—whether they code in a language of firing rate, or in a language of firing synchrony, or in a language of population behaviors. The second dimension concerns their semantic content—what they represent. Given these two dimensions, we can ask two questions of some neural activity: (1) What kind of code is it (analogously, is a given language English or ASL)? (2) What does the code say (what does it mean or represent)? Visual code, for instance, is distinct from other kinds of codes in part because it is localized to particular parts of the brain that are specialize in processing information from the eyes. Additionally, it might rely on firing rate to represent some stimulus properties (e.g., light intensity) and activation of organized populations of neurons to represent other properties. So now we have answers to the two previous questions: these neurons are in a visual code and they represent properties like light intensity and motion.

The first step in Goldman's approach to defining embodied cognitions is now easy to understand. Embodied cognitions are those that (1) use a body code (a *B-code*, or *B-format*) that (2) represents properties of the body. The second condition is straightforward, but the first requires additional clarification. Presumably, B-codes are localized to those portions of the brain that dedicated exclusively to the representation of bodily states and bodily actions. As Goldman (forthcoming: 3) says,

> Proprioception and kinaesthesis give the brain information—couched, presumably, in distinctive formats—about states of one's own muscles, joints, and limb positions. These interoceptive senses are the basis for B-formats of representation. One's own body, or selected parts thereof, is what they *primarily*, or *fundamentally*, represent.

An experience of pain also counts, for Goldman, as an instance of an embodied cognition because the experience depends on activation of areas of the brain with the special function of representing disturbances within the body.

The two dimensions—code format and code content—in some cases come apart. Suppose I look at my hand (Goldman, forthcoming: 3). Although my perception of my hand comes about in part by neural activity that represents a feature of my body, the representation is coded in a *visual* format and is thus not embodied. Conversely, if a given token body code represents something other than a bodily state (and I have no idea whether this is nomically possible), again we must rule against the cognition as being embodied. It has the wrong content.[4]

If Goldman stopped here, embodied cognitions would be limited simply to cognitions about the body (but, again, not all cognitions about the body would be embodied), and one could reasonably doubt that Goldman's definition has captured most of what interests researchers in Embodied Cognition (who, as we saw previously, study topics like language, categorical perception, and metaphor). But suppose that sometimes a B-code that represents facts about the body is used for a purpose other than that for which it originally evolved. This brings us to step two.

The Tin Man, we all know, had a funnel for a hat. This illustrates the obvious point that items made for one purpose might be "reused" for another. An item originally used for pouring liquids into small-mouthed containers gets reused for something else—namely, a hat. Turning from artifacts to organisms, we find that evolution is an expert reuser. The male urethra becomes a conduit for sperm. Reptilian jawbones become components of mammalian ears. A panda's wrist bone becomes a thumb.

Anderson (2007, 2010) defends the hypothesis that brain circuitry shares with other evolved traits a tendency for reuse. One source of evidence for neural reuse employs the so-called subtraction method. A subject's brain is monitored while he or she performs an experimental task A. The subject then performs another task B. Now subtract the portions of the brain active during performance of task A from those active during task B. Left over is the activation of those areas of the brain used only for completion of B. Thus, if both tasks A and B require visual processes, these will be subtracted out. Anderson's interest was in finding those areas of the brain that are reused in distinct kinds of tasks—that would be subtracted out in comparisons of brain activity involved in tasks ranging over different cognitive domains (e.g., "attention, emotion, language, mathematics, memory, and reasoning" [Anderson 2010: 258]). Analysis of the data reveals the following: "(1) Regions of the brain—even fairly small regions—are typically reused in multiple domains. (2) If a region is involved in perception tasks, action tasks, or both, it is more likely to be reused than if it is not involved in such tasks. (3) Regions not involved in such tasks are nevertheless more likely than not to be reused in multiple domains" (ibid.).

Although we will need to consider more exactly the idea of reuse, for now let's simply grant the correctness of Anderson's analysis and agree with his conclusion that many regions of the brain that evolved originally for one purpose (e.g., action planning) get co-opted for other purposes (e.g., perception). We can now introduce the idea that makes Goldman's definition of embodied cognition attractive and interesting. Embodied cognitions needn't be limited to cognitions having to do with pain, limb motions, and bodily orientation, because B-codes that represent states of the body might on occasion be reused in tasks having no obvious connection to the body. If sentence comprehension, for instance, recruits a B-code, or if the memory system does, then these capacities are, by Goldman's definition, embodied.

The two steps to Goldman's position come together in his statement of the "core thesis" of Embodied Cognition:

(Core Thesis) Embodied cognition is a significant and pervasive sector of human cognition because

(1) B-formats in their primary uses are an important part of cognition, and
(2) B-formats are massively redeployed or reused for many other cognitive tasks, including tasks of social cognition. (forthcoming: 10)

The importance of the thesis, Goldman continues, derives from its power to provide "a theoretical unification of the empirical findings that makes systematic sense of these assorted findings" (ibid.).

Goldman cites a few examples that give flesh to his idea. Glenberg and Kaschak (2002) demonstrated an action-sentence compatibility effect. When asked to judge whether a sentence like "Open the drawer" is sensible (in contrast to a sentence like "Hang the coat on the cup"), subjects were slower to respond if their response required a motion in a direction opposite to that entailed by the sentence (pushing a lever for "Open the drawer"; pulling a lever for "Close the drawer"). Goldman summarizes their results: "So, the simple comprehension of a sentence apparently activated action-related representations" (forthcoming: 6).

Next consider Proffitt's work on perception. Bhalla and Proffitt (1999) presented subjects with a hill-judgment task, requiring them to estimate the slant of a long hill extending in front of them. Subjects in the test condition wore a backpack loaded with weights. Bhalla and Proffitt found that these subjects tended to overestimate the hill's slant on verbal and visual measures more than did subjects in the control condition. Goldman agrees with Bhalla and Proffitt's interpretation of these results, taking them to show that B-coded representations (in this case, of the weight on the back) "influence representations of non-bodily objects" (forthcoming: 13).

The experimental work of Glenberg and Proffitt nicely illustrates Goldman's core thesis. In the first case, it appears as if B-coded representations that usually have the function of causing arm movements take on a new use—now they influence judgments about sentence sensibility. In the second case, B-coded representations that usually serve to carry information about the burden on one's back have been redeployed for use in perceptual judgments about hill slant. Language comprehension and perception turn out, quite surprisingly, to be, according to Goldman's definition, embodied.

The Gold in Goldman's Idea

As I detailed previously, anyone who has read enough of the literature in Embodied Cognition will appreciate an effort to unify its various pursuits. Reflecting the range of topics within Embodied Cognition is a wide scattering of views on how, exactly, the body contributes to cognition.[5] Wade through this literature and you'll find that statements of the body's role in embodied cognition are varied, vague, sometimes inconsistent, often trivial.[6]

Helpfully, Clark (1999) distinguishes between simple and radical embodiment. Simple embodiment is the idea that an organism's body *influences* its representational capacities in some manner, perhaps as Lakoff (2003) suggests when he argues that the content of human concepts are constrained by the morphological features of human bodies. *Radical* embodiment, on the other hand, treats the body as a constituent in a cognitive system that extends beyond the brain and sees cognitive processing as involving an interplay between brain, body, and world. Now the body has gone from shaper of cognition to part of cognition proper.

These differences over the significance of the body for cognition are apparent in the ten research areas I mentioned previously. Items (1), (2), (5), (6), (9), and sometimes (10) adopt a radical embodied perspective; (3) and (8) lean toward simple embodiment; and (4) and (7) combine elements of each.

But even if we decide to focus on just simple embodiment, questions remain about *how* a body influences cognitive processes. Lakoff sees the influence moving through metaphorical reasoning. We literally stand tall when in a positive frame of mind and thus explicate concepts like happiness with metaphors like feeling *buoyant*, or *up*, or *high*, or *in seventh heaven*. But this sort of influence is nothing like that which Glenberg describes when he talks about the motor system contributing to sentence comprehension; nor is it like the sensorimotor contingencies that O'Regan and Nöe (2001) discuss, which determine the nature of perceptual experience.

A nice feature of Goldman's idea is that it sidesteps tricky discussions about how to decide whether the body is merely an influence on cognition or a piece of cognition. And if an influence, what sort of influence? If a piece, what kind of piece? That so much debate around these questions persists creates the impression that Embodied Cognition is hopelessly confused.[7] Goldman's definition gives a black-and-white criterion of embodiment. The process either uses a B-code or it doesn't.

Also to its credit, Goldman's definition of Embodied Cognition seems to capture the sense of embodiment at play in some especially prominent research. Glenberg, for instance, writes, "The embodiment claim for language is that sentences are understood by simulating sentence content using neural systems ordinarily used for perception, action, and emotion" (2010: 589). This is essentially Goldman's thesis: language comprehension is embodied because it draws on neural resources that have, among their primary uses, bodily functions like action. Similarly, Pulvermüller (2005) demonstrated that recognition of action words like *kick* and *lick* activates areas of motor cortex that are also active when kicking and licking. And Casasanto and Djikstra (2010) present evidence that a subject's ability to retrieve positive or negative memories involves a motor component (moving marbles upward from a lower platform to a higher one facilitates positive memories; moving marbles downward facilitates negative memories). This is the tip of the iceberg—numerous studies of cognitive capacities implicate the reuse of motor circuitry. Goldman's definition of embodiment would, as he hopes, unify them, explaining when processes of language, perception, memory, and so on are embodied and when not.

Questioning Goldman's Idea

As I noted, Goldman's idea has a number of merits. But one might also harbor suspicions that it's not the right way to think about embodiment. After all, it clearly applies only to two of the ten examples that are commonly cited to illustrate the subject matter of embodied cognition. Relatedly, we might ponder the wisdom of Goldman's insistence that reuse of a B-code be both necessary and sufficient for the embodiment of cognition. Let's begin with general worries.

Embodied Cognition should be a big idea, commensurate with the amount of buzz it has generated over the last twenty or so years. But on Goldman's view, Embodied Cognition is pretty small. Indeed, Goldman appears to recognize the deflationary nature of his project in the title of his paper, "A *Moderate* Approach to Embodied Cognitive Science" (my emphasis). He also notes that his "conception of embodied cognition is fully in sync with existing empirical research and raises no questions, for example, about such staples of traditional cognitive science as mental representation or computational processes" (forthcoming: 1). This alone attenuates what I have called the "why" of Embodied Cognition to an extent that would disillusion many practitioners. With friends like Goldman, who really needs Embodied Cognition?

But the deflationary air of Goldman's definition is nowhere more apparent than in the fact that embodiment, for Goldman, is consistent with the mind's being a brain in a vat. Because the activities of the body are screened off by the activation of B-codes, cognition turns out to be an exclusively neural event. Such a consequence suffices to cast doubt on the adequacy of Goldman's definition, for if anything might be said to capture the spirit of Embodied Cognition, it would be the slogan that brains ain't enough.

Revisiting the ideas Clark introduced, we see an emphasis on devaluing the brain's centrality in cognition. Additionally, we saw that this idea could be embraced across the representational/nonrepresentational divide, making it possible for even the strictest of cognitive purists to reject the brain centrism to which Goldman adheres. Undoubtedly, concepts like nontrivial causal spread, open channel perception, and information self-structuring have been important and inspirational in the growth of Embodied Cognition, and yet neither they nor even less specific kin like situatedness and embeddedness make an appearance in Goldman's account. All this suggests that Goldman's definition of Embodied Cognition omits something very important. Hence, when Goldman suggests that adoption of his version of Embodied Cognition "would mark a major shift in cognitive science as a whole" (forthcoming: 10), I doubt that the shift would be nearly major enough for most fans of Embodied Cognition. They would see it as a mere amendment to traditional cognitive science, requiring nothing terribly new by way of investigative tools or explanatory concepts, and their disappointment would be easy to understand.

But let's now consider more exactly the idea that use of a B-code provides necessary and sufficient conditions for the embodiment of cognition. Casting doubt on the necessity component of this claim is easier, for Goldman's emphasis on codes in the *human* brain carries with it the unattractive suggestion that cognition could not be embodied in anything but a human being. This means that even if one agreed that the activities of one of Brooks' creatures, or of Beer's simulated agent, were the product of cognitive processes, these processes could not, according to Goldman, be embodied.

The obvious rejoinder stipulates that Goldman's definition of embodied cognition is intended to apply only within the human domain. *Human* cognition is embodied if and only if . . . But the appeal of this response depends on its allowing the possibility of embodied cognition in nonhumans as well: *robot* embodied cognition; *simulated agent* embodied cognition; *cricket* embodied cognition; and so on. Now, however, we see a new kind of challenge to the necessity of B-codes. If Goldman is to evade charges of chauvinism, he must explain what it is about robots, simulated agents, and crickets that endows them with embodied cognitions. Must they possess nonneural B-codes? Once we grant the possibility of nonneural B-codes, the question turns to the problem of identifying them. But this invites speculation about why B-codes, or their nonneural analogues, are *necessary* for embodying cognition. Imagine, for instance, a robotic agent with a "brain" that contains no proprietary representational formats, but instead a single format capable of representing visual states, auditory states, *and* bodily states. Perhaps strings of this general code on occasion represent the orientation of the artificial agent's body and that this representation is used in the interpretation of visual data or linguistic data. Processing, in these cases, appears to have a compelling claim on being embodied in keeping with Goldman's suggestion, although in neither case is there anything fitting the description of a dedicated B-code.

This objection might be developed further. If Goldman allows embodied cognitions in our imaginary artificial agent, we must wonder why B-codes are necessary for embodied cognitions even in human beings. The feature of the artificial agent that made it eligible for embodied cognitions was its reuse of representations of the body in cognitive tasks like vision and language comprehension that are not dedicated to the representation of bodily states. But, we saw, Goldman explicitly denies that such cases of reuse suffice to embody cognition, demanding that the representations of bodily states take place in a specialized B-code. This simply reintroduces the problem, however, leaving us to ask whether embodied cognitions ever do occur in nonhuman agents.

Evaluation of the sufficiency requirement depends on empirical specula-tions of a different sort. One source of concern arises when wondering whether it might be possible to quantify the embodiment of a cognition. Presumably, the redeployment of B-codes is not an all-or-nothing affair. Some cognitive tasks might make more extensive reuse of B-codes than others. Perhaps huge amounts of motor circuitry are reused in the sentence comprehension task that Glenberg examined, but only small amounts in the memory retrieval task that Casasanto and Dijkstra studied. In the limiting case, a single string of B-code is reused in a cognitive task that otherwise makes extensive use of, say, the parts of the brain responsible for reasoning. But Goldman's definition of embodiment treats all such cases identically—they all illustrate embodiment.

To be sure, this is not a fatal objection to Goldman's definition, or perhaps not an objection at all. Rather, it is a cry for further research into the extent that B-codes permeate cognition. Nonetheless, once one is open to the possi-bility that some cognitions might turn out to be more embodied than others, questions about the nature of reuse come to the fore. Does reuse of any kind or quantity suffice to embody cognition? Without further qualifications, Gold-man's definition faces several worries.

One such worry arises when entertaining the possibility that *all* cognition, on Goldman's view, might end up embodied. This consequence is surprisingly plausible, and yet, if genuine, would magnify suspicions that Goldman fails to articulate the most salient aspects of embodied cognition—aspects that distinguish embodied approaches to understanding the mind from classically cognitive ones.

So, what speaks in favor of what I shall call *massive embodiment*? Consider first studies like Dijkstra et al. (2005). Dijkstra et al. summarize and collect evidence suggesting that the retrieval of autobiographical memories depends on body posture and facial expressions. Remembering details of your last visit to the dentist is easier when reclining in a chair than when standing straight with your hands on your hips. This work extends earlier studies, such as Rand and Wapner (1967), which found subjects could more easily relearn nonsense syllables when assuming the same posture they had when they initially learned them. Assuming that these studies implicate the redeployment of B-codes, it appears that the more we look for such effects, the more we find them.

Dijkstra et al. also cite, approvingly, Damasio's suggestion that virtually all memory retrieval activates the sensorimotor system. As Damasio (1999: 220) puts it:

> The brain forms memories in a highly distributed manner. Take, for instance, the memory of a hammer. There is no single place in our brain where we will find an entry with the word hammer followed by a

dictionary definition of what a hammer is. Instead ... there are a number of records in our brain that correspond to different aspects of our past interaction with hammers: their shape, the typical movement with which we use them, the hand shape and hand motion required to manipulate the hammer, the result of the action, the word that designates it in whatever many languages we know.

Damasio's vision of distributed memories is in keeping with Anderson's hypothesis of rampant neural reuse. The idea that concepts can be localized to particular centers in the brain is apparently far too simple. Mounting evidence tells a far more complicated story, and one that raises the prospect that B-codes are active in not just a few cognitive processes, but *every* cognitive process.

Again, although the existence of massive embodiment would not provide a counterexample to Goldman's definition of embodiment, it does, I think, threaten to trivialize it. Embodied cognitions should be a special class of cognitions. We should expect that the study of embodied cognition would demand its own set of crucial explanatory concepts and would distinguish itself from the investigations of nonembodied cognitions. That Goldman's definition puts at risk this ideal ought to generate skepticism that he has identified the real essence of embodiment.

Reconsideration of the Tin Man introduces a final note of skepticism about Goldman's sufficiency condition. When the Tin Man decided (and here I'm reading into Baum's novels) to reuse a funnel as a hat, his choice was not motivated by the fact that funnels have the function of easing the transfer of liquids into small-mouthed containers. The funnel could fit over his head and protect it from the sun. That's what made it a good choice. The Tin Man reused the funnel but didn't reuse it *because* it was a funnel. As far as I can tell, the studies Goldman cites in favor of his definition of embodiment are consistent with the possibility that cognitive capacities like sentence comprehension and perception do indeed reuse B-codes but don't reuse B-codes *because* they function to represent the body. Why does this matter?

I suspect that Goldman conceives of reuse as occurring *because* of what B-codes do. Cognitions are embodied when they reuse B-codes *because* B-codes have the function to represent bodily states. But suppose the reuse of B-codes is more like the Tin Man's reuse of a funnel. The properties that make the funnel a good hat—its opacity, its modest weight, its debonair style—are not the properties that make it a good funnel. The problem facing Goldman is that his sufficiency condition fails to distinguish between the two kinds of reuse. Cognitions are embodied, on his account, whether they reuse B-codes *because* B-codes represent conditions of the body, or because they might do other things quite unrelated to their function to represent the body. This, it seems to me, is a distinction that should not be overlooked and is one that places the burden on Goldman to justify his claim that any reuse of B-codes suffices to embody cognition.

Conclusion

Embodied Cognition seems to be a field in need of unification. Whereas chemists, biologists, and traditional cognitive scientists speak with synchronized voices about the whats, whichs, and whys of their respective sciences, conversations among embodied cognition researchers display a disquieting dissonance. I have suggested that the primary dividing line in the subject matter of Embodied Cognition is between capacities that are cognitive in the traditional representational sense and those that are not. Efforts like Clark's to characterize Embodied Cognition straddle this line, doing little to justify why some instances of embodied cognition are cognitive at all. This is not Goldman's problem, for, as we've seen, he continues to view cognition as computational processes over representational states. Rather, Goldman's difficulties reside in his claim that B-codes are necessary and sufficient for the embodiment of cognition. This characterization fails to encompass much, if not most, of the research in Embodied Cognition. Moreover, I've argued that consideration of nonhuman minds, with neural architectures that do not seem to support B-codes, might nevertheless be embodied; and that B-codes that are reused for reasons having nothing to do with their primary function to represent bodily states count, suspiciously on Goldman's account, as sufficient for embodiment.

In closing, we might wonder whether continued progress in Embodied Cognition will show that the search for unity is misguided—that efforts like Goldman's to define the field are pointless. We might decide that ideas like those which Clark describes—and that enjoy widespread acceptance—explain why the examination of *some* instances of cognition requires new concepts and a break from traditional cognitive science. Then we might find that other instances of cognition show heavy reliance on B-codes, making them targets for research that breaks from traditional cognitive science in other ways. Are cognitions of the first or second sort embodied? Does it matter?

Notes

1. I will continue to capitalize "Embodied Cognition" when referring to the field and will use lower case letters when referring to an embodied cognition.
2. In intend this in a colloquial sense of "know," not wishing to inflame debate about the sociology of scientific knowledge.
3. I'm of course not the first to note that many of the capacities studied within Embodied Cognition appear suspiciously noncognitive. Adams and Aizawa (2001, 2008) have argued at length that Embodied Cognition, especially those branches that defend the idea of extending cognition beyond an agent's head, needs to define a "mark" of the mental. Representational capacities of the sort that the brain has "naturally," are for them, a necessary condition of cognition.

4. Goldman's text is not clear on this point. In discussing the idea of reuse, to which we next turn, he says "suppose it turns out that B-formats are also redeployed or co-opted for representing things *other* than one's own bodily parts or states," (forthcoming: 4, his emphasis). This suggests that he would allow B-codes to represent nonbodily states of affairs. However, all his examples of redeployment suggest instead that the reuse of B-codes does not involve new representational functions (they don't come to represent, say, visual information), but instead involve the putting to new *use* of B-codes that continue to have their old representational function of representing bodily parts or states (e.g., representations of the body might play a processing role in capacities unrelated to the body).

5. I am here using "cognition" nonprejudicially, to encompass whatever it is that embodied cognition researchers study.

6. Here's a description, albeit for an audience of nonexperts, of Embodied Cognition in *Scientific American*: Embodied Cognition is "the idea that the mind is not only connected to the body but that the body influences the mind, [and] is one of the more counter-intuitive ideas in cognitive science" (McNerney 2011). Counterintuitive? It's about as counterintuitive as the idea that pennies fall when dropped. Of course the mind is "connected" to the body; of course the body influences the mind. No cognitive scientist would object to either claim, and so this description does nothing to distinguish Embodied Cognition from plain, old-fashioned cognitive science.

7. For a taste of this debate, see Block's comments on Nöe and the discussions of cause versus constituent in Adams and Aizawa (2008), Rupert (2004, 2009), and Shapiro (2011).

References

Adams, F., and Aizawa, K. (2001). "The Bounds of Cognition." *Philosophical Psychology* 14: 43–64.

Adams, F., and Aizawa, K. (2008). *The Bounds of Cognition* (Malden, MA: Blackwell Publishing).

Anderson, M. (2003). "Embodied Cognition: A Field Guide." *Artificial Intelligence* 149: 91–103.

Anderson, M. (2007). "The Massive Redeployment Hypothesis and the Functional Topography of the Brain." *Philosophical Psychology* 21: 143–174.

Anderson, M. (2010). "Neural Reuse: A Fundamental Organizational Principle of the Brain." *Behavioral and Brain Sciences* 33: 245–313.

Ballard, D., Hayhoe, M., Pook, P., and Rao, R. (1997). "Deictic Codes for the Embodiment of Cognition." *Behavioral and Brain Sciences* 20: 723–767.

Beer, R. (2003). "The Dynamics of Active Categorical Perception in an Evolved Model Agent." *Adaptive Behavior* 11: 209–243.

Bhalla, M., and Proffitt, D. (1999). "Visual-Motor Recalibration in Visual Slant Perception." *Journal of Experimental Psychology: Human Perception and Performance* 25: 1076–1096.

Brooks, R. (1991). "Intelligence without Representation." *Artificial Intelligence* 47: 139–159.

Casasanto, D., and Dijkstra, K. (2010). "Motor Action and Emotional Memory." *Cognition* 115: 179–185.

Chemero, A. (2009). *Radical Embodied Cognitive Science* (Cambridge, MA: MIT Press).

Clark, A. (1997). *Being There: Putting Brain, Body and World Together Again* (Cambridge. MA: MIT Press).

Clark, A. (1999). "An Embodied Cognitive Science." *Trends in Cognitive Sciences* 3: 345–351.

Clark, A. (2008). *Supersizing the Mind: Embodiment, Action, and Cognitive Extension* (Oxford: Oxford University Press).

Collins, S., Ruina, A., Tedrake, R., and Wisse, M. (2005). "Efficient Bipedal Robots Based on Passive-Dynamic Walkers." *Science* 307: 1082–1085.

Damasio, A. (1999). *The Feeling of What Happens: Body and Emotion in the Making of Consciousness* (NewYork: Harcourt Brace).

Dijkstra, K., Kaschak, M., and Zwaan, R. (2005). "Body Posture Facilitates Retrieval of Autobiographical Memories." *Cognition* 102: 139–149.

Glenberg, A. (1997). "What Memory Is For." *Behavioral and Brain Sciences* 20: 1–55.

Glenberg, A. (2010). "Embodiment as a Unifying Perspective for Psychology." *WIREs Cognitive Science* 1: 586–596.

Glenberg, A. M., and Kaschak, M. P. (2002). "Grounding Language in Action." *Psychonomic Bulletin & Review* 9: 558–565.

Goldman, A. (2012). "A Moderate Approach to Embodied Cognitive Science." *Review of Philosophy and Psychology 3*: 71–88.

Kelso, J. (1995). *Dynamic Patterns: The Self-Organization of Brain and Behavior* (Cambridge: MIT Press).

Lakoff, G. (2003). "How the Body Shapes Thought: Thinking with an All Too Human Brain." In A. Sanford and P. Johnson-Laird (eds.), *The Nature and Limits of Human Understanding: The 2001 Gifford Lectures at the University of Glasgow* (Edinburgh: T. & T. Clark Publishers, 49–74).

Lakoff, G., and Johnson, M. (1999). *Philosophy in the Flesh: The Embodied Mind and Its Challenge to Western Thought* (New York: Basic Books).

Lund, H., Webb, B., and Hallam, J. (1998). "Physical and Temporal Scaling Considerations in a Robot Model of Cricket Calling Song Preference." *Artificial Life* 4: 95–107.

McNerney, S. (2011). "A Brief Guide to Embodied Cognition: Why You Are Not Your Brain." Guest Blog for *Scientific American*. Available at: http://blogs.scientificamerican.com/guest-blog/2011/11/04/a-brief-guide-to-embodied-cognition-why-you-are-not-your-brain/.

O'Regan, J., and Noë, A. (2001). "A Sensorimotor Account of Vision and Visual Consciousness." *Behavioral and Brain Sciences* 24: 939–1031.

Pulvermüller, F. (2005). "Brain Mechanisms Linking Language and Action." *Nature Reviews: Neuroscience* 6: 576–582.

Rand, G., and Wapner, S. (1967). "Postural Status as a Factor in Memory." *Journal of Verbal Learning and Verbal Behavior* 6: 268–271.

Rupert, R. (2004). "Challenges to the Hypothesis of Extended Cognition." *The Journal of Philosophy* 101: 1–40.

Rupert, R. (2009). *Cognitive Systems and the Extended Mind* (New York: Oxford University Press).

Shapiro, L. (2007). "The Embodied Cognition Research Programme." *Philosophy Compass* 2: 338–346.

Shapiro, L. (2011). *Embodied Cognition* (New York: Routledge).

Shapiro, L. (2012). "Embodied Cognition." In E. Margolis, R. Samuels, and S. Stich (eds.), *The Oxford Handbook of Philosophy of Cognitive Science* (New York: Oxford University Press, 118–147).

Spivey, M. (2007). *The Continuity of Mind* (New York: Oxford University Press).

Thelen, E., and Ulrich, B. (1991) "Hidden Skills: A Dynamic Systems Analysis of Treadmill Stepping During the First Year." *Monographs of the Society for Research in Child Development* 56: 1–97.

Varela, F., Thompson, E., and Rosch, E. (1991). *The Embodied Mind: Cognitive Science and Human Experience* (Cambridge, MA: MIT Press).

Wilson, M. (2002). "Six Views of Embodied Cognition." *Psychological Bulletin and Review* 9: 625–636.

Wilson, R., and Foglia, L. (2011). "Embodied Cognition." *Stanford Encyclopedia of Philosophy*. Available at: http://plato.stanford.edu/entries/embodied-cognition/.

Ziemke, T. (2003). "What's That Thing Called Embodiment?" In R. Alterman and D. Kirsh (eds.), *Proceedings of the 25th Annual Conference of the Cognitive Science Society* (Mahwah, NJ: Lawrence Erlbaum, 1134–1139).

CHAPTER 4

The Bodily Formats Approach to Embodied Cognition

ALVIN I. GOLDMAN

Chapter Overview

In the past few decades, many practitioners of cognitive science and philosophy of mind have staked out programs and positions under the label of "embodied cognition" (EC). They have widely differing views, however, of what embodiment consists in and why a program of embodied cognition might be an improvement over classical cognitivism. Frederique de Vignemont and I have recently proposed a general characterization of embodied cognition (Goldman & Vignemont, 2009), and I have expanded on the ramifications of this conception when one adds to it evolutionary considerations and a certain attractive conception of neuroarchitecture (Goldman, 2012). On this occasion, I review the definitional proposal in the context of other conceptions of embodiment and show how an assortment of empirical evidence lends strength to our proposal. Finally, I reply to Lawrence Shapiro (this volume, Chapter 3), who raises a series of challenges for our conception.

Existing proposals for EC can be divided into two general categories: proposals predominantly derived from computer science, artificial intelligence (AI), and robotics; and proposals predominantly derived from cognitive psychology and cognitive neuroscience. In the first section, I look at samples of both kinds of proposals. The second section then reviews the definition of embodiment we have proposed and how extensive the range of embodiment is likely to be given the empirical findings that have already emerged. Finally, in the third section, I reply to Shapiro's comments.

Embodied Cognition: Highlights of Alternative Conceptions

A chief impetus for the embodied cognition approach in AI—as Michael Anderson (2003) tells the story—is in terms of a reaction by selected AI practitioners to good old-fashioned artificial intelligence (GOFAI). As Anderson explains, the story is usefully begun with Descartes's philosophy. Descartes drew a sharp distinction between animals and humans. He regarded animals as mere automata, having sensations but no thought or language. True intelligence is to be identified with higher-order reason and language. These ideas were revived in the twentieth century by GOFAI and the classical cognitivist movement in general. EC in computer science and AI is substantially a reaction to these ideas.

A fundamental feature of classical cognitivism is the thesis that thought is fundamentally the manipulation of abstract symbols in accord with explicit rules. In contrast to this high-level or top-down approach to intelligence, Rodney Brooks (1999) has advocated an approach to intelligence that proceeds from the bottom up, and specifically urges us to recall our evolutionary heritage. Human beings are largely continuous with our forebears, from whom we inherited a substrate of systems for coping with the environment. Brooks therefore advocates the following, decidedly un-Cartesian idea: "The study of that [inherited] substrate may well provide constraints on how higher-level thought in humans could be organized" (1999: 135). Brooks argues that representation is the wrong unit of abstraction for building the bulkiest parts of intelligent systems. A substrate of perceptual and behavioral capacities must be established in order to *ground,* or give meaning to, any and all mental symbols. Ungrounded abstract symbols cannot by themselves constitute intelligence.

These ideas echo themes from several philosophers, such as Heidegger (1962) and Merleau-Ponty (2002), whose work is widely cited in the EC literature. Heidegger contended that "being in the world"—involving practical agency and interactive coping—is essential to intelligence and mindedness. Merleau-Ponty argued that representations are "sublimations" of bodily experience, and the employment of such representations "is controlled by the acting body itself, by an 'I can', not an 'I think that'" (as explained by Hilditch, 1995: 108–109).

Unfortunately, the precise role of the body in this literature is mainly gestured at rather than clearly delineated. Moreover, it is difficult to pinpoint the empirical support for the theses that one can sink one's teeth into. These are among the principal reasons why I find them less satisfactory or persuasive than the styles of support for EC to be found in other branches of cognitive science, specifically cognitive psychology and neuroscience. Particular strands of research in these fields disclose much more specificity vis-à-vis phenomena that are crucial to EC and its empirical viability. However, Brooks's emphasis on our evolutionary heritage and the low-level substrate it leaves with us is an emphasis prominently retained in the positive web I shall weave.

Another important theme that carries over from the AI conception of EC is the idea that thought and language must be grounded in low-level cognition, specifically, in sensorimotor cognition (which is commonly equated with embodied cognitions). The traditional idea of classical cognitivism is that pure, amodal cognition occupies a level of cognition entirely segregated from perception and motor execution. The latter types of cognition are executed via an assortment of special-purpose modules that are encapsulated from information in higher-level cognition (Fodor, 1983). Such amodal cognition, or symbol systems, does not need—or cannot get—grounding in modal cognition. Embodiment-leaning researchers, by contrast, adduce evidence that purports to show that high-level cognition—even language (generally assumed to be at the apex of cognitive capacities)—is deeply interwoven with sensorimotor cognition. Even the semantic content of verbs referring to bodily actions are said to be understood—at least partly—in terms of modal cognitions. This provides alleged support for an embodied grounding thesis. Whether it is adequate support, and whether semantic grounding should be considered the crucial test of embodiment, remains to be seen.

There are two entirely different ways of formulating and/or interpreting EC theses. On one interpretation, the *body itself* (and its various parts) plays a crucial role in cognition, a much more pervasive role than classical cognitivism recognizes. On the second interpretation, it is *representations* of the body and its parts that are so pervasive and important to cognition. Theorists like Brooks (1999), Thelen and Smith (1994), and others contend that cognition is significantly mediated by the body's interaction with its environment, where this interaction does not take the form of the mind's *representation* of the body.[1] This sort of thesis lies at the heart of the nonrepresentationalist form of EC. On the other side stands a large and growing group of investigators who focus on the prevalence in cognition of representations of the body's condition and activity. This important difference sometimes goes unremarked, whereas I take it to be critical to a clear elucidation of the kind of approach to EC one means to develop.[2]

Consider the work of George Lakoff and Mark Johnson (Lakoff, 1987; Lakoff & Johnson, 1999). Their dominant theme is the pervasive use of body-related metaphor in language and thought. The core idea here is the intensive use of representations of (parts of) the body in metaphor and associated uses of language. In *Philosophy in the Flesh*, for example, they describe how we use bodily "projection":

Bodily projections are especially clear instances of the way our bodies shape conceptual structure. Consider examples such as in front of and in back of. The most central senses of these terms have to do with the body. We have inherent front and backs. We see from the front, normally move in the direction the front faces, and interact with objects and other people at our fronts . . .

We project fronts and backs onto objects. What we understand as the front of a stationary artifact, like a TV or a computer or a stove, is the side we normally interact with using our fronts. (Lakoff & Johnson,1999: 34)

Although the beginning of this passage speaks of *bodies* (per se) as shaping our conceptual structure, the core message of the passage is that our *conceptual structure* is pervaded by representations of our bodies. Our conceptualization of objects is dominated by how we conceptually relate other objects to our own bodies. This is all, fundamentally, about representation. Similarly, Lakoff and Johnson's talk of "projecting" the body onto other objects is really addressed to how we *think* about other objects—namely, by conceptually relating them to representations of our own body.

The centrality of representation is also transparent in many EC arguments that address the grounding problem. Lawrence Barsalou is a leading proponent of this theme (1999; see also Prinz, 2002). He develops the idea that abstract thought—generally referred to as *amodal* symbols—is grounded in the experience of perceptual, motor, and other forms of nonabstract thought—referred to as *modal* symbols. Indeed, amodal thought does not merely originate in modal thought, according to Barsalou, but ultimately reduces to *simulations* of (i.e., the revival and re-cycling of) the same modal experiences that previously occurred during perception. Since all modal experience is subsumed under the heading of "embodied," it emerges that all amodal thought is also embodied. This, of course, contrasts sharply with classical cognitivism. Here is an example of how Barsalou (2008) expounds these ideas. First, the classicist account of higher-order thought in language comprehension is rendered as follows:

> During language comprehension, hearing the word for a category (e.g., "dog") activates amodal symbols transduced from modal states on previous occasions. Subsequent cognitive operations on category knowledge, such as inference, are assumed to operate on these symbols. Note that none of the modal states originally active when amodal symbols were transduced . . . are active during knowledge representation. . . . Instead, amodal symbols are assumed to be sufficient, with modal states being irrelevant. (Barsalou, 2008: 12)

His own preferred approach—a grounded cognition approach—is then explained as follows:

> On experiencing a member of a category (e.g., "dogs"), modal states are again represented as activations in the visual system, auditory system,

motor system, somatosensory system, and so on. . . . Higher-order cross-modal associations then integrate conjunctive neurons in lower-order association areas to establish a multimodal representation of the experience. . . . [H]earing the word for a category (e.g., "dog") activates conjunctive neurons in higher-order cross-modal association areas that have previously encoded experiences of the respective category. In turn, these conjunctive neurons activate lower-order conjunctive neurons that partially reactivate modal states experienced previously for the category. These neural reenactments attempt to simulate the modal states likely to occur when actually encountering category members. . . . [T]hese reenactments[are] referred to as *simulations,* given that they result from the brain attempting to simulate previous experience. (2008: 13)

The heavy appeal to simulation supports an embodiment thesis not because simulation per se is associated with embodiment, but because what is simulated is *bodily* experience.

Much of Barsalou's writing is heavy on the theoretical side. The empirical side is not neglected, but this work is less striking. For more striking experimental findings in support of the theory that higher-order thought is grounded in lower-level cognition, consider the neuroimaging findings of Friedemann Pulvermuller and colleagues (Hauk, Johnsrude, & Pulvermuller, 2004; Pulvermuller, 2005). Pulvermuller and colleagues conducted experiments concerning the link between language comprehension and activation of cortical areas dedicated to action. Traditionally, cortical systems for language and for action control were thought to be paradigms of independent and autonomous functional systems or modules. These systems have different cortical bases in circumscribed areas: motor and premotor cortex in the case of action and left perisylvian areas in the case of language. They are fully dissociable by neurological disease—paralysis and apraxic action deficits versus aphasic language deficits. And they can themselves be subdivided into finer functional subsystems—subsystems for movement of different body parts in the case of action systems and subsystems for speech production versus comprehension, or phonology versus syntax versus semantics, in the case of language (Pulvermuller, 2005: 576). Traditionally, a strict modular organization of language and the action systems, respectively, was supported by the inability of patients who have had a stroke to move one extremity while all other motor and language functions remain relatively intact, or the predominant loss of usage of one category of words.

Modern theoretical perspectives, however, offer a different view, says Pulvermuller. Cortical functions might be served by distributed interactive functional systems rather than by local encapsulated modules. Many links have been demonstrated between the premotor and language areas where they are adjoined, in the inferior frontal cortex, and through long-distance cortico-cortical connections (see Figure 4.1). There are multiple links between the superior temporal

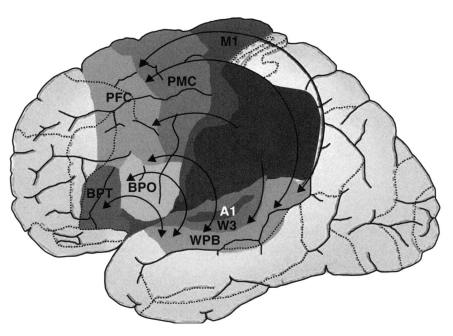

Figure 4.1 Connections between the language and action systems. The arrows indicate long-distance cortico-cortical links.

language areas and the motor system, for example, rendering information flow possible between the cortical systems for language and those for action.

Furthermore, Pulvermuller reports, the motor cortex has a somatotopic organization, with the mouth and articulators represented close to the Sylvian fissure, the arms and hands at dorsolateral sites, and the feet and legs projected to the vertex and interhemispheric sulcus (see Figure 4.2). This semantic somatotopy model of action words implies that there are differently distributed networks for the English words *lick*, *pick*, and *kick*. Crucial predictions about the semantic somatotopy model include the following. First, the perception of spoken and written action words should activate cortical areas involved in action and execution in a category-specific somatotopic fashion. Second, the spread of activation is fast, so that specific sensorimotor areas should be activated early in the course of spoken and written word comprehension. Third, activation of the sensorimotor cortex should not require people to attend to language stimuli but should instead be automatic.

Functional imaging experiments in Pulvermuller's laboratory have provided ample support to all of these predictions. Hauk et al. (2004) reported that when participants were instructed to silently read action words that related to the face, arm, and leg, a predicted somatotopic pattern of activation emerged

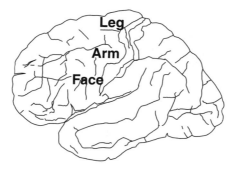

Figure 4.2 Somatotopy of the motor and premotor cortex: the approximate location of the face/articulators, arm/hand and foot/leg representations.

along the motor strip. A similar experiment was carried out with action words embedded in sentences. For example, participants heard action descriptions such as "the boy kicked the ball" or "the man wrote the letter" while their brain was imaged. Specific premotor areas reflecting the different involvement of body part information were found to be active. Hearing different sentences involving *lick*, *pick*, and *kick* activated motor areas that control the tongue, the fingers, and the leg, respectively. These striking findings corroborate earlier findings by Martin, Wiggs, Ungerleider, and Haxby (1996) that the processing of action-related words correlates with the activation of premotor cortex.

Pulvermuller concedes that even if action word processing activates the motor system in a somatotopic fashion, this does not necessarily imply that the motor and premotor cortex influence the processing of action words (2005: 579). But further studies show, he says, that this somatotopy reflects referential word meaning. He concludes as follows:

> Action meaning seems to be not only necessary, but also highly relevant for language. Verbs form the grammatical backbone of sentences, and the majority explicitly refer to actions. Tool words, for example, relate to actions for which the tools are made, and words that denote internal states, such as "pain" or "disgust," can be understood only because both speaker and listener can relate them to similar motor programs that are, by genetic endowment, associated with the expression of pain or disgust. Understanding language means relating language to one's own actions, possibly because the automatic and extremely rapid linkage of sensory and motor information in our brains benefits comprehension and learning processes. (2005: 661)

All of this lends at least prima facie support to the notion that higher-level thought is grounded in low-level representations of motor actions in the motor or premotor cortices. However, this support for the language-grounding hypothesis has not escaped criticism by other cognitive neuroscientists. Mahon and Caramazza (2008) take issue with the contention that Pulvermuller's findings establish that "conceptual content is reductively constituted by information that is represented within the sensory and motor systems—the embodied cognition hypothesis" (2008: 59). Mahon and Caramazza go on to equate the grounding theses with the *embodied cognition* hypothesis as a whole. "According to the embodied cognition hypothesis, understanding is sensory and motor simulation" (2008: 59). This hypothesis is contrasted with what they call the "disembodied cognition hypothesis"; namely, "conceptual representations are 'symbolic' and 'abstract', and as such, qualitatively distinct and entirely separated from sensory and motor information" (2008: 59). In effect, then, they see the debate over the truth or falsity of the grounding thesis as equivalent to the debate between the embodied and disembodied cognition approaches, where the latter seems to be equated with classical cognitivism. Mahon and Caramazza side with classical cognitivism:

> Concepts of concrete objects (e.g., HAMMER) could plausibly include, in a constitutive way, sensory and motor information. But consider concepts such as JUSTICE, ENTROPY, BEAUTY or PATIENCE. For abstract concepts there is no sensory or motor information that could correspond in any reliable or direct way to their "meaning." The possible scope of the embodied cognition framework is thus sharply limited up front: at best, it is a partial theory of concepts since it would be silent about the great majority of the concepts that we have. (2008: 60)

Mahon and Caramazza also offer additional rebuttals of the embodied cognition (i.e., grounding) thesis as advanced by Pulvermuller and colleagues. Quoting directly from Pulvermuller, they stress the fact that the somatotopic activation of the motor system according to the meaning of action words, while interesting in its own right, does not resolve the issue of whether meaning is embodied. This is because "it is unknown whether the motor system becomes activated *prior to*, or rather only *subsequent to*, access to an 'abstract' conceptual representation" (2008: 62). If the motor system becomes activated only subsequent to an abstract conceptual representation, it may be that the motor system's activation isn't crucially constitutive to the meaning of the concept. That meaning might be supplied by the abstract conceptual representation, not by the motor activations. Addressing the issue in connection with another experimental finding—namely, the action-sentence compatibility effect (Glenberg & Kaschak, 2002)—Mahon and Caramazza make the same sort of point. "According to the embodied cognition hypothesis, the motor system is activated because that activation is causally involved in the semantic analysis of the sentence. According to the disembodied cognition hypothesis, the observed motor activation is due to information spreading throughout the system" (2008:63). The latter possibility—which has not been excluded—does not imply that the motor system is helping to supply the meaning or content of the concepts in question. So the findings of motor activation do not settle the question in favor of an embodied cognition hypothesis.

I conclude this section with the following summary. First, there are interesting and challenging empirical findings (only a tiny sampling of which have been reported here) that are highly congenial to some forms of embodied cognition. However, depending on exactly how an EC thesis is formulated, this evidence may or may not be close to *establishing* such a thesis. It is extremely important to be quite clear about what, exactly, the EC thesis is supposed to be. Of course, we cannot expect a unique meaning of an EC thesis to be dropped to us from heaven. We must consider definitional options for embodied cognition, and once we choose a particular definition for consideration, we should revisit the question of how strong or weak that evidence is (given the definition). This is exactly what will be undertaken in the next section.

A New Approach to Embodied Cognition: The Bodily Formats Approach

The first task is to specify the kind of definitional question that I think needs to be addressed by EC theorists. How shall we even formulate the problem? We might start with the question, "Under what conditions would it be true to say that cognition is embodied?" This formulation appears to assume, however, that the question is whether cognition *as a whole* is embodied or not. An alternative possibility is to hold that *parts* of cognition are embodied and other parts are not; in other words, that some *tokens* of cognition are embodied and other tokens are not. In that case, we should ask the question, "What property of a token cognition C renders it embodied?" In other words, what is *constitutively* necessary and sufficient for a token cognition to qualify as embodied? This is the "analytical" or "definitional" question I shall initially address.

For reasons already sketched, I prefer a representationalist approach to this question. But a simple-minded representationalist definition is clearly inadequate. Here is what I mean by a "simple-minded" representationalist definition:

(SMR) Cognition (token) C is embodied if and only if C represents a body or part of a body.

This cannot be what EC theorists are after. When a perception or thought is about *another* person's body, this is not a sufficient reason to view it as embodied. The proposal should at least be amended as follows:

(SMR') Cognition (token) C is embodied if and only if C represents the cognizer's *own body* or part of his/her body.

But this too seems on the wrong track. "Outer" senses like vision and hearing can be used to perceive one's own body; one can see one's own arm or hear one's own vocalization. But such perceptions do not smack of embodiment. It is only the use of "inner" senses, or systems of inner bodily monitoring, which introduces the notion of embodiment (at least on the approach we favor). There is ample reason, moreover, to suspect that we share such systems with our animal cousins, as part of our evolutionary heritage. For example, the Parma group that discovered mirror neurons in monkeys began by identifying a "motor vocabulary" in monkey premotor cortex, where individual cells or populations of cells code for particular hand actions such as holding, grasping, breaking, and so forth. (Rizzolatti & Sinigaglia, 2006). In other words, monkeys have a system for internally representing their own movements, just as we do. Systems of bodily representation of these "inner" kinds are what we regard as the key to embodied cognition. Specifically, embodied cognition is the application of *special* systems, systems *dedicated* to inner bodily representation. The study of such systems—not always characterized in these terms—has become a major growth area of cognitive science in the last several decades. These new developments include an impressive array of cases in which systems for bodily representation are also utilized for tasks that go considerably beyond the representation of the body *simpliciter*. Thus, they may provide a *substructure* for higher-level cognitive activities. This is what Pulvermuller's findings, for example, seem to suggest. Whether these findings support a "grounding" conclusion in the sense of a semantic reduction of linguistic terms to bodily activity terms is a side issue. This question should not usurp attention from other legitimate questions about the organization of cognition.

In our 2009 article, de Vignemont and I drew attention to the (moderate) popularity within cognitive science of the notion of mental *codes* or *formats*. Within a modularist framework (which we did not embrace), there is the idea that each module has its own proprietary format, which may consist in a distinctive vocabulary, syntax, and/or set of computational procedures. Such formats might also have a distinctive array of *contents*, arising from the basic function the code is called on to play. If one disapproves of the "code" or "format" terminology, as being too language-like (which is not intended in the present context), one might speak instead—as I did previously—of representational *systems*. In this chapter, I shall use the terms *format* and (representational) *system* approximately synonymously.

Helping ourselves, then, to the notion of multiple formats or representational systems in the brain, we further postulate that a subset of these systems are (originally) dedicated to representing *bodily* subject matters, in particular, representing bodily states and bodily activity from an *internal* point of view. These are representations of "inner sense" rather than "outer sense." Now, most bodily representations (and formats of representation) involve descriptive contents. That is, they have contents like "Area A of my body is currently in state Σ, or is undergoing change G." But some classes of representation have imperatival, or "instructional," contents such as "Effector E: move to the left," or "Effector F: curl." Motoric areas, in particular, have representational contents of the imperatival kind. Thus, the premotor and motor areas discussed by Pulvermuller utilize bodily codes the primary function of which is to send messages with imperatival contents. Some of these areas send messages to the mouth or tongue, some to the fingers and arms, and some to the legs.[3]

Many other systems are dedicated to various other body-oriented topics. The primary somatosensory cortex is dedicated to representing the condition of (all parts of) the surface of the body. The so-called pain matrix is a complex system consisting of two functionally specialized networks (see de Vignemont & Jacob, 2012). The sensory-discriminative component represents the intensity of pain and its bodily location. The affective component represents the unpleasantness of a painful experience. It recruits the anterior insula, the anterior cingulate cortex, the thalamus, and the brain stem. In relatively recent work, Craig (2002) explores a system of representation of the entire body that he calls "interoception" (a distinct species of inner sense). This system, the lamina I spinothalamocortical system, conveys signals from small-diameter primary afferents that represent the physiological status of all bodily tissues. Lamina I neurons project to the posterior part of the ventromedial nucleus, or VMpo. Craig calls the VMpo "interoceptive cortex" and argues that it contains representations of distinct, highly resolved sensations, including different types of pain, tickle, temperature, itch, muscular and visceral sensations, and sensual touch.

The most interesting part of the EC story I wish to tell, however, does not reside in the primary functions of these body-representing systems. Rather, it resides in the ways such systems are exploited for *other* cognitive tasks. A theoretical background for understanding these exploitative developments is presented by Anderson (2007, 2008, 2010). Anderson presents a principle of the mind/brain that he called the "massive redeployment hypothesis." The underlying idea is that, over evolutionary time, or even in ontogeny, neural circuits originally established for one purpose are exapted, recycled, and redeployed for different uses, without necessarily losing their original function. Evidence for this thesis arises from the fact that neural structures we can study now are activated by different tasks across multiple cognitive domains. For example, Broca's area is not only involved in language processing but also in action-related and imagery-related tasks such as movement preparation, action sequencing, and action recognition. In other words, different cognitive functions are supported by putting many of the same neural circuits together in different arrangements. This is the consequence (largely) of evolution, in which the reuse of existing components for new tasks is favored over the more "expensive" development of additional circuits de novo.[4]

Anderson (2010) reviews numerous examples of the massive redeployment hypothesis (some of which I review in Goldman [2012]). Such redeployments can be expected to result in the reuse of bodily formats—originally dedicated to ancient tasks—in the execution of new tasks, for example, the use of motoric representations for language comprehension. Pulvermuller's identification of a large circuit running from language areas to the motor and premotor cortices is an excellent example of the redeployment of an older (motoric) system, featuring a bodily format, to help execute tasks of language comprehension. Exactly what this "help" consists in remains controversial. But it looks like a lovely example of the reuse of bodily formatted circuits for novel purposes.

Let us now return to the task of providing a definition of an embodied cognition (which was dropped abruptly earlier in the section). I now propose the following. If a cognition C uses an internal bodily format in the process of executing some cognitive task T, then even if task T is in no recognizable sense a bodily task (but rather a higher-level task of some kind), C still qualifies as an embodied cognition. In other words, our proposed definition of an embodied cognition is a B-format linked definition:

> (BFC) Cognition (token) C is a specimen of embodied cognition if and only if C uses some (internal) *bodily format* to help execute a cognitive task (whatever the task may be).[5]

This definition alone, of course, does not speak to the question of how extensive a part of human cognition is embodied. However, the experimental literature is chock full of cases of bodily codes being redeployed for non-bodily tasks. In the action-sentence compatibility task, for instance, Glenberg and Kaschak (2002) found that it took longer to respond to a sentence that makes sense when the action described runs counter to the required response motion. So, the simple comprehension of a sentence apparently activated action-related representations. A second category of examples is the reuse of motor control circuits for memory. Casasanto and Dykstra (2010) found bidirectional influence between motor control and autobiographical memory. Participants retrieved more memories and moved marbles more quickly when the direction of movement was congruent with the valence of the memory (upward for positive memories and downward for negative memories.). Many of the much-discussed findings in the mirror-neuron literature are also cases of applying motor codes to nonstandard tasks, for example, not using them to guide one's own actions but to represent the actions of others. Combining this wide-ranging literature with the definition provided previously makes for a robust case of embodied cognition (even if not a "totalizing" conclusion to the effect that *all* cognition is embodied).

Shapiro on the Bodily Formats Approach: Some Replies

Lawrence Shapiro (this volume, Chapter 3) provides an instructive overview of the state-of-play in research on embodied cognition, which also serves as illuminating background to the considerations I had in mind in advancing a new approach to the subject (Goldman, 2012; see also Goldman & de Vignemont, 2009). I particularly appreciate his framing of my proposal in the context of the history of science. However, although Shapiro has understood and expressed my aims with considerable accuracy, his articulation of them is a bit off track in one important respect. I did not mean to formulate an approach to EC that meshes with the favored approaches of *all* players in the field and could therefore be expected to appeal to them all. My aim was less ecumenical than Shapiro supposes.

Shapiro characterizes my proposal as an "effort to look for a consensus within Embodied Cognition" (this volume, Chapter 3), in order to exemplify the situation in many branches of science where practitioners agree on which are the fundamental problems and assumptions of their field. Shapiro finds such consensus lacking in the current state of play in EC. He sees me as offering a proposal intended to attract the "crowd" of EC enthusiasts and thereby precipitate the desired consensus. He fears, however, that my aim will fall short. But hold on! I never entertained this aim. I am fully aware that my proposal will leave many self-styled EC theorists unmoved and unimpressed. Their vision of the field is too remote from the one I wish to plow. So, I never had any illusion of being able to forge a union with them. Nonetheless, I contend that the field I am carving up (along with Frederique de Vignemont and with Gallese & Sinigaglia [2011]) is one that could well attract many members of the cognitive science community, in particular, practitioners of orthodox cognitive neuroscience. It should attract them, I believe, because it provides unity to an impressive array of empirically established phenomena with roots in bodily cognition. Yes, I would indeed hope to precipitate a unified vision of this subfield of cognitive science at some point down the road. But I do not expect this consensus to include all of the current proponents of EC, including all those represented by Shapiro's list of ten examples. The orientation of roboticists and dynamic systems theorists, for example, is quite disparate from mine. It is unlikely that we would achieve a shared conception of our problems and assumptions. One need not agree with Shapiro, however, that his ten examples are ideally selected to identify the "essence" of EC. I could easily assemble quite a different ten-item list from those whose work I endorsed in the first two sections of this chapter. As Shapiro himself acknowledges, the history of science is replete with cases in which a scientific field (e.g., alchemy) displays shared assumptions at one point in time about the phenomena worthy of study, yet these assumptions are ultimately abandoned and replaced by others (e.g., those of modern chemistry). This scenario could easily be replicated in the area of EC.

Shapiro's discontent with my approach seems to be triggered partly by its moderation and partly by its brain-centrism. I see no reason to apologize for its moderation. (For many cognitive scientists, moreover, it is already too radical.) A first point to make about its brain-centrism is that such features emphasized by other embodiment theorists as nontrivial causal spread, situatedness, and embeddedness are also compatible with EC as I present it. I don't address these topics in the target article, but neither am I forced to reject them. (They might stand on their own without any linkage to my sense of embodiment.) Also worth mentioning—obvious though it is—is that, as far as anything I discuss goes, it is certainly possible (indeed, likely) that the *contents* of mental representation are very much a function of what they causally interact with. So envatted brain states would not have the same contents as brain states of ordinary embodied brains.

Shapiro's principal complaint, perhaps, is that my way of framing EC, with its adherence to brain-centrism, threatens to divest the embodiment movement of its most exciting and distinctive departure from orthodox cognitive science. Perhaps; but excitement isn't everything, especially in science. In any case, I think there is a pretty exciting and unorthodox theme in my story, which may be crystallized in the exaggerated slogan: "In the beginning, what we represent is our own body." Spelled out more cautiously, it's the thesis that a significant amount of human cognition has its origin in representations of one's own body.[6] This is not a trivial thesis. Indeed, most contemporary mainstream cognitive scientists probably reject it, and it certainly was not on the horizon for the first several decades of cognitive science. If it currently lacks shock value, this is because many relevant findings in cognitive science (and especially cognitive neuroscience) are already in the literature and comprise a firm empirical foundation on which I am trying to erect a sound theoretical edifice. The existence of those findings reduces the shock value of the thesis, but they also contribute mightily to its epistemic support, to its probability of being true. This firm empirical foundation is hardly a shortcoming. Sheer novelty is not the aim of science.

Moving forward in Shapiro's discussion, we come to his question of whether B-code use is indeed both necessary and sufficient for embodiment. Shapiro begins this phase of his discussion by disputing the necessity contention. However, he attributes to me the view that "cognition could not be embodied in anything but a human being" (this volume, Chapter 3). What leads Shapiro to interpret me in this fashion? He does not quote any passage from my target article to support this interpretation. True, the focus throughout the paper was human cognition, but this does not warrant the inference that I intended to restrict EC to the human species.[7]

Shapiro envisages a cognition-endowed creature that does not use dedicated B-formats. What about this class of creatures? he asks. Would they have embodied cognitions? I say that these creatures would not have embodied cognitions. This follows directly from the proposed definition of embodied cognition. If a creature has no B-formats, it has no embodied cognitions. The divide between embodied and nonembodied cognition, as I seek to draw it, is in terms of B-formats. Of course, other theorists might wish to draw the line between embodied and nonembodied cognitions differently. They might want to draw a distinction, for example, between mental tokens that represent states of the body and mental tokens with no such representational content—ignoring entirely the codes, formats, or systems that are used. This is certainly a possible demarcation criterion; it just isn't as interesting a divide when it comes to the central scientific aim of cognitive science—namely, to understand the architecture of human cognition. Because, as the evidence I have assembled indicates, human cognition *does* involve the massive redeployment of cognition systems originally used for bodily representation but applied instead to a variety of tasks.

Having probed the issue of whether B-formats are *necessary* for embodiment, Shapiro next turns to whether they are *sufficient* for embodiment. In the very next sentence, however, he turns to a different question: whether embodiment shouldn't be treated as a graded category rather than a dichotomous one. This is surely a possibility, though not an easy one to manage, I suspect. Nonetheless, it is a matter we should definitely put on the agenda for future consideration. Different ways of measuring greater and lesser embodiment should be explored, to see how they might be used to broaden the approach.

Yet a different worry is expressed in Shapiro's worry that perhaps *all* cognition is embodied on the criterion I am proposing. Here we contemplate a very high degree of embodiment not for individual tokens of cognition but for the class of cognition tokens as a whole. Here again Shapiro surprises me with the following reaction to the prospect that *all* cognitions are embodied:

> This consequence is surprisingly plausible, and yet, if genuine, would magnify suspicions that Goldman fails to articulate the most salient aspects of embodied cognition—aspects that distinguish embodied approaches to understanding the mind from classically cognitive ones. (this volume, Chapter 3)

I don't quite follow this suggestion. Exactly why should a "totalizing" upshot—*all* cognitions are embodied—magnify suspicions about my proposal? Maybe the thought is better articulated a few paragraphs later, where Shapiro says that massive (universal?) embodiment would threaten to *trivialize* the notion of embodiment.

Why would universal embodiment threaten to trivialize the embodiment notion? Admittedly, a definition of embodiment should leave *conceptual* room for both embodied and nonembodied cognitions. And that is clearly accomplished by my definition (both the one in Goldman [2012] and the one offered above, BFC). But leaving conceptual room for both doesn't and shouldn't preclude the possibility that all cognitions are in fact embodied. An appropriate analogy here is the notion of the physical. A definition of "physical" should leave conceptual room for the possibility that both physical and nonphysical things exist. Still, it might turn out to be the case, as a factual matter, that all existing things are physical. Each of the putatively nonphysical things (God, numbers, thoughts, etc.) might turn out either (i) not to exist or (ii) to be physical after all. Why would this trivialize the notion of the physical?

Shapiro's final comment features a positive proposal to strengthen the proposed notion of EC. Instead of saying that it suffices for a cognition to qualify as embodied that it reuse a B-code, the test for embodiment (via reuse) should require both that the cognition reuse a B-code *and* that it reuse the B-code in question *because* this B-code has the function of representing certain bodily states.[8] This might indeed be a helpful addition. However, I suspect that the addition wouldn't make a big difference to the extension of cognitions that qualify as embodied, simply because the proposed extra condition would almost invariably be satisfied when the original condition of reuse is satisfied.

Notes

1. A related thesis is the "extended mind" thesis, which construes the representing mind as including what is usually considered part of the environment. This approach is developed by Andy Clark and David Chalmers (Clark, 1997; Clark &Chalmers, 1998). However, I view this thesis as somewhat orthogonal to the embodied cognition thesis and won't try to work it into my discussion.
2. It is easy to find writers in the embodied cognition mold who, in the same work, vacillate between characterizations of their thesis in terms of the role of the body per se and some sort of *knowledge* or *representation* of bodily interrelationships. For example, Noe (2004) sometimes characterizes his "enactive" approach as the view that "perceiving [is] a way of acting" (2004: 1) and the view that "perception is a species of skillful bodily activity" (2004: 2). However, on the very same page of the latter quotation, he characterizes his view as holding that our ability to perceive "is constituted by . . . our possession of sensori-motor *knowledge*" (2004: 2, italics added). This formulation strongly implies that *representations* of sensorimotor relationships are what comprise perception.
3. That they are also activated in connection with language comprehension was a surprise, and the question of their function in this connection was the subject of the debate with Mahon and Caramazza considered previously. That this seems to be an *added* function is a topic to which we shall return.
4. Similar theories have been advanced in the literature, Anderson notes, by at least three other researchers or pairs of researchers: (1) Gallese and Lakoff's (2005) "neural exploitation" hypothesis; (2) Hurley's (2008) "shared circuits" model; and (3) Dehaene's (2005) "neuronal recycling" theory.
5. This is a somewhat improved formulation of the definition stated in Goldman (2012: 73).
6. This thesis is quite clearly presented by Antonio Damasio (2003). See especially chapter 3 on feelings.
7. I do want to avoid species chauvinism, as Shapiro suspects. But that is easily done with the recognition that other types of species, with different, non-neural material substrates, might have bodily formats and might reuse them for other purposes.

8. I give a tweak to Shapiro's proposal because I think it (slightly) enhances the appropriateness of the added condition.

References

Anderson, M. L. (2003). Embodied cognition: A field guide. *Artificial Intelligence* 149: 91–130.

Anderson, M. L. (2007). The massive redeployment hypothesis and the functional topography of the brain. *Philosophical Psychology* 21 (2): 143–174.

Anderson, M. L. (2008). Circuit sharing and the implementation of intelligent systems. *Connection Science* 20 (4): 239–313.

Anderson, M. L. (2010). Neural reuse: A fundamental organizational principle of the brain. *Behavioral and Brain Sciences* 33: 245–266.

Barsalou, Lawrence W. (1999). Perceptual symbol systems. *Behavioral and Brain Sciences* 22: 577–609.

Barsalou, Lawrence W. (2008). Grounding symbolic operations in the brain's modal systems. In G. R. Semin and E. R. Smith, eds., *Embodied Grounding: Social, Cognitive, Affective, and Neuroscientific Approaches* (pp. 9–42). Cambridge: Cambridge University Press.

Brooks, Rodney. (1999). *Cambrian Intelligence: The Early History of the New AI.* Cambridge, MA: MIT Press.

Casasanto, D., and Dykstra, K. (2010). Motor action and emotional memory. *Cognition* 115 (1): 179–185.

Clark, Andy. (1997). *Being There: Putting Brain, Body, and World Together Again.* Cambridge, MA: MIT Press.

Clark, A., and Chalmers, D. (1998). The extended mind. *Analysis* 58 (1): 7–19.

Craig, A.D. (2002). How do you feel? Interoception: The sense of the physiological condition of the body. *Nature Reviews Neuroscience* 3: 655–666.

Damasio, Antonio. (2003). *Looking for Spinoza: Joy, Sorrow and the Feeling Brain.* Orlando, FL: Harcourt.

Dehaene, S. (2005). Evolution of human cortical circuits for reading and arithmetic: The "neuronal recycling" hypothesis. In S. Dehaene, J.-R. Duhamel, M.D. Hauser, and G. Rizzolatti, eds., *From Monkey Brain to Human Brain* (pp. 131–157). Cambridge, MA: MIT Press.

de Vignemont, Frederique and Jacob, Pierre. (2012). What is it like to feel another's pain? *Philosophy of Science* 79(2): 295–316.

Fodor, Jerry A. (1983). *The Modularity of Mind.* Cambridge, MA: MIT Press.

Gallese, Vittorio, and Lakoff, George. (2005). The brain's concepts: The role of the sensory-motor system in conceptual knowledge. *Cognitive Neuropsychology* 22 (3–4): 455–479.

Gallese, Vittorio, and Sinigaglia, Corrado. (2011). What is so special about embodied simulation? *Trends in Cognitive Sciences* 15 (11): 512–519.

Glenberg, A.M., and Kaschak, M. F. (2002). Grounding language in action. *Psychonomic Bulletin and Review* 9: 558–565.

Goldman, Alvin I. (2012). A moderate approach to embodied cognitive science. *The Review of Philosophy and Psychology* 3 (1): 71–88.

Goldman, Alvin I., and de Vignemont, Frederique. (2009). Is social cognition embodied? *Trends in Cognitive Sciences* 13 (4): 154–159.

Hauk, O., Johnsrude, I., and Pulvermuller, F. (2004). Somatotopic representation of action words in human motor and premotor cortex. *Neuron* 41: 301–307.

Heidegger, Martin. (1962). *Being and Time.* New York: Harper Collins.

Hilditch, D. (1995). At the heart of the world: Merleau-Ponty and the existential phenomenology of embodied and embedded intelligence in everyday coping. PhD thesis, Department of Philosophy, Washington University, St. Louis, MO.

Hurley, S.L. (2008). The shared circuits model: How control, mirroring, and simulation can enable imitation, deliberation, and mindreading. *Behavioral and Brain Sciences* 31 (1): 1–58.

Lakoff, George. (1987). *Women, Fire, and Dangerous Things: What Categories Reveal about the Mind.* Chicago: University of Chicago Press.

Lakoff, George, and Johnson, Mark. (1999). *Philosophy in the Flesh: The Embodied Mind and Its Challenge to Western Thought.* New York: Basic Books.

Mahon, B. Z., and Caramazza, A. (2008). A critical look at the embodied cognition hypothesis and a new proposal for grounding conceptual content. *Journal of Physiology—Paris* 102: 59–76.

Martin, A., Wiggs, G. L., Ungerleider, L. G., and Haxby, J. V. (1996). Neural correlates of category-specific knowledge. *Nature* 379: 649–652.

Merleau-Ponty, Maurice. (2002). *The Phenomenology of Perception.* New York: Routledge.

Noe, Alva. (2004). *Action in Perception.* Cambridge, MA: MIT Press.

Prinz, Jesse. (2002). *Furnishing the Mind: Concepts and Their Perceptual Basis.* Cambridge, MA: MIT Press.

Pulvermuller, F. (2005). Brain mechanisms linking language and action. *Nature Reviews Neuroscience* 6: 576–582.

Rizzolatti, G. and Sinigaglia, C. (2006). *Mirrors in the Brain: How Our Minds Share Actions and Emotions.* Oxford: Oxford University Press.

Thelen, E., and Smith, L. (1994). *A Dynamic Systems Approach to the Development of Cognition and Action.* Cambridge, MA: MIT Press.

Suggestions for Further Reading

Adams, Fred, and Ken Aizawa. 2001. "The Bounds of Cognition." *Philosophical Psychology* 14: 43–64.
This article defends a more traditional conception of cognition as occurring entirely in the head; the argument is based on considerations pertaining to the demarcation of cognition (the "mark of the mental").

Clark, Andy, and David Chalmers. 1998. "The Extended Mind." *Analysis* 58: 7–19.
This article offers a first explicit and rigorous argument (relying on a thought-provoking thought experiment) for the notion that some mental states are "extended": they do not occur "in the head" and indeed are partially outside the organism's physical body.

Goldman, Alvin I. 2012. "A Moderate Approach to Embodied Cognitive Science." *Review of Philosophy and Psychology* 3: 71–88.
This article offers an interpretation of claims to the effect that cognition is "embodied," which both takes account of pertinent empirical evidence and retains conceptual continuity with traditional cognitive science.

O'Regan, Kevin, and Alva Noë. 2001. "What It Is Like to See: A Sensorimotor Approach to Perceptual Experience." *Synthese* 129: 79–103.
This article argues that the subjective feel of conscious experience is "enactive"; it is characterized first and foremost by the kinds of interactions with the outside world it involves or enables.

PART III

Consciousness
Representationalism and the Phenomenology of Moods

CHAPTER 5

The Case against Representationalism about Moods

AMY KIND

Chapter Overview

According to representationalism, the phenomenal character of a mental state reduces to its intentional content. Although representationalism seems plausible with respect to ordinary perceptual states, it seems considerably less plausible for states like moods. Here the problem for representationalism arises largely because moods seem to lack intentional content altogether. In this chapter, I explore several possible options for identifying the intentional content of moods and suggest that none of them is wholly satisfactory. Importantly, however, I go on to argue that the plausibility of representationalism should not be seen to rest on the question of whether moods have intentional content but rather on the question of whether the intentional content of moods, were there any, would be sufficient to determine their phenomenal character. As I argue, even if we concede to the representationalist that moods have intentional content, their phenomenal character outstrips their intentional content; thus, the representationalist reduction cannot succeed. Ultimately, then, I conclude that moods do indeed pose a serious objection to the representationalist theory.

Despite the enormous neuroscientific progress of the last half century, the phenomenon of consciousness remains largely a mystery. Fortunately, with respect to one large class of unanswered questions about consciousness, unraveling the mystery looks to be only a matter of time. Questions broadly relating to the information-processing side of consciousness, for example, all look eventually answerable in neuroscientific or computational terms. Such questions thus constitute what are often called the *easy problems* of consciousness. Although such questions may well take us decades to solve, they do not seem beyond the realm of our standard physicalist framework. Contrast such questions, however, with what's known as the *hard problem* of consciousness, the problem of conscious experience. Our inner life is filled with vivid sensations of color and sound, with pulsing pains, with deeply felt emotions and moods. Consider the experience of seeing the rich hues of a peacock's plumage, of hearing the sonorous tones of a grandfather clock, of stubbing a toe against the wall, of overflowing with happiness, or of sinking deeper into an all-encompassing depression. With respect to conscious experiences such as these, it looks considerably less likely that standard scientific explanations will eventually be forthcoming. No matter how much we learn about a given neural process, it seems that we still won't have explained how the process gives rise to *this* particular conscious experience—or why it gives rise to any conscious experience at all. Conscious experience—often referred to as *phenomenal experience* or *phenomenal consciousness*—threatens to escape our physicalist net and potentially remain entirely outside the domain of scientific inquiry.[1]

Over the past couple of decades, many philosophers have attempted to defuse this threat by showing that phenomenal consciousness can be understood in terms of the technical notion of *intentionality*. The philosophical terminology is somewhat unfortunate here, since this sense of "intentional" has nothing to do with the ordinary notion of being purposively brought about. Rather, to say that a mental state is intentional in this technical sense—stemming from the Latin *intendere*, which means "to aim at," as with a bow—is to say that it is *directed at* or *about* something (i.e., that it is representational). Beliefs, desires, and perceptions are all paradigmatic examples of intentional states. My visual perception of the can of Diet Coke on my desk, my belief that it is half full, and my desire to have a sip from it, are all intentionally directed at the can on my desk. Importantly, mental states can have intentionality even if they're intentionally directed toward something that does not exist. My belief that Vulcan is a planet is about Vulcan, even though no such heavenly body exists.

Giving an acceptable physicalist account of intentionality is no trivial matter, but most philosophers believe that this task can eventually be accomplished. If they are right, then the successful reduction of a state's phenomenal character to its intentional content would in turn provide a solution to the hard problem of consciousness.[2] The theory of consciousness that attempts this reduction is known as *representationalism*, or more specifically, *strong representationalism*. Some proponents of this theory call their view *strong intentionalism*, but the two terms are used interchangeably in the literature, and in what follows, I adopt the former terminology.

Strong representationalism contrasts with *weak* or *nonreductive representationalism*. While strong representationalists attempt to reduce phenomenal character to intentional content, weak representationalists claim only that phenomenal character supervenes on intentional content (see, e.g., Crane 1998; Chalmers 2004). Weak representationalism, however, does not aim to provide a theory of what phenomenal character *is* and, correspondingly, does not offer a solution to the hard problem of consciousness. In what follows, my discussion will be directed at strong representationalism, the reductive version of the view.[3] As is common in the literature surrounding this theory, I will hereafter drop the qualifier "strong" and refer to the view in question simply as *representationalism*.

Representationalism seems comparatively plausible with respect to ordinary perceptual experiences: when I look at a sunflower, the fact that my visual experience has the particular yellowish phenomenology that it does seems closely tied to the fact that it represents the yellow sunflower.[4] It's perhaps for this reason that much of the work on representationalism has concerned perception and, specifically, visual perception. But most representationalists nonetheless endorse an unrestricted version of the theory: for *any* state with phenomenal character, the state's phenomenal character reduces to its intentional content. Only unrestricted representationalism can offer us a theory about the nature of phenomenal character in general, and it thus seems that the plausibility of the view hinges in large part on its applicability across all phenomenal states.[5]

Much of the debate about the viability of unrestricted representationalism has focused on phenomenally conscious states that seem to lack intentionality altogether. Since a state's phenomenal character will not be reducible to its intentional content if the state does not have any intentional content, any nonintentional states serve as counterexamples to an unrestricted representationalist thesis. Despite Brentano's famous claim that intentionality is the *mark of the mental*—that all mental states have intentional content—there nonetheless seem to be examples of phenomenally conscious states that lack intentionality altogether. When I press on my eyeball, thereby creating a phosphene experience, that experience does not seem to be about anything. And while bodily sensations like pain might be intentional, representing bodily damage, it is less clear how we could identify intentional content for bodily sensations like tickles and orgasms. Finally, consider mood states like generalized elation or depression, or free-floating anxiety. Although oftentimes I am elated, depressed, or anxious about particular things or happenings in the world, it seems that sometimes these states can occur without being directed or about anything at all.

In this essay, I explore this last category of potential counterexamples to representationalism. Moods have long proven to be a particularly thorny problem for representationalists, and even some of the staunchest among them have simply thrown up their hands when trying to identify a plausible candidate for the intentional content of moods. Fred Dretske, for example, hedges his bets when claiming that all mental facts are representational facts by adding the phrase "plus or minus a bit." The qualifier is needed, he notes, because there are some "experiences—a general feeling of depression, for example—about which I do not know what to say" (Dretske 1995, xv).

My investigation into the plausibility of representationalism as applied to moods will require me first to explore what exactly moods are, and whether and how they are to be differentiated from other affective states like emotions. This leads in turn to a discussion of the intentionality of moods. Although moods have often been claimed to be nonintentional, I will concede to the representationalist that this claim should be rejected. To my mind, the plausibility of representationalism turns not on the question of whether moods have intentional content, but rather on whether the intentional content of moods is sufficient to determine their phenomenal character. I will argue that it does not. Ultimately, then, I conclude that moods do indeed pose a serious objection to the representationalist theory.

Moods versus Emotions

The contemporary philosophical literature contains surprisingly little philosophical discussion of moods, and even less devoted to moods in and of themselves.[6] What little discussion there is tends to occur in the context of discussing emotion. This is perhaps not surprising given the deep similarities between moods and emotions. For every mood state, there seems to be a corresponding emotion state, often identified by the very same term. Compare being in an anxious mood with one's anxiety about a particularly steep segment of a hike, or being in a fearful mood with one's fear when a rattlesnake suddenly appears on the trail ahead, or being in an elated mood with one's elation upon reaching the mountain summit.

In fact, there is considerable disagreement about whether emotions and moods should be classified together or treated separately as different kinds of mental states. For some philosophers, the difference between emotion and mood is just, as Peter Goldie puts it, "a matter of degree" (2000, 17), where moods are simply more diffuse or "generalized" emotions.[7] My own inclination, however, lies with the philosophers who separate out moods from the class of emotions—that is, who insist that a proper classification of our mental states not lump emotion and mood together.[8] In most cases, the argument for drawing a distinction relies on the fact that moods and emotions play different functional roles and/or have different functions in our mental life as a whole. Carolyn Price, for example, contrasts the functional roles played by the emotion of fear and a fearful mood: while experiencing the emotion of fear has the function of enabling a subject to deal effectively with an occurrent threat, being in a fearful mood has the function of adapting the subject to an environment in which a threat is likely (2006, 57). For Paul Griffiths (1997), moods contrast with emotions in virtue of being higher-order functional states.[9]

In the empirical literature on affect, researchers tend to draw a sharp distinction between moods and emotion, although there is not widespread agreement on the exact characteristics that distinguish them.[10] Among the numerous criteria proposed, one of the most common concerns the duration of the state in question. Emotions are thought to be affective states of relatively brief duration, while moods are affective states of more sustained duration. The duration criterion, which is echoed in the philosophical literature as well, enjoys considerable intuitive plausibility, as it matches up well with typical episodes of both emotions and moods: emotions are fleeting, lasting sometimes just mere seconds and at most a few minutes, while moods tend to last for a considerably longer periods of time. In evaluating this criterion, however, we must ask whether this is *always* the case. Although moods are *typically* long-lasting, there are plausible cases in which they are relatively brief. An unexpected act of deep kindness, for example, might shake someone from her gloomy mood very shortly after its onset. Conversely, although emotions are *typically* short-lasting, there do seem to be cases where they are sustained over a considerable period of time. Might not a strong-willed child fume with anger for hours? Or consider a mild claustrophobic trapped in an elevator for an entire morning. Can't we easily imagine her terror lasting the entirety of the episode? It thus seems unlikely that duration is either necessary or sufficient to differentiate moods from emotions.[11]

A second criterion commonly offered in both the psychological and philosophical literature, and one that is especially relevant for our overall purposes here, concerns the intentionality of these states. Emotions are thought always to be directed at something determinate. When we're fearful, or angry, or disgusted, there's always some particular thing—an object, a person, an event, a state of affairs—at which our fear, anger, or disgust is directed.[12] This gives us a claim I'll call the *directedness of emotions*:

(DE) Emotions are always directed at something particular.

Moods, in contrast, lack the kind of intentional determinateness that is characteristic of emotions. As the psychologist Nico Frijda puts in, moods are distinguished by their "absence of orientation around an object" (1993, 381). This seems clearest, perhaps, when considering states like free-floating anxiety or ennui, but it holds broadly across the whole spectrum of moods from ebullience to depression. This gives us a claim that I'll call the *undirectedness of moods*:

(UM) Moods are typically not directed at anything particular.

Sometimes in the literature one finds an even stronger claim, what I'll call the *strong undirectedness of moods*:

(SUM) Moods are never directed at anything particular.

Proponents of SUM include Julien Deonna and Fabrice Teroni. As they argue, it does not make sense to restrict the attribution of a mood to a particular object or objects: "One is in a gloomy, grumpy or joyful mood, never gloomy or grumpy about Mike or about the rich" (Deonna and Teroni 2012, 4).[13]

Initially, it may seem that SUM is too strong. Isn't it perfectly natural to describe someone as being grumpy about having lost a hard-fought soccer match or joyful about the birth of a child? Can't moods in this way be connected with particular incidents or things, just as emotions can? To my mind, the proponent of SUM has two natural ways to respond to these putative counterexamples. First, she might note that in some such cases we are not really picking out a person's mood but rather the corresponding emotion. Second, in cases where we really have identified a grumpy or joyful mood and not simply a grumpy or joyful emotion, she might note that the particular incident or thing pointed to is best understood as the *cause* of the mood rather than what the mood is directed toward—mood reports use the causal and not the intentional sense of "about." To say that someone is grumpy about having lost a close soccer game, for example, is to say that her grumpiness was caused by the loss; now ensconced in a state of grumpiness, her mood seems no more directed at the soccer game in particular than it is at anything else in the world.

Whether this defense of SUM is successful is fortunately not a matter we need to settle here. In what follows, I will assume only the weaker UM, a claim about which there is a widespread consensus.[14] But what about DE, the claim that emotions are always directed at something in particular? Although there is widespread agreement about the truth of this thesis as well, it's not clear that DE is immune to counterexample. One might all of a sudden be panicky, or angry, without being panicky or angry about anything in particular.[15] Or consider the emotions aroused by listening to music—the exaltation brought on by various marches or the yearning brought on by romanticist chamber music. In an interesting discussion, Joel Kupperman notes that such emotions seem to have a peculiarly free-floating quality; when listening to a Brahms quartet piece, for example, the bittersweet feelings aroused do not seem to be about the music itself, nor about anything at all (Kupperman 1995).

If any of these purported examples of nonintentional emotions were to hold up to scrutiny, they would serve as counterexamples not only to DE but to representationalism as well. Since I lack the space here to explore these cases in any detail, I will refrain from relying on them in my case against representationalism; in what follows, I will simply grant the truth of DE.

The Intentionality of Moods

Previously, we saw that there is widespread consensus that moods, unlike emotions, are typically not directed at anything in particular. But some philosophers move quickly from UM to a further claim that I'll call the *nonintentionality of moods*:

(NIM) Moods are typically nonintentional.

The move from UM to NIM is unusually explicit in the following passage from Deonna and Teroni:

> Moods, like emotions, have a characteristic phenomenology. . . . Unlike emotions, however, and this is the principled distinction between the two types of affective phenomena, *moods do not appear to be intentional in that they never target specific objects.* (2012, 4; my emphasis)

But Deonna and Teroni are not alone in making this move. Consider John Searle's influential treatment of intentionality:

> Beliefs, fears, hopes, and desires are Intentional; but there are forms of nervousness, elation, and undirected anxiety that are not Intentional. A clue to this distinction is provided by the constraints on how these states are reported. If I tell you I have a belief or desire, it always makes sense for you to ask, "What is it exactly that you believe?" or "What is it that you desire?"; and it won't do for me to say, "Oh I just have a belief and a desire without believing or desiring anything." But my nervousness and undirected anxiety need not in that way be *about* anything. (1983, 2)

For Searle, it's when moods are not directed at anything in particular that they become classified as nonintentional.[16]

If moods—or at least some moods—are as these philosophers describe them, then representationalism would be false for such states; the phenomenal character of a state cannot be reduced to its intentional content if the state has no intentional content. The truth of NIM, in other words, would make the antirepresentationalist case an easy one. Unfortunately, things are not quite this simple. Several different kinds of proposals in the literature suggest ways that, despite the truth of UM, moods might have intentional content. Here I discuss each in turn.

Moods as Generalized Representations (Outward Directedness)

In moving from UM to NIM, the philosophers quoted previously seem to be working with an object-oriented conception of intentionality; that is, they take intentionality to consist in *object-directedness*. It seems implausible, however, that the kind of directedness involved in intentionality must be understood in such a narrow way. Once we broaden our conception of intentionality, moods can be seen to have intentional content even if they are not directed at anything particular.

Consider, for example, the fact that moods are often described—puzzlingly so—as being directed at both nothing and everything.[17] The apparent puzzle quickly dissipates once we realize that what's meant is that moods are directed at nothing *in particular* by being directed instead at everything *altogether*. In contrast to the experience of an emotion which is directed at a specific target, moods have a more generalized directedness. But how should we understand the notion of generalized directedness?

This rough idea has been most commonly spelled out in two different ways, although I think they are often run together in the literature.[18] Consider, for example, the following two passages:

> Euphoria, melancholy, and depression are not about anything in particular (though some particular incident might well set them off); they are about the whole of our world, or indiscriminately about anything that comes our way, casting happy glows or somber shadows on every object and incident of our experience. (Solomon 1976, 173)

> We are often unaccountably depressed, on days when for no reason everything seems black; but pointless depression is not objectless depression, and the objects of depression are the things which seem black. (Kenny 1963, 61)

One strand in these passages consists in the idea that the focus of moods varies widely through time—first the mood is directed on one thing, then another, and then another. Consider someone in the grips of ennui. Whatever she turns her attention to—first the food on the table in front of her, then the show playing on the television, then the book she's trying to read—strikes her as dull and uninteresting. And there's nothing special about ennui. If she were suffering from depression instead, then these same things might seem black, as Kenny suggests, or overcast with Solomon's "somber shadows"; in a euphoric mood, they might all seem bright and wonderful, infused by Solomon's "happy glows."[19]

A second strand in these passages, and in the literature as a whole, consists in the idea that moods are directed not at a changing series of objects over time but broadly at the world at large; as William Lyons says, moods are "aimed out at the world" without coming to rest "in any one spot or on any one thing" (1980, 104). We see this idea in the previous passage from Solomon when he talks of moods being directed at the "whole of our world." It is also reflected in Annette Baier's claim that moods have "near all-inclusive and undifferentiated objects" (1990, p. 14).[20]

Not everyone is convinced that all cases of moods fit into one of these two categories. As Mendelovici argues, some cases of anxiety or elation do not seem to be directed either at the world as a whole or at a changing series of objects; in such cases, one simply feels anxious or elated, full stop. Although Mendelovici thinks that we should take seriously the fact that such experiences appear to lack an intentional object, she does not think that this requires us to deny that moods have intentional content. Moods might lack an intentional *object* yet nonetheless be intentionally directed insofar as they represent *properties*.

This suggestion is best understood in relation to Mendelovici's account of the intentionality of emotions (this volume, Chapter 6). Consider the fear I experience when I unexpectedly encounter a rattlesnake. My fear, in being intentionally directed toward the rattlesnake, represents the snake as SCARY. According to Mendelovici, the property of scariness—like rosiness, bleakness, and other properties represented by emotions—is a sui generis emotion property, distinct from ordinary physical or dispositional properties, and not reducible to any other kinds of properties. To avoid confusion going forward, I will indicate these properties with an asterisk: scariness*, rosiness*, and so forth. In Mendelovici's view, then, my fear of the snake represents the snake as being scary*, a different property from the one picked out by the thought "The snake is scary."

Since it is implausible that objects in the world actually have the emotion properties that our experiences represent them as having, Mendelovici embraces a form of projectivism about these properties. More specifically, she adopts the view known as *figurative* projectivism: it's not that these properties are instantiated somewhere else, but that they are not instantiated at all. We mistakenly attribute these emotion properties to objects to mark the fact that the objects have significance for us. On her view, we should think of the different emotions as analogous to different highlighter colors—joy at the birth of a baby highlights the baby with a certain emotion property, while sadness at the illness of a beloved friend highlights the friend with a different emotion property.

Now consider a mood like free-floating anxiety, which does not appear to be intentionally directed at any object.[21] For Mendelovici, such a mood represents the same kind of emotion property that the corresponding object-directed emotion does, but in this case, the emotion property is represented as unbound (i.e., not bound to any object). Moods, then, should be thought of as analogous to the color of the ink in a highlighter—in experiencing a mood, we experience the color of the ink though no particular thing or group of things is "highlighted." Mendelovici in this way gives us a third way to think of the generalized, outward-directedness of moods—such experiences strike us as more diffuse or generalized than emotions because they are not tied to particular objects or even series of objects. The free-floatingness of moods can be explained by the fact that they represent free-floating properties.

I will return to all three of these views in the subsequent section "Against Reductive Representationalism." For now, however, what's important to note is that if any of these three views provides a plausible understanding of the generalized directedness of moods, NIM would turn out to be false.

Moods as Sensory Representations of Bodily States (Inward Directedness)

Suppose at this point we were simply to dig in our heels and deny that all moods must be outwardly directed. There might be a mood, a feeling of elation perhaps, that is not about a changing series of objects in the world, or the world as a whole, or even about unbound elatedness. Although it might seem that such a mood would have to be nonintentional, many philosophers have denied this claim. Even if we grant that there could be such a mood entirely lacking in *outward* directedness, the mood might still have a kind of inward directedness.

Here it's instructive to compare recent discussion of the intentionality of pain. A long tradition in philosophy had classified pain—along with other bodily sensations, and also states like both emotions and moods—as nonintentional. Consider, for example, Louise Antony's suggestion that "things like pleasures, pains, moods and emotions don't, on the face of it, appear to be about anything at all" (1997, 25).[22] Against this tradition, many philosophers have recently argued for a perceptual account of bodily sensations: just as a visual experience provides us with perceptual awareness of the world, a sensation provides us with perceptual awareness of the body. Pain can thus be understood as a sensory representation, one that represents a particular bodily disturbance. When you cut your finger, your pain represents the tissue damage in that finger; after a strenuous workout, your aches represent the condition of your muscles.[23] In some cases, we might be in pain without any corresponding bodily damage, but such cases are simply instances of misrepresentation.

Thus, insofar as pains carry information about the states of our body they can, contra Antony, be understood as intentional. This general analysis might then be extended to emotions and moods. First consider emotions. Instances of emotions typically are associated with various physiological changes, from flushed cheeks and sweaty palms to a racing pulse and shortness of breath. Different philosophical theories of the emotions explain this association in different ways. William James, for example, famously argued that emotions are to be *identified* with the experiences of physiological changes; as natural as it might be to think that my pulse is racing and I'm short of breath *because* I'm afraid, in fact it's the experience of these bodily changes in which my fear consists (James 1884). In recent years, James's theory has largely fallen into disfavor—among other problems, it's not at all clear that the physiological profiles of differing emotions are sufficient to individuate them. But even assuming there is more to emotion than just the experience of physiological changes, it's nonetheless plausible to suppose that emotions are—at least in part—representations of such changes.[24]

Moods, unlike pains and emotions, are not associated with specific or easily identifiable physiological changes. Yet like pains and emotions, they seem to be importantly tied to our bodies. In attempting to flesh out this thought, it might be claimed that moods have a more general representational function—namely, to represent the overall state of one's body. As Tye has argued, our moods are representations of physical changes to our "bodily landscapes":

> For each of us, there is at any given time a range of physical states constituting functional equilibrium. Which states these are might vary from time to time. But when functional equilibrium is present, we operate in a balanced, normal way without feeling any particular mood. When moods descend on us, we are responding in a sensory way to a *departure* from the pertinent range of physical states. (1995, 129)

Certainly more would need to be said to make this analysis a plausible one. But if it could be developed, NIM—the claims that moods are typically nonintentional—would be falsified. Even if moods can fail to be directed outward to the world or to objects or properties within it, they would nonetheless have a sort of inward directedness by representing something about our physiology.

Interestingly, this kind of inward directedness is best described as generalized in a way reminiscent of the previous subsection. In contrast to emotions, which are inwardly directed at particular bodily changes and are thus specific sensory representations, moods are inwardly directed more generally at the body overall and are thus generalized sensory representations. This parallels the difference between moods and emotions with respect to outward directedness. Whatever intentional content moods may have, whether it be inward or outward, it seems to be of a more diffuse or generalized nature than the intentional content of emotions.

Hybrid Theories

Of course, the two accounts just considered—moods as generalized representations of the world and moods as (generalized) representations of the body—are not mutually exclusive. In discussing the intentionality of moods, several philosophers have recently offered what we might call *hybrid* views— views that see the intentionality of moods as consisting in both outward and inward directedness. One particularly well-developed hybrid theory has been offered by Peter Goldie, who claims that mood experiences involve two kinds of feelings, what he calls *bodily feelings* and *feelings toward*.[25] For Goldie, both of these are intentional. A bodily feeling is intentional in being inwardly directed toward one's body and the changes that it is undergoing. A feeling toward, in contrast, is outwardly directed—it is an "unreflective emotional engagement with the world beyond the body" (Goldie 2002, 241).[26]

What then, are we to make of NIM, the claim that moods are typically nonintentional? The discussion throughout this section makes this claim look increasingly implausible. Despite the truth of UM, that is, despite the fact that moods are typically not directed at anything in particular, it seems implausible that they are typically nonintentional. NIM should thus be rejected.

While the truth of NIM would have made our case against representationalism an easy one, it's important to note that the falsity of NIM does not settle the issue in favor of the representationalist picture. There remain several argumentative strategies available to the antirepresentationalist.

First, even if moods are *typically* intentional, there could still be isolated cases where they are nonintentional. Consider a weaker version of NIM, the *weak nonintentionality of moods*:

(WNIM) Moods are sometimes nonintentional.

WNIM would still be enough to falsify the representationalist treatment of moods (and thus unrestricted representationalism more generally). To develop our antirepresentationalist case, then, we might explore whether some instances of moods, be they cases of generalized depression or free-floating anxiety or something else altogether, are best understood as being about nothing at all (as opposed to just nothing in particular).

Though I think this strategy has considerable potential, I will leave this fight for another day. In what follows I want to pursue a different line of attack against representationalism. Going forward, I'll simply grant the representationalist that moods have—not just typically, but always—the kind of generalized intentionality (either outward, inward, or both) detailed previously. But just as we might agree that perceptual experiences are always intentional while rejecting representationalism about perception, so too we can agree that moods are always intentional while rejecting representationalism about moods. For representationalism to be true of moods, it must be the case not only that moods have intentional content, but also that their phenomenal content reduces to this intentional content. It is this latter claim that I will explore—and dispute—in what follows.

Against Reductive Representationalism

For the representationalist, a state's phenomenal character is nothing over and above its intentional content; what it is like to be in a certain state is just a matter of what the state represents. So consider what this representationalist picture means for moods. Previously, we saw three different ways to understand the intentional content of such a state—as outwardly directed, inwardly directed, or a hybrid of the two. Broadly speaking, then the representationalist has the following three options:

Outward Directedness: What it is like to be in mood M is to have a certain kind of outwardly focused representational content.

Inward Directedness: What it is like to be in mood M is to have a certain kind of inwardly focused representational content.
Hybrid Directedness: What it is like to be in mood M is to have both a certain kind of outwardly focused representational content and a certain kind of inwardly focused representational content.

In the section "Moods as Generalized Representations (Outward Directedness)," we distinguished three different ways that moods might be outwardly directed: as directed at a changing series of objects, as directed at the world as a whole, or as directed at unbound properties. Thus, there are three different ways of pursuing the first option and correspondingly three different ways of pursuing the third hybrid option. To my mind, however, all of these options fail. Even on the assumption that moods have intentional content, this content does not seem able to account for the phenomenology. As William Lycan has put the point, when it comes to mental states like moods, the intentional content "does not loom very large in the overall phenomenal character of the mental state in question" (2006).

This strikes me as especially clear with respect to inward directedness. Granted, if one has adopted a theory that sees moods on a continuum with emotions, the fact that the phenomenology of emotions might plausibly be (at least partly) explained in terms of inward intentional content makes it tempting to suppose that the phenomenology of moods should also be explainable (at least partly) in terms of inward intentional content. But this temptation must be avoided. When I am briefly overcome with anger after a driver cuts me off on the freeway, I am often vividly aware of the changes my body undergoes—I feel my face getting flushed, my heart beating faster, and the trembling in my hands. Things seem quite different when, over the course of several hours, or several days, I am in an irritable mood. I feel on edge, prone to snap, and not quite myself. But this phenomenology does not seem rooted in the state of my body, even in some generalized way. Though my body may indeed be in a different physiological condition from its baseline, this physiological fact is not something of which I am aware, let alone vividly so. In short, even if my physiological condition is represented by my mood, this intentional content is far too minimal to capture the rich phenomenological aspects of what it's like to be in irritable mood. The point seems to apply just as strongly—or perhaps even more so—when we reflect on other moods, like states of free-floating anxiety or generalized elation. In contrast to the inward intentional content of emotions, the inward intentional content of moods is too impoverished to do the work that it is being assigned.[27]

The situation initially looks better for the representationalist with respect to outward directedness, since here the intentional content is somewhat more robust. Even here, however, the intentional content is insufficient to capture the phenomenology. For the representationalist, the phenomenal character of moods *reduces to* the intentional content—that's simply what the phenomenal character *is*. Importantly, this means that there can be no change in the intentional content of a mood without a corresponding change in the phenomenal character, and likewise, that there can be no change in the phenomenal character of a mood without a corresponding change in the intentional content. As I will suggest, neither of these claims is plausible.

Let's start with the suggestion that moods are intentionally directed at a changing series of objects in the world. As noted previously, when someone is depressed, everything to which she turns seems awful and black; when she's elated, everything to which she turns seems wonderfully rosy. So now consider a few moments in the life of an elated person. As she walks along outside, she encounters an ever-changing landscape of sights, sounds, and smells. Today, given her mood, the storefront across the way doesn't seem nearly as shabby as it usually does; the face of her taciturn neighbor doesn't strike her as quite as menacing; the car horns fail to disturb her and likewise for the odors emanating from the overflowing dumpster at the curb. Today, everything she passes seems wonderful and new. Insofar as her mood is directed at a changing series of things in the world, the intentional content of her mood is constantly changing. But what of the phenomenological character of her mood? Is there any reason to suppose that this must be changing as well? Granted, as she walks along, there will be changes to her visual phenomenology, and likewise to her auditory and olfactory phenomenology. But these sorts of changes are distinct from the phenomenology of the mood itself, which need not vary as she makes her way out in the world.[28]

In saying this, I do not mean to suggest that the phenomenology of moods always remains completely static. We often refer to moods as waxing and waning, and I take these to be phenomenological descriptors. Over the course of a day in which one feels elated, the elation might be felt more deeply, more intensely, at one moment than at another. But what's important is that these changes do not seem at all tied to the changing series of worldly objects at which one's mood is directed. Thus, not only do we have changes in the intentional content of the mood that are not reflected in corresponding changes in the phenomenal character of the mood, but we also have changes in the phenomenal character of the mood that are not reflected in corresponding changes in the intentional content.

Faced with this latter point, I envision the representationalist responding along the following lines: "An elated mood represents worldly objects as being rosy and wonderful. When my mood waxes, I'm representing the relevant worldly object as being rosier and more wonderful; when my mood wanes, I'm representing it as being less rosy and wonderful." This suggestion, however, does not seem faithful to our experience of moods. Consider a new father who has been in an elated mood for hours, ever since his child was born. As he rocks his daughter to sleep in his arms, his elation deepens. Must we suppose that as this happens, his daughter starts to seem rosier and more wonderful to him? If his elation lessens, must we suppose that she starts to seem less rosy and wonderful to him? The point here is not one about *concepts*. Even if we suppose, along with many representationalists, that the representational content of experience is nonconceptual content, my claim still holds: a person's mood can change phenomenally even when there is no change to the way the object of the mood seems to that person.

The fact that the phenomenology can change without any corresponding changes to the intentional content shows why the representationalist is no better off supposing that the mood is directed at the world as a whole, rather than at a changing series of objects in the world. Insofar as the phenomenology of a mood can change without the world seeming different, the representationalist's reduction will be no more successful here than on the previous way of spelling out outward directedness.

Granted, since on this second view the mood is continually directed at the same object, the world, it does seem better able than the previous view to explain situations in which a mood's phenomenology remains constant. But I think even here there are problems for the view. After all, the following claims seem perfectly coherent, and (unless we're in the grips of a theory) I don't see why we shouldn't take them at face value:

My depression hasn't worsened since yesterday, but today everything seem blacker.

My fearfulness hasn't lessened any, but the world seems less scary today.

Compare also claims like the following, which likewise seem perfectly coherent:

The world doesn't seem any more worrying today, yet somehow my anxiety has intensified.

The world doesn't seem any blacker today, yet I find myself sinking deeper into depression.

All of these claims serve to falsify the suggestion that the phenomenal character of a mood reduces to the mood's representing the world in a certain way.

That brings us to the third way of spelling out outward directedness—namely, Mendelovici's suggestion that a mood's intentional content be explained in terms of sui generis unbound emotion properties. Emotion experiences are hypothesized to represent these properties as bound to objects—so, for example, when I am scared of a snake, my experience of fear represents the snake as scary*. In contrast, when I am in a fearful mood, my mood represents scariness* as unbound.

One clear advantage of Mendelovici's view is its ability to account for the fact that moods often present themselves phenomenally as free floating in nature. But while it gets right the fact that fearful moods, for example, don't seem to represent anything in particular as scary*, it's not clear that this means that they represent unbound scariness* instead. In large part, this is because it's not entirely clear what it is to represent unbound scariness*. Perhaps it might it be something like the representation: *there's scariness* about.* But this seems less a case where scariness* is unbound than a case in which we're representing scariness* as bound to something unidentified or unidentifiable, a situation more like a representation of scariness* bound to we know not what. Thus, the plausibility of this view rests in part on whether we can be given an adequate explanation of the suggestion that properties can be represented unbound.

Even given such an explanation, however, some of the same problems we raised previously for the other versions of outward directedness arise again here. To account for the fact that moods vary in their phenomenology over time, Mendelovici will have to identify appropriate changes in the intentional content. There are not many options here. Since the emotion properties are hypothesized to occur unbound, there is no intentional object to change. Presumably, then, there will have to be different emotion properties represented at different times—mild scariness*, moderate scariness*, and so on. Perhaps the proliferation of properties is not itself something to worry about. But what *is* worrying is the fact that it seems we can experience phenomenal changes to our mood without corresponding intentional changes of this sort.

Consider again the father rocking his newborn to sleep in his arms. Previously, in arguing against a different version of outward directedness, I suggested that it was implausible to suppose that his daughter must seem different to him—slightly more wonderfully rosy—as his elation deepens. Since on Mendelovici's view, his generalized feeling of elation does not represent his daughter, she can avoid this implausible supposition. But the victory is short lived. Her view commits her to something equally implausible, since one's deepening elation doesn't seem to need to correspond to a change from rosiness* to deeper rosiness*—that is, from unbound-rosiness* seeming to unbound-deeper-rosiness* seeming. The point seems to apply to other moods as well. Must the degree of my fearful mood correspond to the degree of unbound-scariness* seeming? Must the degree of my depression correspond to the degree of unbound-blackness* seeming? In my view, the answer to both these questions is clearly "no." In short, the switch to unbound properties does not seem to improve the representationalist's chances for a successful reduction of phenomenological character to intentional content.[29]

What then of hybrid theories? Although inward directedness and outward directedness are individually problematic, one might naturally think that the representationalist could solve the problems mentioned previously by synthesizing the two in some way. In particular, one might think the inward and outward intentional content of a mood might be jointly sufficient to capture its phenomenal character even if neither such content is individually so.

In evaluating this suggestion, it's first important to note the unified nature of the phenomenal character of moods. Unless the inward and outward content can be integrated in some way, a hybrid view will not get off the ground.[30] But even if some sort of unification can be achieved, other problems remain. For example, the addition of inward intentional content to outward intentional content will be of no help to the representationalist if the phenomenal character of a mood can stay the same even while the outward intentional content changes. Thus, the hybrid view looks to have no more promise than the other views we have here considered.

The Failure of Transparency

The discussion of the previous section suggests that the representationalist reduction fails with respect to moods. Even if we concede that NIM in false—that is, even if moods are typically intentional—the representationalist needs to do more than simply identify some intentional content associated with moods. The intentional content that she finds must be such that the phenomenal character of moods could plausibly be said to reduce to it. And this she has not done.

My discussion thus far has not ruled out that the representationalist might light upon some source of intentional content not yet discussed that would account for the phenomenal character of moods. In this concluding section, however, I would like to offer at least one compelling reason to think that this won't happen. We noted at the start of the chapter that the driving motivation for representationalism has been its promise to solve the hard problem of consciousness. This motivation, however, is loaded. It does not help to show that the theory might be true; after all, the hard problem might simply be unsolvable. In arguing for their theory, representationalists thus tend to rely on a second, less loaded motivation: the so-called transparency of experience.

Experience is said to be transparent in the sense that we "see" right through it to the object of that experience, analogously to the way we see through a pane of glass to whatever is on the other side of it. Considerations of this sort were introduced into the contemporary debate about by Gilbert Harman. In a now famous passage, Harman claimed:

> When Eloise sees a tree before her, the colors she experiences are all experienced as features of the tree and its surroundings. None of them are experienced as intrinsic features of her experience. Nor does she experience any features of anything as intrinsic features of her experiences. And that is true of you too. There is nothing special about Eloise's visual experience. When you see a tree, you do not experience any features as intrinsic features of your experience. Look at a tree and try to turn your attention to intrinsic features of your visual experience. I predict you

will find that the only features there to turn your attention to will be features of the presented tree . . . (1990, 667)[31]

If representationalism were true, then we would have a clear explanation of transparency: the reason that we cannot attend to intrinsic features of our experience is that there are none; rather, there are only representational features.[32] In this way, intuitions about transparency play a key role in building a case for the representationalist view.

What exactly it means to say that experience is transparent, and whether the way in which it is transparent really does support representationalism, has recently been the subject of much debate.[33] Importantly, however, there is a wide consensus that some version of the transparency thesis seems plausible with respect to ordinary visual experiences. Things are quite different when it comes to moods. Defenders of transparency about visual experiences have rarely attempted to extend the transparency thesis to mood experiences, presumably because in this domain the thesis has no purchase.[34] Many would go further and claim that it has no purchase even for emotions. As Ronald De Sousa has noted, in comparison with perceptual experience, emotions are relatively opaque: when someone tries to focus her attention on her jealousy or anger or joyfulness, her attention doesn't go out into the world; in contrast, when she tries to focus her attention on the world, she often ends up focusing only on her own state of mind (2004, 64).[35]

For transparency to be true of moods, it would have to be the case that whenever one tried to focus one's attention on a mood itself, one's attention would slip right through the experience to something else—perhaps worldly objects, or perhaps the state of one's body.[36] But this isn't at all what happens. It might be that in attending to my experience of blueishness, I don't (or even can't) attend directly to the blueishness of my experience itself. But in attending my experience of elation, it seems most natural to describe what I'm attending to as the elation itself. I'm not simply attending to some feature of the world, or to a feature of a changing series of things, or even to some unbound feature. Rather, I focus directly on what it feels like to be elated.

If this is right, if I can focus directly on what it feels like to be elated—on the felt quality of the mood, an *intrinsic* feature of it—then representationalism about moods faces a serious threat. On a representationalist view, there are no such intrinsic features. Thus, the problem for the representationalist is not a matter of fine-tuning their specification of the intentional content of moods. No matter how the intentional content is specified, the failure of transparency suggests that there is more to the phenomenology than can be captured by that content.

Undoubtedly, the representationalist will have something to say in response to the previous line of argument. But even if I have not yet shown that transparency is false with respect to moods, the reflections of this concluding section make clear that transparency is by no means *obviously* true with respect to moods. And even this much weaker conclusion plays an important role in the case against representationalism. In the perceptual sphere, transparency is taken to be an obvious phenomenological fact in need of explanation and thus is invoked to show not just that representationalism is a viable option but that it must be true. With respect to moods, in contrast, transparency is not an obvious phenomenological fact. We thus have no special reason to think that representationalism about moods has any promise.

In short, even if the representationalist were able to explain away the seeming failure of transparency with respect to moods, the key motivation for her theory would have been undermined. This result, combined with the reflections in the previous section suggesting the failure of existing representationalist theories, provides compelling reason to think that the representationalist reduction of moods cannot be achieved.

Notes

1. The *easy/hard* terminology derives from David Chalmers. Much of the contemporary discussion of the hard problem of consciousness owes to his work (see, e.g., Chalmers 1995).

2. Charles Siewert provides a particularly clear explanation of the motivation behind strong representationalism: "One may believe that it offers us the only hope for a natural scientific understanding of consciousness. The underlying thought is that a science of consciousness must adopt this strategy: first conceive of intentionality (or content or mental representation) in a way that separates it from consciousness, and see intentionality as the outcome of familiar (and non-intentional) natural causal processes. Then, by further specifying the kind of intentionality involved (in terms of its use, its sources, its content), we can account for consciousness. In other words: 'naturalize' intentionality, then intentionalize consciousness, and mind has found its place in nature" (2006).

3. Although I here target only strong representationalism, some of my criticisms apply to weak representationalism as well.

4. This should not be taken as an endorsement of representationalism with respect to perceptual experiences. See, for example, Kind (2008) for arguments against representationalism even in the perceptual case.

5. There is agreement on this point by both representationalists and nonrepresentationalists. For example, I make this point in Kind (2007) in the context of arguing against representationalism, while Byrne (2001) and Mendelovici (this volume, Chapter 6) make this point in the context of arguing for representationalism.

6. Three notable exceptions include Lormand 1985, Griffiths (1989), and Sizer (2000).

7. Solomon uses the term "generalized emotion" (Solomon 1993, 71); Frijda refers to moods as "diffuse" (Frijda 1994, 60). Other philosophers who treat moods as a subclass of emotions include Prinz (2004, 182–188), Fish (2005), DeLancey (2006), and Mendelovici (this volume, Chapter 6).

8. Although going forward I will assume that emotions and moods are distinct, this assumption is not critical for my argument; the failure of representationalism to account for moods is just as problematic for the theory if moods are merely a subclass of emotions than if they form a distinct class of mental state.

9. Other philosophers who explicitly distinguish moods from emotions include Lormand (1985), Montague (2009), De Sousa (2010), and Sizer (2000). In presenting her computational analysis of moods, Sizer challenges not only the assumption that moods and emotions are essentially the same type of state, but also the assumption that "one theory or explanatory apparatus can be applied to all types of affect" (2000, 748).

10. See, for example, Davidson and Ekman (1994, 94).

11. For related considerations against the duration criterion, see Lazarus (1994) and Prinz (2004, 183).

12. This does not mean that we must always be able to correctly identify the objects of our emotions. Awoken by a strange sound in the middle of the night, I might have a feeling of fear without quite knowing what I am fearful about.

13. See also Thalberg (1964). According to Thalberg, states like depression, euphoria, total apathy, and free-floating anxiety, and so forth, cannot take objects.

14. One philosopher who objects even to the weaker UM is Craig Delancey. According to Delancey, the fact that we cannot identify the particular object of a mood does not mean that there is no such object: "Since the only evidence for the lack of objects for moods is phenomenological, then the fact that moods sometimes *appear* to lack an object is not a distinguishing feature. They could have an object of which we are unaware; and they may have a series of objects, including unrelated objects. The same is true of emotions: they often do not have an object we can identify, and in fact, an emotion can occur and have measurable effects on us, even effects we are aware of, without our knowing we are in the emotional state" (2006, 533).

15. For discussion of objectless panic and objectless rage, see Price (2006, 52).

16. See also George Graham's (1990, 405–406) distinction between two kinds of depression, *depression with intentionality* and *depression without intentionality*.

17. See, for example, Goldie (2000, 18), De Sousa (2010), and Sizer (2000, 747).

18. One place where they are very clearly distinguished is Tye (2008).

19. See also Tye (2008) and Sizer (2000) for discussions of elation and melancholy, respectively, along these lines.

20. See also the psychologist Richard Lazarus's claim that moods reflect "the existential background of our lives" (1994, 84).

21. As noted above in the first section, Mendelovici thinks of moods as a subclass of emotions and correspondingly refers to them as the *undirected emotions*. In explaining her view, I have modified her terminology to correspond with the terminology I am using here.

22. See also Colin McGinn's claim that "bodily sensations do not have an intentional object in the way perceptual experiences do" (1991, 8–9).

23. See, for example, Tye (1995, 111–116) and Crane (1998).

24. Moreover, the representationalist aims to identify the phenomenal character of emotion with this representational content. See, for example, Tye (1995).

25. Although Goldie is concerned primarily with the intentionality of emotions, recall that for him the difference between emotion and mood is simply one of degree.

26. Tye (2008) also offers a hybrid account.

27. Here also it's worth briefly noting that one woman's modus ponens is another's modus tollens. Given the phenomenological similarity between emotions and moods, representationalists are inclined to think that the inwardly directed account that they've offered for emotions can be applied, mutatis mutandi, to moods. In my view, however, the discovery that this account cannot be easily applied to moods gives us reason to call into question this treatment of emotions as well. But I do not have the space here to pursue this point.

28. Perhaps there might be some component of the intentional content that remains unchanged as her mood is directed at a changing series of objects of the world. My suspicion is that this thought is best worked out in connection with Mendelovici's view of moods as representing unbound emotion properties (see subsequent discussion).

29. Another way to put these points is to return to Mendelovici's highlighter analogy, discussed previously. As our mood waxes and wanes, it does not seem that there need to be corresponding changes to the shade of the highlighter ink. Likewise, as the shade of the highlighter ink changes, it does not seem that there need to be corresponding changes to the felt intensity of the mood.

30. Mendelovici (this volume, Chapter 6) pushes this point against hybrid views.

31. See also Tye (1995, 30).

32. It is generally assumed in this discussion that representational features are nonintrinsic.

33. See, e.g., Kind (2003).

34. Here Michael Tye is a striking exception (e.g., Tye 1995).
35. See also Deonna and Teroni (2012, 68–69).
36. Transparency seems especially hard to make out on a view like Mendelovici's. Given her analysis of the intentional content of moods, it looks like she would have to claim that whenever one attends to one's mood one's attention slips through and one ends up attending to unbound properties instead. But what could it mean to attend to an unbound property?

References

Antony, Louise. 1997. "What It's Like to Smell a Gardenia." *The Times Literary Supplement* 4897 (February 7).

Baier, Annette. 1990. "What Emotions Are About." *Philosophical Perspectives* 4: 1–29.

Byrne, Alex. 2001. "Intentionalism Defended." *Philosophical Review* 110: 199–240.

Chalmers, David. 1995. "The Puzzle of Conscious Experience." *Scientific American*, 273: 80–86.

Chalmers, David. 2004. "The Representational Character of Experience." In *The Future for Philosophy*, ed. Brian Leiter (pp. 153–181). Oxford: Oxford University Press.

Crane, Tim. 1998. "Intentionality as the Mark of the Mental." In *Contemporary Issues in the Philosophy of Mind*, ed. Anthony O'Hear, 136–157. Cambridge: Cambridge University Press.

Davidson, Richard, and Paul Ekman. 1994. "Afterword: How Are Emotions Distinguished from Moods, Temperament, and Other Related Affective Constraints?" In *The Nature of Emotion*, ed. Paul Ekman and Richard Davidson, 94–96. Oxford: Oxford University Press.

DeLancey, Craig. 2006. "Basic Moods." *Philosophical Psychology* 19: 527–538.

Deonna, Julien A., and Fabrice Teroni. 2012. *The Emotions: A Philosophical Introduction*. New York: Routledge.

De Sousa, Ronald. 2004. "Emotions: What I know, What I'd Like to Think I know, and What I'd Like to Think." In *Thinking About Feeling*, ed. Robert C. Solomon, 61–75. Oxford: Oxford University Press.

De Sousa, Ronald. 2010. "Emotion." *Stanford Encyclopedia of Philosophy, ed.* Edward Zalta. Available at URL = <http://plato.stanford.edu/archives/spr2013/entries/emotion/>.

Dretske, Fred. 1995. *Naturalizing the Mind*. Cambridge, Mass.: The MIT Press.

Fish, William. 2005. "Emotions, Moods, and Intentionality." In *Intentionality Past and Future*, ed. G. Forrai and G. Kampis, 25–35. New York: Rodopi Press.

Frijda, Nico. 1993. "Moods, Emotion Episodes, and Emotions." In *Handbook of Emotions*, ed. J. Haviland and M. Lewis, 381–403. New York: Guilford.

Frijda, Nico. 1994. "Varieties of Affect: Emotions and episodes, moods and sentiments." In *The Nature of Emotion*, ed. Paul Ekman and Richard Davidson, 59–67. Oxford: Oxford University Press.

Goldie, Peter. 2000. *The Emotions*. Oxford: Oxford University Press.

Goldie, Peter. 2002. "Emotions, Feelings, and Intentionality." *Phenomenology and the Cognitive Sciences* 1: 235–254.

Graham, George. 1990. "Melancholic Epistemology." *Synthese* 82: 399–422.

Griffiths, Paul E. 1989. "Folk, Functional, and Neurochemical Aspects of Mood." *Philosophical Psychology* 2: 17–30.

Griffiths, Paul E. 1997. *What Emotions Really Are: The Problem of Psychological Categories*. Chicago: The University of Chicago Press.

Harman, Gilbert. 1990. "The Intrinsic Quality of Experience." In *The Nature of Consciousness*, eds. Ned Block, Owen J. Flanagan, and Güven Güzeldere, 663–75. Cambridge, Mass.: The MIT Press, 1997.

James, William. 1884. "What Is an Emotion?" *Mind* 9: 188–205.

Kenny, Anthony. 1963. *Action, Emotion and Will*. London: Routledge & Kegan Paul.

Kind, Amy. 2003. "What's So Transparent about Transparency?" *Philosophical Studies* 115: 225–244.

Kind, Amy. 2007. "Restrictions on Representationalism." *Philosophical Studies* 134: 405–427.

Kind, Amy. 2008. "How to Believe in Qualia." In *The Case for Qualia*, ed. E. O. Wright, 285–298. Cambridge, Mass.: MIT Press.

Kupperman, Joel. 1995. "An Anti-Essentialist View of the Emotions." *Philosophical Psychology* 8: 341–351.

Lazarus, Richard. 1994. "Appraisal: The Long and the Short of It." In *The Nature of Emotions*, ed. P. Eckman and R. J. Davidson (pp. 208-215). Oxford: Oxford University Press.

Lormand, Eric. 1985. "Towards a Theory of Moods." *Philosophical Studies* 47: 385–407.

Lyons, William. 1980. *Emotion*. Cambridge: Cambridge University Press.

Lycan, William. 2006. "Representational Theories of Consciousness." *Stanford Encyclopedia of Philosophy*, ed. Edward Zalta. Available at http://plato.stanford.edu/entries/consciousness-representational/

McGinn, Colin. 1991. "Consciousness and Content." In *The Nature of Consciousness*, Ned Block, Owen J. Flanagan, and Güven Güzeldere, eds., 295–307. Cambridge, Mass.: MIT Press, 1997.

Montague, Michelle. 2009. "The Logic, Intentionality, and Phenomenology of Emotion." *Philosophical Studies* 145: 171–192.

Price, Carolyn. 2006. "Affect without Object: Moods and Objectless Emotions." *European Journal of Analytic Philosophy* 2: 49–68.

Prinz, Jesse. 2004. *Gut Reactions: A Perceptual Theory of Emotion*. Oxford: Oxford University Press.

Searle, John R. 1983. *Intentionality*. Cambridge: Cambridge University Press.

Siewert, Charles. 2006. "Consciousness and Intentionality." *Stanford Encyclopedia of Philosophy*, ed. Edward Zalta. Retrieved from http://plato.stanford.edu/entries/consciousness-intentionality/

Sizer, Laura. 2000. "Towards a Computational Theory of Mood." *British Journal for the Philosophy of Science* 51: 743–769.

Solomon, Robert. 1976. *The Passions*. New York: Anchor Press/Doubleday.

Solomon, Robert. 1993. *The Passions: Emotions and the Meaning of Life*. Indianapolis: Hackett.

Thalberg, Irving. 1964. "Emotion and Thought." *American Philosophical Quarterly* 1: 45–55.

Tye, Michael. 1995. *Ten Problems of Consciousness*. Cambridge, Mass.: MIT Press.

Tye, Michael. 2008. "The Experience of Emotions: An Intentionalist Theory." *Revue Internationale de Philosophie* 62: 25–50.

CHAPTER **6**

Pure Intentionalism about Moods and Emotions

ANGELA MENDELOVICI

Chapter Overview

Moods and emotions are sometimes thought to be counterexamples to *intentionalism*, the view that a mental state's phenomenal features are exhausted by its representational features. The problem is that moods and emotions are accompanied by phenomenal experiences that do not seem to be adequately accounted for by any of their plausibly represented contents. This chapter develops and defends an intentionalist view of the phenomenal character of moods and emotions on which (1) directed moods and emotions represent intentional objects as having sui generis affective properties, which happen to be uninstantiated, and (2) at least some moods represent affective properties not bound to any objects.

Introduction

According to intentionalism, a mental state's phenomenal features are determined by its representational features. All there is to the phenomenal experience of seeing blue is the visual representation of blueness. An experience of blueness does not involve "raw feels" or blue qualia; its phenomenal nature is exhausted by the represented blueness.

Moods and emotions throw a wrench in the intentionalist project. The problem is that they really seem like "raw feels" or mere qualia. Even though they are sometimes *directed* at particular objects, their phenomenal character does not seem to be adequately captured by any of the features they seem to represent their objects as having. Moods, such as sadness, elation, and irritation, pose an

135

even greater problem; they seem to be entirely *undirected,* lacking intentional objects entirely. They pervade our experience without attaching to any particular objects or other targets.

This chapter develops and defends an intentionalist theory of the phenomenal character of moods and emotions. On the view I will defend, (1) emotions and some moods represent intentional objects as having sui generis affective properties that happen to be uninstantiated, and (2) like concepts, but unlike most perceptual representations, affective representations can be tokened without binding to any object representations, yielding undirected moods.

The chapter proceeds as follows: the section "Moods, Emotions, and Intentionalism" clarifies some key notions, the section "Emotions" provides an intentionalist account of emotions, and the section "Moods" provides an intentionalist account of directed and undirected moods.

Moods, Emotions, and Intentionalism

Emotions are affective states that seem to be directed at something. Examples include fear of a dog, joy about an upcoming event, and guilt about a wrong one has committed. Emotions tend to be fairly short-lived and are usually caused by a specific stimulus, which may or may not be what they are directed at. *Moods* are affective states that do not seem to be directed at anything. Examples include happiness, sadness, and anxiety. Moods tend to be longer lasting than emotions and are usually not associated with a specific stimulus.[1] For most moods, there is a corresponding phenomenally similar emotion. For example, an anxious mood is phenomenally similar to anxiety about something, say an upcoming event.[2]

Intentionalism is the view that a mental state's phenomenal features are reducible to, supervenient on, type or token identical to, or determined by its representational features. Loosely, the idea is that phenomenal consciousness is nothing over and above mental representation.

Intentionalist views can be categorized based on purity. *Pure intentionalism* is the view that phenomenal character is reducible to, supervenient on, type or token identical to, or determined by representational content *alone* (Mendelovici, 2010, chap. 7). *Impure intentionalism* is the view that phenomenal character is reducible to, supervenient on, type or token identical to, or determined by representational content *together with some other features.* These other features are usually functional roles (Tye, 2000) or perceptual or other modalities (Lycan, 1996; Crane, 2003; Chalmers, 2004).

In what follows, I defend a type identity version of intentionalism, on which phenomenal features are identical to certain representational features.[3] The identity version of intentionalism arguably faces the greatest challenges in accounting for moods and emotions. It must maintain that the phenomenal characters of moods and emotions are identical to, rather than merely supervenient on or determined by, their representational contents. If this version of intentionalism can offer a plausible account of emotion, then other, weaker, versions should also be defensible on similar grounds. For brevity, "intentionalism" will be taken to refer to the type identity version of intentionalism.[4] Since the view I will defend does not appeal to nonrepresentational features, it is a type of pure intentionalism about emotions, which makes it compatible with both pure and impure intentionalism about phenomenal states in general.

Intentionalism is at least initially plausible for experiences such as color experiences, shape experiences, and sound experiences. In the case of shape, intentionalism claims that the phenomenal character of a shape experience is exhausted by the representation of shape properties. This is somewhat plausible at least largely because there are suitable candidate represented properties that adequately "match" shape experiences' phenomenal characters. For example, the represented property *circle* is similar enough to the phenomenal character of an experience of a circle to be plausibly identified with it. As this example illustrates, intentionalism about an experience is at least initially plausible when there is a suitable candidate represented content that adequately "matches" the experience's phenomenal character. When there is no suitable candidate, intentionalism is significantly less plausible.[5]

In the case of moods and emotions, however, it seems that there are no suitable candidate represented contents to "match" the states' distinctive phenomenal characters. First, it is not even clear what moods and emotions represent, or if they represent anything at all. Second, it is not at all clear that any of their candidate representational contents adequately match their distinctive phenomenal characters. For example, no candidate representational content plausibly attributed to joy seems to adequately match its phenomenal character.

The special challenge for intentionalism posed by emotions is that of accounting for the *distinctive* phenomenal character of moods and emotions. On many views, moods and emotions involve visual, auditory, cognitive, or other states that might contribute to their overall phenomenal character. If such views are correct, then the intentionalist must account for all these phenomenal characters in order to provide a complete account of the phenomenal character of moods and emotions. However, visual, auditory, cognitive, and other such phenomenal characters don't pose a *special* challenge for intentionalism about emotions. Presumably the intentionalist must already account for the phenomenal character of these experiences. Moods and emotions pose a *special* problem for intentionalism because they seem to have phenomenal characters that outrun visual, auditory, and so forth phenomenal characters. These are the distinctive phenomenal characters of anger, fear, sadness, disgust, and so forth. One way to get a grip on these phenomenal characters is to consider the case of two different emotions directed at the same intentional objects represented in the same modality, for example, excitement and anxiety directed at the same upcoming event represented in thought. The two states' different phenomenal characters are the distinctive phenomenal characters of excitement, on the one hand, and anxiety, on the other. In what follows, I will be concerned with offering an account of the *distinctive* phenomenal characters of moods and emotions.

There have been few explicit endorsements of intentionalism about moods and emotions. Peter Goldie (2000, 2002) has a view of moods and emotions that arguably anticipates intentionalism about emotions. On his view, moods and emotions consist in both an awareness of bodily states and a "feeling toward" particular objects. Both of these components account for the phenomenal character of emotions. "Feelings toward" are representational states that are automatically imbued with phenomenal character, much as the intentionalist would like. For Goldie, moods differ from emotions in that they are directed toward general or nonspecific objects.

Michael Tye (2008) specifically aims to offer an intentionalist account of emotions. On his view, the phenomenal character of emotions is determined by their representation of objects as (1) having evaluative features, such as threateningness, and (2) causing or accompanying certain physiological or bodily disturbances. Tye (1995) offers an intentionalist view of moods on which their phenomenal character is accounted for by the representation of departures from the "range of physical states constituting functional equilibrium" (p. 129). William Seager (2002) offers a similar account of emotions on which emotions' phenomenal characters are determined by the representation of evaluative properties and bodily states. Seager suggests that moods are "reflections of the base or average" evaluative features (2002, p. 678).

As we will see, these views offer useful insights. However, I will argue that they do not get things quite right. Instead, I will suggest that the distinctive phenomenal character of moods and emotions is best explained by the representation of sui generis affective properties. The next section develops the view for emotions, while the section "Moods" develops the view in the case of moods.

Emotions

Emotions are affective states that seem to be directed at objects. An intentionalist account of the phenomenal character of emotions must specify which of the contents of emotions account for their distinctive phenomenal characters. After canvassing various options, this section suggests that the representational contents that account for directed emotions' distinctive phenomenal characters are sui generis affective properties.

Bodily States

On many views of emotions, emotions involve the awareness or perception of bodily states. On the James-Lange theory, for instance, emotions involve the awareness of bodily states such as one's heart racing or one's blood pressure rising (James, 1884; Prinz, 2004, 2005, 2006). The intentionalist might suggest that emotions' representation of bodily states accounts for their distinctive phenomenal characters; call this the *bodily states view.*

The James-Lange view is currently out of fashion, and the reasons for this are instructive for assessing the bodily states view. A common objection is that the same physiological processes, and presumably the awareness of the same physiological processes, is associated with different emotions (Cannon, 1929). For example, physiological arousal caused by an injection of epinephrine can be associated with both anger and euphoria (Schacter and Singer, 1962). While there may in fact be subtle differences in the physiological reactions associated with these emotions (LeDoux, 1996), it seems doubtful that awareness of these subtly different physiological reactions is sufficient to account for their different phenomenal characters as the bodily states view would require.

The bodily states view also faces a challenge in accounting for the experienced directedness of directed emotions. Fear of a dog seems to be in some way directed at *the dog*, and this directedness is reflected in emotion's distinctive phenomenology. While the bodily states view allows that emotions exhibit directedness toward bodily states, this is not the type of experienced directedness we're after. We're after directedness toward dogs and other extrabodily entities.

One way to see the worry is to consider the following phenomenal contrast case: Compare (1) visually experiencing a dog and a raccoon while fearing the dog, and (2) visually experiencing a dog and a raccoon while fearing the raccoon. Suppose the visual experience, the level of fear, and the physiological response to the fearful object are the same in both cases. It is still plausible that there is a phenomenal difference between (1) and (2). But the bodily states view treats the two cases alike. They both involve the same visual experience and the same physiological response of which we are presumably aware.[7] Thus, the representation of bodily states does not fully account for the phenomenal character of emotions.

Intentional Objects

Emotions are usually directed at something. It is quite plausible that emotions involve the representation of these things, and so we might call them *intentional objects.* One might suggest that emotions' intentional objects explain their distinctive phenomenal characters; call this the *intentional objects view.*

Emotions can be directed toward a diverse range of intentional objects belonging to a diverse range of ontological categories, such as concrete particulars (fear of a dog), events (anxiety about an upcoming performance), propositions (happiness that one has achieved a goal), regions of space-time (fear of the dark alley at night), and ourselves (embarrassment at oneself). An emotion's intentional object need not be the object that caused it (e.g., workplace stress can cause one to become irritated at an innocent friend). These intentional objects need not even exist (one can be afraid of monsters under the bed). Intentional objects can be represented in various modalities. For example, fear can be directed at a dog represented in various perceptual modalities, or in imagination or thought.[8]

Although it is quite plausible that emotions represent intentional objects, this doesn't yet explain emotions' *distinctive* phenomenal characters. A perceptual experience of a dog and a fear of a dog have the same intentional object represented in the same modality (e.g., vision), but the emotion has a distinctive phenomenal character that the perceptual experience lacks. Thus, the intentional objects view fails.[9]

Affective Properties

Perhaps the intentionalist can find the contents that determine emotions' distinctive phenomenal characters not in the generic representation of emotions' intentional objects, but rather in some special *affective* properties they represent their intentional objects as having; call this the *affective properties view.* It does seem that emotions somehow *qualify* their intentional objects, or present them in certain *ways.* This qualification goes beyond the ways nonemotional perception, imagination, and thought qualify these same intentional objects. For example, when we fear a dog, we not only experience the dog as brown, moving, barking, and so forth, but we also experience the dog as *scary.* When we are frustrated at a situation, we experience the situation as *frustrating.* When we experience joy at the thought of an upcoming event, the event itself is experienced as *joyous.* But what do these properties of being scary, frustrating, and joyous amount to?

Ordinary Physical Properties

One option is that affective properties are just ordinary physical properties, like those of having a certain mass or being a table. Presumably, these would be subject-independent physical properties that are at least sometimes had by the intentional objects of fear, frustration, joy, and so forth, such as dangerousness or threateningness. Call this the *ordinary properties view.*[10]

The problem with the proposal is that it is not at all clear which ordinary physical property scary dogs and scary economies can be said to have in common that can be identified with scariness. The physical properties that tend to elicit emotions form a complex and disjunctive set. These complex and disjunctive properties are foreign to the phenomenology of fear, which makes them poor candidates for the properties fear represents. Further, and perhaps more obviously, they are poor candidates for the contents of fear that determine its phenomenal character. Something similar can be said about directed elation, anxiety, and other emotions.

There are two standard moves that can be made to defend the claim that experiences represent properties that appear foreign from a phenomenological perspective: first, one might claim that the apparently foreign properties are represented under a particular (less foreign) mode of presentation.[11]

There are several problems with this strategy. First, we are now owed an account of the relevant modes of presentation. Modes of presentations are generally thought to be types of contents. For example, the distinct modes of presentation of our concepts morning star and evening star correspond to their involving distinct contents—namely, the last heavenly body to disappear in the morning sky and the first heavenly body to appear in the night sky, respectively. But what contents play the role of modes of presentation for affective properties? The problem is that the intentionalist must find contents that plausibly account for emotions' phenomenal characters, which is just the challenge originally facing the intentionalist. By saying that emotions represent ordinary properties under a special mode of presentation we haven't made much progress. Note also that if this strategy can be made to work, then modes of presentation would be doing all the work in accounting for the phenomenal character of emotions, since *they* are what match the phenomenologically familiar intentional and phenomenal aspects of emotion. The representation of the affective properties themselves would be doing no work in accounting for the distinctive phenomenal characters of emotion.

Perhaps there are nonrepresentational ways of understanding modes of presentation, for example, as functional or other features of the states that do the representing. On one way of understanding this strategy, these nonrepresentational modes of presentation do all the work in accounting for the phenomenal character of emotion. Representational content drops out of the picture. But this would no longer count as a version of intentionalism.

If, instead, we say that the nonrepresentational modes of presentation *together* with representational contents do the work, then we have a version of impure intentionalism, since representational and nonrepresentational factors together fix phenomenal character. The problem with this view is that much more will have to be said about how these modes of presentation transform the phenomenologically foreign representational contents of emotions into their phenomenologically familiar phenomenal characters. Whereas it's somewhat plausible that the content *circle* yields the phenomenal character associated with seeing circles, it's not at all clear how the phenomenologically foreign contents of emotion representations together with a special impure element yield the distinctive phenomenal character of emotions.[12]

The second strategy in defense of phenomenologically foreign content attributions is to claim that the relevant contents are represented *nonconceptually*. This strategy has been utilized by Tye (2000) to argue that color experience represents phenomenologically foreign surface reflectance properties and that pains represent phenomenologically foreign bodily damage and is utilized by Tye (2008) again to argue for similar claims in the case of emotion. The basic idea is that nonconceptual representation allows us to represent contents for which we do not have concepts. Although Tye aims to remain somewhat neutral on how to understand the notion of nonconceptual content, he does suggest the following account: a state has *nonconceptual content* just in case its subject can entertain its content without possessing the concepts involved in specifying that content, where one *has a concept* of P when, perhaps among other things, one is able to identify instances of P on multiple occasions (Tye, 2000, pp. 62–63). For example, my perceptual representation of a particular shade of blue, $blue_{421}$, has nonconceptual content because if I were to see $blue_{421}$ again, I would not recognize it as the same shade of blue.

This appeal to nonconceptual content is unconvincing. It's unclear how representing a property in a way that doesn't allow me to reidentify it on multiple occasions entirely occludes its representational content from me, making it phenomenologically foreign. It's also unclear how, on a view like Tye's, the phenomenologically familiar phenomenal characters of emotions arise from the occluded representation of phenomenologically foreign properties. The problem here is the same as the problem facing the modes of presentation theorist who maintains that a combination of phenomenologically foreign content and nonrepresentational modes of presentation accounts for the distinctive phenomenal character of emotions: it's unclear just how this proposal can be made to work.

Since being nonconceptual is arguably a nonrepresentational feature of mental states,[13] Tye's view is a version of impure intentionalism. The problem is that it is hard to see how such impure elements transform the phenomenologically foreign representation of surface reflectance properties, bodily damage, and ordinary properties like dangerousness into the phenomenologically familiar phenomenal experience of colors, pain, and fear, respectively. The intentionalist focuses her efforts on showing that representational content is relevant to phenomenal character, but if she is to appeal to impure factors, she must motivate the relevance of those factors as well. In cases where the representational contents attributed to a state are phenomenologically foreign, she must make plausible the claim that impure factors can turn the phenomenologically foreign contents into phenomenologically familiar phenomenal characters. It's difficult to see how this can be motivated in the case of Tye's nonconceptual contents, and one might worry that it is likely to be similarly difficult to motivate other attempts to make impure elements do similar work.

The source of the problem with identifying the phenomenal character of emotions with phenomenologically foreign contents is, very simply, that the two seem distinct. Absent a plausible story involving impure elements, this results in an empirically inadequate account of emotion's phenomenal character. Of course, one might bite the bullet and maintain that despite appearances, emotion's phenomenal character is identical to phenomenologically foreign contents. One might argue that the ordinary properties view is supported by distinct theoretical considerations, such as considerations arising from one's theory of mental representation. For example, *tracking theories of mental representation,* on which mental representation is a species of causal or other tracking relation (Stampe, 1977; Dretske, 1981, 1995; Millikan, 1984; Fodor, 1987), might predict that emotions represent ordinary physical properties, and this might motivate the ordinary properties view. However, this does nothing to address the apparent mismatch between ordinary properties and the phenomenal character of emotions. The ordinary properties view is still empirically inadequate, so we will resume our search for the contents of emotions that determine their phenomenal character.

Response-Dependent Properties
Instead of identifying affective properties with ordinary physical properties, we might opt for a response-dependent account on which emotions represent objects as having some effect on us. For example, affective properties might be dispositions of objects to cause certain mental, behavioral, or other effects on us, or the manifestation of such dispositions.[14]

This account also seems phenomenologically inaccurate: when we experience a dog as scary, our fear does not seem to represent the dog as being disposed to cause certain states, reactions, or behaviors in us. Rather, our experience of the dog seems to qualify *the dog itself* independently of our relationship to it. The dog itself seems scary independent of any relation to us. Further, and perhaps more obviously, the phenomenal character of fear does not seem to be adequately captured by these fairly sophisticated dispositional contents.[15]

To be clear, I am not claiming that a response-dependent account of the content of emotion-related *concepts* is implausible. Emotion-related concepts are concepts such as the concept scary that is involved in the thought expressed by "*The Exorcist* is SCARY." Perhaps the concept scary has as its content a dispositional property, such as that of being disposed to cause experiences of fear in certain subjects. My claim, however, is that a response-dependent account of the content of *emotions* is not plausible.

Edenic Properties
So far, we have examined and dismissed views on which the properties represented by emotions are everyday physical or dispositional properties on the grounds that such views are phenomenologically inadequate. My suggestion, instead, is that affective properties are sui generis, perhaps primitive or basic (scariness, annoyingness, joyfulness, etc.). By describing affective properties as "sui generis," I mean that, as a group, they are not reducible to other types of properties.[16] This view takes emotions at face value and attributes to them representational contents that exactly fit the intentional/phenomenal bill. Affective properties are exactly those familiar qualities we experience when we are angry, sad, and so forth. They are akin to David Chalmers's (2006) Edenic color, shape, and sound properties. Chalmers argues that the phenomenal

content of experience—a type of content that is intimately related to phenomenal character—involves the properties our experiences, taken at face value, present us with (e.g., primitive redness, primitive squareness, and primitive loudness). My suggestion is that the kind of contents that can be identified with the phenomenal character of emotions are analogous *Edenic affective properties.* Call this the *Edenic view.*[17]

Objects need not actually have the affective properties our emotions represent them as having. On Chalmers's view, objects do not really have Edenic colors. Instead, they have properties that reliably cause us to have color experiences. In the case of emotions, it is quite implausible that objects ever actually have Edenic affective properties. Though Edenic affective properties are phenomenologically familiar, they are foreign to our scientific understanding of the world and we have no emotion-independent evidence for their instantiation. The most plausible view here is that they are never actually instantiated. Instead, some kind of *projectivism* might be true of our emotion experiences. On one version of projectivism, which Sydney Shoemaker (1990) calls *literal projectivism*, we mistakenly attribute properties of ourselves or our mental states to represented objects. On a different version, which Shoemaker calls *figurative projectivism*, we mistakenly attribute to objects properties that they don't really have, but that we only represent them as having as a result of our own interests, mental features, or constitution. On literal projectivism, the properties in question are instantiated, although not where we represent them to be instantiated, while on figurative projectivism, the properties in question need not be instantiated at all. One might argue that there is no good reason to attribute sui generis affective properties to ourselves, and so figurative projectivism is preferable. In any case, the intentionalist should opt for figurative projectivism, since the affective properties the literal projectivist posits look a lot like qualia and it is hard to see how we might offer an intentionalist-compatible account of them.

To put it somewhat metaphorically, we can think of represented affective properties as qualifying our internal world in ways that do not veridically reflect external reality, but that are only relevant to us, much as when we highlight important lines of text in documents based on our own needs and interests. When we highlight lines of text, the highlighting signifies importance, but the highlighted lines need not have any objective property of importance. Similarly, dogs, governments, landscapes, and the like are "highlighted" as scary, irritating, or euphoric, but they need not actually have the property we highlight them with. We can think of different types of emotions as analogous to different highlighter colors. Although the highlighted objects have significance for us and are important for us to keep track of, the world itself need not contain these highlights. As long as our highlighting objects (e.g., as scary) allows us to react appropriately to them (e.g., with avoidance), it does not matter if they do not actually have this property but instead only have other properties (eg., being disposed to harm us).

The case of emotions is one of *reliable misrepresentation*: emotions misrepresent, but they misrepresent in the same way all or most of the time. This misrepresentation is *reliable* because the same emotions are caused by the same kinds of environmental features on different occasions. These environmental features are something like the ordinary physical properties previously discussed in the section "Ordinary Physical Properties." In other words, while emotions might represent uninstantiated Edenic affective properties, they quite plausibly *track* complex and disjunctive actually instantiated properties that are important for survival and flourishing. These tracking relations help account for why emotions are so useful despite misrepresenting. As long as our mental highlighting *corresponds* to features of the environment that are important for our survival and flourishing, we can use our highlighting to appropriately guide our behaviors. For example, while our emotions might misrepresent a dog as SCARY, they might also track certain properties the dog actually has, such as the property of being likely to cause harm. As long as we react to scary things in the way that it is appropriate to react to things that are likely to cause harm, our misrepresentation can be just as useful as a veridical representation of the dog as likely to cause harm. Indeed, perhaps it is more efficient for us to misrepresent the dog as having the simpler property of scariness rather than to veridically represent it as having the more complex property of being likely to cause harm.

The main advantage of the Edenic view over other versions of intentionalism about emotions is that it gets the phenomenology right. By taking emotion experiences at face value, it delivers affective properties that are phenomenologically familiar. Another advantage of the Edenic view is that it can automatically account for the phenomenal difference between emotions and emotion-related thoughts. Consider the cases of fearing a dog, on the one hand, and believing that a dog is scary, on the other. On both the ordinary physical properties view and the response-dependent view, both mental states arguably attribute the same properties to the same object. We have a case of two experiences that are intentionally alike but phenomenally different, which is a counterexample to intentionalism. A typical response to this kind of counterexample is to restrict intentionalism so as not to apply to thoughts on the grounds that factors other than intentional content are relevant to phenomenal character and those factors are absent in thoughts—that is, to adopt an impure version of intentionalism. For Tye (2000, 2008), having *nonconceptual* content is one such further requirement for having phenomenal character that thoughts do not satisfy. Someone like Goldie (2000, p. 60) might instead appeal to differences in modes of presentation to partly determine phenomenal characters. Both strategies, however, end up invoking extra ingredients whose relevance to phenomenal character might be challenged in the ways described earlier. My pure intentionalist treatment of emotions, in contrast, naturally allows for the view that emotions and thoughts involving emotion-related concepts have different contents: emotions represent sui generis Edenic affective properties, while thoughts represent dispositional or ordinary physical properties. This neatly accounts for the phenomenal difference between the two states without appealing to nonrepresentational factors.[19,20]

In summary, I have argued that the Edenic view offers the most viable intentionalist account of emotions. On the Edenic view, emotions represent intentional objects as having sui generis affective properties. The representation of affective properties accounts for the distinctive phenomenal character of emotions.

Moods

Moods are affective states that seem not to be directed at any intentional object.[21] They tend to last longer than emotions and lack isolable causes. Most moods have a corresponding phenomenally similar emotion. For example, a happy mood is phenomenally similar to directed happiness (e.g., happiness about an upcoming event), and generalized fear is phenomenally similar to directed fear. Such similarities suggest that it might be possible to offer a unified intentionalist account of moods and emotions. However, unlike emotions, moods don't seem to have intentional objects, and so, it might be thought, they don't represent at all.

Some intentionalist treatments of moods maintain that they do in fact have intentional objects. These intentional objects might be bodily states or unusual external objects. I will consider these views before offering an account on which moods need not have intentional objects at all.

Us and Our Bodies

We rejected the bodily states view of emotions on the grounds that it fails to capture the phenomenal character associated with the directedness of emotions toward their intentional objects, which are usually not bodily states. However, moods fail to exhibit such directedness, so perhaps an analogue of the bodily states view can work for them.

According to the *bodily states view of moods*, the phenomenal character of moods is determined by the representation of bodily states. Tye (1995) endorses a version of this view: emotions represent departures from the "range of physical states constituting functional equilibrium" (p. 129). When our bodies are in functional equilibrium, we don't experience any moods. When our bodies depart from functional equilibrium, we represent this, and this accounts for the distinctive phenomenal character of moods.

It is plausible that we are sometimes aware of the bodily changes that are involved in moods. However, as in the case of the bodily states view of emotion, it's not clear that there are enough bodily states to account for all the distinct moods we experience. This problem is exacerbated by the fact that many of the bodily changes that are strongly linked to moods are changes we do not seem to represent at all. While we are sometimes aware of our hearts racing, we are not aware of the secretion of hormones, such as cortisol, which play a central role in certain moods. Even if such changes are in fact represented in some way, they do not seem to match anything in the phenomenal character of moods; they are phenomenologically foreign to experience, and so they are not of much use to the intentionalist.[22] Another way to put the problem is that at least some of the distinctive phenomenal characters of moods don't seem to be matched by the bodily changes of which we are aware. For example, in an anxiety attack, one might experience difficulty breathing, sweating, and a racing heart. However, representation of such bodily states does not fully capture the *anxiousness* present in the experience, something like a feeling of unsettledness or urgent discomfort. If there are phenomenal characters involved in moods that do not seem to be matched by any contents involving changes in bodily states, then such contents cannot account for them.[23]

Another problem with the bodily states view is that, if we accept the view of emotions I have proposed, it doesn't easily accommodate the observed phenomenal similarity between moods and their corresponding emotions. Unless we accept the bodily states view of emotions, moods and emotions have different contents, so we would expect them to have different phenomenal characters, which is contrary to our observation.[24]

Another possible view is that moods represent not our bodies, but *us* as having certain properties. For example, one might feel oneself as *afraid*. However, representing oneself as afraid is not the same thing as being in a fearful mood. Representing oneself as afraid might involve, say, a reflective awareness of oneself and one's fear, while being in a fearful mood needn't involve any such awareness. While there is plausibly such thing as feeling oneself as afraid, this does not account for all the cases of apparently undirected fear.

Special Intentional Objects

Another intentionalist strategy is to maintain that moods have a special kind of intentional object. For instance, one might maintain that moods represent *everything, something*, or *the world as a whole* as having certain properties. Variants of this strategy are proposed by Goldie (2000), Seager (2002), and Tye (2008).[25] A pervasive feeling of elation might represent the world as a whole as positive or good. An apparently undirected fear might represent something, though nothing in particular, as scary. Another related suggestion is that at least some moods have frequently changing intentional objects (Tye, 2008).[26] For example, road rage might be best understood as an affective state directed at different cars or drivers at different times.

A virtue of these suggestions is that they explain the observed similarity between moods and emotions. Moods and their corresponding emotions represent the same affective properties. The representation of these affective properties accounts for their distinctive phenomenal characters. This explains why moods and their corresponding emotions have the same distinctive phenomenal characters.

These suggestions might account for a broad range of cases, but there are also cases that escape their characterizations. While some cases of apparently undirected anxiety are, upon closer examination, directed at the world as a whole or frequently changing intentional objects, other cases don't seem to be directed at anything at all. They are cases of merely feeling anxious. And while some cases of sudden elation represent the world as a whole as good, other cases of sudden elation don't seem to be directed at the world or anything else, not even an unspecified object. One just feels elated. Such experiences appear to lack an intentional object altogether. They do not seem to "say" that anything has the relevant affective properties. These are *undirected moods*. Undirected moods not only *appear* to be undirected; they *are* undirected.

The intentionalist might deny that there are undirected moods and maintain that the states I have in mind do indeed represent the world as a whole or some such, but this overintellectualizes the states in question. In order to experience moods, one must be able to represent particular objects, the world as a whole, or unspecified objects, which seems to be too sophisticated a requirement for having the states in question. Further, it seems that there is a phenomenal difference between mere elation and elation directed at the world as a whole (the kind of state that is expressed by, "Everything's great!"). The most natural explanation of this difference is that the former state is an undirected mood whereas the latter is a directed mood whose intentional object is the world as a whole. It is not clear how the intentionalist who denies the existence of genuinely undirected moods can comfortably account for this difference.

Unbound Affective Properties

While I think there are many cases of moods that are directed at ourselves, the world as a whole, or indeterminate or changing objects, I also want to allow for genuinely undirected moods. Undirected moods seem to be a lot like directed moods and emotions, except that they lack intentional objects. I suggest that we accept this appearance at face value. My proposal is that moods are what we get when we have an emotion without an intentional object: a representation of a mere affective property.

My suggestion is that, unlike, for example, the contents of color representations, the contents of affective representations can occur without attaching to any object. In the case of color representations, we typically cannot experience a color property without experiencing something as having that property, but in the case of affective properties, we *can* experience free-floating, or *unbound*, instances of the properties. Undirected moods can be thought of as analogous to the color of the ink in the highlighter. When we experience moods, no particular thing or group of things is "highlighted," but we experience the mere color of the ink. We feel the fear, elation, or anxiety, but we don't feel it as bound to or qualifying anything.

The claim that we can represent mere properties might seem strange. We are used to thinking of representational states as having an object-property structure: they attribute properties to objects. I am claiming that some representational states represent mere properties, without attributing them to objects. At this point, it is worth reminding ourselves that despite our experiential and perhaps theoretical familiarity with the representation of properties qualifying objects, we do not yet have a fully satisfactory psychological account of just how representational states come to represent properties as binding to objects.[27] Our lack of a fully satisfying account might suggest that our relative comfort with mental states having an object-property form and our relative discomfort with mental states lacking such form doesn't track explanatory difficulty or costliness, or metaphysical queerness.

In any case, there are familiar cases of representation of unbound properties. The contents of concepts can occur unbound. We can use our concept cat to think *cat* without thinking that anything is a cat. This would presumably involve tokening the concept cat without binding its content to the contents of any other representations. Thus while the capacity of affective representations to have their contents occur unbound is very unlike the capacities of most perceptual representations, such unbound occurrences occur regularly and unproblematically in the case of concepts. More controversially, some perceptual experiences might arguably involve unbound representations. For instance, the experience of Mark Johnston's (2004, p. 141) brain gray, the color we experience when our eyes are closed, might be an example of an experience of an unbound color property.[28]

Amy Kind (this volume, Chapter 5) objects that it is unclear just what it is to represent unbound properties. She suggests that the representation of unbound scariness might amount to the representation of the content *there's scariness around*. However, she rightly claims that this would be a case in which scariness is "bound to something unidentified or unidentifiable" rather than a case of genuine unbound representation of scariness. This is not what I intend. Instead, I intend the representation of unbound scariness to be just like the representation of unbound cathood. In the case of the unbound representation of the content *cat*, what "runs through our heads" is just *cathood*, where cathood is the same feature that sometimes binds to our representation of particular cats. Similarly, when we represent unbound scariness, we represent *scariness*, where scariness is the same feature that sometimes binds to dogs, snakes, and possible election results.

One virtue of the unbound properties account of undirected moods is that it explains the similarity between undirected moods and their corresponding emotions. Since both kinds of affective states involve the representation of the same affective properties, and affective properties determine phenomenal character, moods and their corresponding emotions have the same distinctive phenomenal characters.

The unbound properties view is arguably quite attractive regardless of one's independent attraction to intentionalism. The view explains the phenomenal similarity between moods and emotions, the directedness of emotions and directed moods, and the lack of directedness of undirected moods. The phenomenal similarity between moods and emotions is explained by the fact that they literally share components. These shared components are representations whose contents can occur unbound. Since these shared components are *representations*, they are of the right format to bind to object representations to yield directed emotions. And since these shared components *can occur unbound*, they are able to occur in undirected moods, which do not involve intentional objects.

In summary, while some moods might in fact be directed at intentional objects of some sort, some moods lack intentional objects altogether. Undirected moods involve the unbound representation of the same affective properties that are represented in emotions. Unlike emotions, these affective properties are not represented as qualifying any objects, and this accounts for the apparent lack of directedness in undirected moods.[29]

Objections

Changing Moods

Kind (this volume, Chapter 5) argues that the unbound properties view has trouble accounting for changes in the force or intensity of one's undirected moods. Our undirected moods wax and wane. For example, an undirected feeling of sadness can get stronger or weaker throughout the day. On my view, this change is a change in the representation of unbound properties. Kind claims that this is implausible. It just does not seem that we undergo such representational changes when our moods change. Kind considers an example of a father experiencing undirected happiness after the birth of his newborn daughter. As he rocks his newborn to sleep, his happiness deepens. Yet it does not seem that he goes from representing *happiness* to representing *strong happiness*.[30]

A first reaction to this objection is to insist that the father's representational state does in fact change as required. Of course, he needn't come to represent a new way that the world is. For instance, as Kind rightly points out, he needn't suddenly come to see his daughter as more wonderful. And he needn't come to see the world as a whole as a better place. On my view, undirected moods don't represent full-fledged propositions, so a change in mood doesn't imply a change in which propositions are represented. Still, changes in mood involve a representational change analogous to the change one undergoes when one thinks *cat* and then thinks *octopus*. The property before one's mind's eye changes.

The Transparency of Experience

Kind (this volume, Chapter 5) argues that the transparency of experience, one of the main motivations for intentionalism, fails for moods, making intentionalism about moods implausible. In this paper, my aim was not to argue for intentionalism about affective states, but rather to develop and defend the best version of the view. However, if the main motivation for intentionalism does not apply moods, this might be taken to be indicative of a failure of intentionalism about moods. Perhaps moods are importantly different from other mental states for which intentionalism is better motivated.

I agree with Kind that the transparency of experience does not *directly* support intentionalism about moods. However, I claim that, on a suitable construal of transparency, it *indirectly* supports the view.

Everyone agrees that moods have certain salient affective qualities that are available to introspection and that we call "sadness," "happiness," and so forth. The disagreement between the intentionalist and the opponent of intentionalism is over whether these affective qualities are represented contents, as the intentionalist claims, or "raw" phenomenal characters, as the opponent of intentionalism claims.

In the case of visual and other perceptual experiences, the intentionalist claims that transparency intuitions derived from introspection support her view that the qualities of experiences are represented contents. For example, when we introspect on our visual experiences, it seems that the color-related qualities we are aware of are qualities of external objects, if anything. This is the transparency intuition. If this is right, then introspection supports the view that color qualities are represented contents, rather than mere phenomenal characters. This is one way, though not the only way, of understanding the transparency of experience and how it is supposed to support intentionalism. In short, we can tell from introspection that color qualities *behave* like represented contents—they qualify represented objects. This supports the claim that they *are* represented contents.[31]

But the affective qualities of undirected moods don't introspectively seem to qualify anything at all. So it seems that transparency intuitions derived from introspection cannot be used to support intentionalism about undirected moods in the same way in which they can be used to support intentionalism about color experience. This is why it might seem that the newborn's father's undirected moods can change without any of his representational states changing. From introspection alone, we have no reason to think that his changing mood is a matter of a changing representational state.[32]

I fully agree that transparency intuitions derived from introspection do not directly support intentionalism about moods. Instead, I think they play an indirect role as follows: a reason to take the affective qualities of undirected moods to be represented contents is that (1) the very same affective qualities involved in undirected moods are also involved in (directed) emotions, and (2) in emotions, these qualities seem to qualify objects (this is the transparency observation about emotions). Only represented properties can qualify represented objects in the way observed, so affective qualities are represented properties. Intentionalism about moods does not rest on transparency intuitions about moods, but it is indirectly supported by the introspection of moods and transparency intuitions about emotions.

Objections to Sui Generis Properties

Another type of objection concerns my claim that affective properties are sui generis. One might worry that appealing to the sui generis involves positing new entities and thereby inflating our ontology, something that should generally be avoided. However, this objection is mistaken. I am merely claiming that our experiences *represent* these Edenic affective properties, not that they are actually instantiated or even that they exist. If the objection to the sui generis stems from resistance to positing new entities, then it does not apply to my proposal, since my proposal does not posit any new entities.

One might instead object that, all else being equal, content attributions appealing to familiar instantiated properties are preferable to content attributions appealing to unfamiliar uninstantiated properties. However, it's not obvious why our view of mental contents should be constrained in this way. And even if we accept this constraint, it is not clear that it offers a basis for rejecting the Edenic view. As I have argued, all else is not equal. Edenic affective properties are well equipped to play the role required by intentionalism about moods and emotions, and other candidate properties are not.

Objections to Reliable Misrepresentation

One might object to my claim that emotions reliably misrepresent on the grounds that it entails that our affective properties are in error: they represent objects other than as they are. This may be thought to be problematic for several reasons. First, it is contrary to common sense. Second, it might appear to fail to account for the usefulness of emotions. I have already addressed the second worry in arguing that reliably misrepresenting emotions can be useful for survival and flourishing, so I turn to the first worry.

The first worry is not very troubling. It's not clear why we should expect our common sense view of emotions to be correct. In any case, even if being contrary to common sense weighs against a view, it's far from clear that it outweighs the virtues of the view, including that it respects the phenomenology.

One might further object that classifying all emotions as nonveridical obliterates useful normative distinctions between different token emotions. For example, one might be *appropriately* afraid of a rabid Doberman, but *inappropriately* afraid of a sleeping three-legged poodle. One way to cash out the difference between appropriate and inappropriate emotions is in terms of veridicality: the first emotion is veridical, while the second is not. This way of explicating the distinction is not available to the view I'm defending, since it claims that all emotions are nonveridical. However, there are other ways to explicate the distinction between appropriate and inappropriate emotions. In the first case, one's emotion is in line with one's interests and well-being, while in the second case, it is not. In the first case, one's emotion is triggered by environmental features that fear usually tracks, while in the second case, it is not. For those who insist on distinguishing between the two kinds of cases on the basis of veridicality, there are some strategies available that are compatible with my view. While I have focused on emotions' representational content that determines their distinctive phenomenal character, I allow that emotions have other intentional contents. For example, they might regularly include beliefs or judgments. The relevant beliefs or judgments might be veridical in the rabid Doberman case but not in the sleeping poodle case.

Conclusion

I have proposed and defended an intentionalist view of the phenomenal character of moods and emotions. My view takes phenomenal character at face value. Moods and emotions represent Edenic affective properties. These affective properties can be represented as qualifying a wide range of intentional objects, yielding emotions and some kinds of moods. They can also be represented without being bound to any intentional objects, yielding undirected moods.[33]

Notes

1. What distinguishes moods from emotions is a matter of some controversy. The various criteria proposed for distinguishing between them (their duration, whether they exhibit directedness, and whether they are connected to a specific stimulus) can come apart (see Kind, this volume, Chapter 5). For most purposes, it might be best to assume that moods and emotions are natural kinds and to fix reference on them partly ostensively by use of examples or typical features. Since my goal is to provide an intentionalist account of all affective states, everything I say should apply equally well to different ways of distinguishing between moods and emotions.
2. Moods and emotions are arguably complex states involving all or many of bodily, behavioral, neural, cognitive, normative, and phenomenal components. However, since intentionalism is a theory of phenomenal character, it is the phenomenal component that primarily concerns it. Thus, the intentionalist's explanandum is the phenomenal character of moods and emotions, not moods and emotions in their entirety, and intentionalism about moods and emotions is a view specifically about the phenomenal character of moods and emotions.
3. This version of intentionalism is favored by many intentionalists, for example, Gilbert Harman (1990), Fred Dretske (1995), Michael Tye (1995, 2000, 2009), Alex Byrne (2001b), and Frank Jackson (2004, 2005). It is in a good position to provide a satisfying theory of

consciousness, since it claims that phenomenal features of mental states are identical to their representational features, rather than merely supervenient on them or in some way determined by them that might leave open the possibility that phenomenal features are something over and above representational features.

Introspection also provides some initial support for an identity version of intentionalism. For many phenomenal characters, there is a matching represented property, and the two do not appear to be distinct. For example, there is something it is like to have a visual experience of the blackness of the letters on this page. This phenomenal character has a matching represented property, *blackness*. But there do not seem to be two blackness-related mental features, a phenomenal blackness and a represented blackness. Introspectively, there appears to be only one blackness, which may be correctly described as both a represented property of the letters and a phenomenal character. The same holds for other aspects of experience. Introspection provides evidence for only one mental feature, and this provides some support for the identity version of intentionalism.

4. The identity version of intentionalism is compatible with there being representational features that are not identical with phenomenal features, but if we deny this, then the view also counts as a version of the *phenomenal intentionality theory*, the view that a state's intentional features are type or token identical, reducible to, supervenient on, or determined by its phenomenal character (see, e.g., Horgan & Tienson, 2002). Sometimes intentionalists endorse the further claim that the intentional is explanatorily or ontologically prior to the phenomenal, in which case their version of intentionalism would not compatible with the phenomenal intentionality theory.

5. This is seen most clearly in the case of the identity version of intentionalism. This version of the view is an identity claim, and identity claims seem more plausible when the items that are to be identified appear similar. Phenomenal circularity and represented circularity seem similar, so it is at least somewhat plausible that they are in fact one and the same thing.

6. This is somewhat surprising given that many views of emotion involve representational states (see Charland [1995], who proposes a representational framework for situating these theories).

7. One might suggest that the phenomenal difference between the two cases is a difference in attention, detail in the representation of the raccoon versus the dog, or some such. While there probably are such accompanying differences, it is implausible that they exhaust the phenomenal difference between the two cases. It seems introspectively obvious that experienced fear in some sense attaches to the objects that it is directed toward.

8. Intentional objects might be *singular contents*, contents involving individual entities as direct constituents, or they might be property clusters or some such. There is much debate surrounding how perception and thought represent intentional contents, but we need not take a stand on it. Indeed, since it seems that the objects of emotion are generally provided by other types of mental states, such as perceptual states and thoughts, one might look to considerations concerning those types of states to settle these questions. Of course, which of these views about intentional objects is correct will affect what phenomenal characters intentional objects can contribute to an experience. However, the intentional objects view fails on all these views, or so I will argue.

9. Recall that one reason to think that there are such distinctive phenomenal characters that outrun the phenomenal character of the ordinary representation of intentional objects is that phenomenally different emotions can be directed toward the same intentional objects. The same perceptual experience of the same dog barking in the same way can be provide the object of fear, the object of joy, or the object of irritation.

10. The ordinary properties view encompasses views on which emotions represent evaluative properties and evaluative properties are understood as ordinary properties (e.g., as in Tye, 2008).

11. Although Goldie does not seem to have the present worry in mind, his view appeals to something much like modes of presentation. Goldie's "feelings toward" represent properties objects at least sometimes have, such as dangerousness and threateningness. But Goldie claims that the contents of emotions differ from the contents of thoughts attributing the

same properties to the same objects. "The difference between thinking of X as Y without feeling and thinking of X as Y with feeling . . . [at least partly] lies *in* the content . . ." (Goldie, 2000, p. 60; italics original) These two contents, according to Goldie, have the same referent (Goldie, 2002), but they present their referents in a different way. One way of understanding this view is as claiming that emotions represent ordinary properties under special modes of presentation. An alternative way of understanding this is as claiming that emotions have something like descriptive contents that pick out ordinary properties.

12. The view that modes of presentation are qualia or "raw feels" is not open to the intentionalist for the additional reason that these are precisely the kinds of entities she seeks to avoid positing.

13. Tye seems to have a state view of the conceptual/nonconceptual distinction, on which the difference between conceptual and nonconceptual contents has to do with features of the states doing the representing, rather than the contents of those states (though see Byrne [2001a] for discussion). See Heck (2000) for the distinction between content and state views of the conceptual/nonconceptual distinction.

14. One of Tye's (2008) components of the contents of emotion is response dependent: emotions represent their intentional object as causing or accompanying a certain physiological or bodily disturbance.

15. As in the case of the previous proposal on which affective properties are ordinary physical properties, one might use modes of presentation or nonconceptual content to respond to this worry. But these strategies are unsatisfactory for the same reasons as those mentioned previously.

16. It is an open question whether some affective properties reduce to other affective properties. It is also an open question whether these sui generis properties can be organized in a representational space.

17. Views on which emotions represent evaluative properties that are not reducible to ordinary physical properties or other kinds of properties count as versions of the Edenic view.

18. In Mendelovici (forthcoming), I have argued that reliable misrepresentation can be just as useful as veridical representation for performing certain tasks.

19. The pure intentionalist about emotions faces a few challenges. It seems that she must implausibly maintain that we cannot represent Edenic affective properties in thought, for if we can, they should give rise to the phenomenal character distinctive of emotions, and it seems that thoughts never give rise to such phenomenal characters. Thanks to Daniel Stoljar for raising this worry. My preferred response is to agree that Edenic affective properties are never genuinely represented in thought. However, they might be *derivatively* represented in thought, in much the same way that sentences derivatively represent in virtue of their relations to nonderivatively representational states (Bourget, 2010; Mendelovici, 2010, chap. 10). Another worry is that pure intentionalism about emotions does not allow for nonconscious emotions. Again, I think the intentionalist should bite the bullet here and either claim that nonconscious emotions are merely derivatively representational (Kriegel, forthcoming), or that they are not representational at all (Mendelovici, 2010, chap. 7).

20. For the pure intentionalist, however, this is only a minor victory, since the same kinds of problems arise for intentionalism about perceptual experiences. For example, it seems that color concepts and visual experiences of colors represent some of the same contents but differ phenomenally. For a treatment of these problems along the same spirit as my proposed treatment in the case of emotions, see Mendelovici (2010, chap. 7 and §10.5).

21. Depending on how we distinguish moods from emotions (see note 1), it might turn out that some emotions apparently lack intentional objects. The discussion in this section would also apply to such cases.

22. One might claim that moods represent the likes of cortisol levels *nonconceptually* or *under a certain mode of presentation*. This is unsatisfactory for the reasons listed in the section "Ordinary Physical Properties."

23. The worries with the bodily states view of moods described in this section also apply to the bodily states view of emotions.

24. Recall that I aim to defend a type identity version of intentionalism. A token identity version of intentionalism, however, can allow that phenomenal character types can be realized by distinct representational content types, so such a view is compatible with the observed phenomenal similarity between moods and their corresponding emotions. However, it does nothing to *explain* this similarity, and as we will soon see, other views are able to offer an explanation.
25. One might complain that existential and universal generalizations do not have intentional objects. This issue is merely terminological. I choose to count existential and universal generalizations as having intentional objects since they predicate properties of things that may or may not exist.
26. Tye considers these states to be types of apparently undirected emotions, rather than moods. This terminological issue is irrelevant for our purposes, which is to offer an intentionalist account of apparently undirected affective states, regardless of how we choose to classify them. See note 1.
27. This problem has various facets, including the problem of the unity of the proposition and the binding problem.
28. This case is controversial. One might suggest that brain gray is experienced as qualifying a particular region of space-time.
29. Could there be undirected emotions? I take emotions to be affective states that seem to be directed at intentional objects. I suppose there could be cases where these appearances are misleading, though I cannot think of such a case. (Of course, on other definitions of "emotion," such as on a definition on which emotions are short-lived affective states, there are clear examples of undirected emotions.)
30. Kind's worry is not that changes in intensity will require multiple distinct sui generis unbound properties (e.g., mild elation, elation, strong elation, very strong elation, etc.) But for those readers who are worried about the plethora of affective properties that will be required by my account, this can be rendered less bizarre if we suppose that these affective properties can be organized in an affective space with a limited number of dimensions, in much the same way that color properties can be organized in a color space with a limited number of dimensions. Being amenable to this kind of organization does not prevent affective properties from being sui generis any more than it prevents color properties from being sui generis.
31. See Harman (1990) and Tye (2000) for defenses of transparency and Kind (2003; this volume, Chapter 5) for a critique.
32. In other words, introspection provides positive evidence for a quality's being a represented content (though a lack of such evidence cannot tell us very much on its own). If we encounter a quality that qualifies a represented object, then this is evidence that the quality is a represented content. But if we encounter a quality that does not qualify a represented object, this is easily compatible both with its being a "raw feel" and with its being an unbound represented quality.
33. Thanks to David Bourget, Uriah Kriegel, Daniel Nolan, and Daniel Stoljar for helpful comments and discussion on previous drafts of this paper. Thanks also to audiences at Wayne State University, the July 2011 meeting of the Australasian Association of Philosophy, Charles Sturt University in Wagga Wagga, the Australian National University's Women's Work-in-Progress Seminar, and the Princeton Philosophical Society for helpful discussion.

References

Bourget, D. (2010). Consciousness is underived intentionality. *Noûs*, 44 (1): 32–58.
Byrne, A. (2001a). Don't PANIC: Tye's intentionalist theory of consciousness. *A Field Guide to the Philosophy of Mind* symposium on Tye's *Consciousness, Color, and Content* <http://host.uniroma3.it/progetti/kant/field/tyesymp_byrne.htm>
Byrne, A. (2001b). Intentionalism defended. *Philosophical Review*, 110 (2): 199–240.
Cannon, W. (1929). *Bodily Changes in Pain, Hunger, Fear and Rage*. 2nd ed. New York: Appleton.

Chalmers, D. J. (2004). The representational character of experience. In Leiter, B., editor, *The Future of Philosophy*, 153–181. Oxford: Oxford University Press.

Chalmers, D. J. (2006). Perception and the fall from Eden. In Gendler, T. S., and Hawthorne, J., editors, *Perceptual Experience*, 9–125. Oxford: Oxford University Press.

Charland, L. C. (1995). Feeling and representing: Computational theory and the modularity of affect. *Synthese*, 105(3): 273–301.

Crane, T. (2003). The intentional structure of consciousness. In *Consciousness: New Philosophical Perspectives*. New York, NY: Oxford University Press, 33-56.

Dretske, F. (1981). *Knowledge and the Flow of Information*. Cambridge, MA: MIT Press.

Dretske, F. (1995). *Naturalizing the Mind*. Cambridge, MA: MIT Press.

Fodor, J. A. (1987). *Psychosemantics*. Cambridge, MA: MIT Press.

Goldie, P. (2000). *The Emotions: A Philosophical Exploration*. New York, NY: Oxford University Press.

Goldie, P. (2002). Emotions, feelings and intentionality. *Phenomenology and the Cognitive Sciences*, 1(3): 235–254.

Harman, G. (1990). The intrinsic quality of experience. *Philosophical Perspectives*, 4: 31–52.

Heck, R. (2000). Nonconceptual content and the "Space of Reasons." *The Philosophical Review*, 109: 483–524.

Horgan, T., and Tienson, J. (2002). The intentionality of phenomenology and the phenomenology of intentionality. In Chalmers, D. J., editor, *Philosophy of Mind: Classical and Contemporary Readings*. Oxford: Oxford University Press, 520–533.

Jackson, F. (2004). Representation and experience. In Hugh Clapin, Phillip Staines & Peter Slezak (eds.), *Representation in Mind: New Approaches to Mental Representation*, 107–124.

Jackson, F. (2005). Consciousness. In Frank Jackson and Michael Smith (eds.), *The Oxford Handbook of Contemporary Philosophy*. New York, NY: Oxford University Press, 310–333.

James, W. (1884). What is an emotion? *Mind*, 19: 188–204.

Johnston, M. (2004). The obscure object of hallucination. *Philosophical Studies*, 120: 113–183.

Kind, A. (2003). What's so transparent about transparency? *Philosophical Studies*, 115: 225–244.

Kriegel, U. (forthcoming). Towards a new feeling theory of emotion. *European Journal of Philosophy*.

LeDoux, J. (1996). *The Emotional Brain*. New York: Simon and Schuster.

Lycan, W. (1996). *Consciousness and Experience*. Cambridge, MA: MIT Press, Bradford Books.

Mendelovici, A. (2010). Mental representation and closely conflated topics. PhD thesis, Princeton University, Princeton, NJ.

Mendelovici, A. (Forthcoming). Reliable misrepresentation and tracking theories of mental representation. *Philosophical Studies*. DOI: 10.1007/s11098–012–9966–8.

Millikan, R. G. (1984). *Language, Thought and Other Biological Categories*. Cambridge, MA: MIT Press.

Prinz, J. J. (2004). *Gut Reactions: A Perceptual Theory of the Emotions*. New York: Oxford University Press.

Prinz, J. J. (2005). Are emotions feelings? *Journal of Consciousness Studies*, 12(8–10): 9–25.

Prinz, J. J. (2006). Is emotion a form of perception? *Canadian Journal of Philosophy*, 36(5S): 137–160.

Schacter, S., and Singer, J. (1962). Cognitive, social and physiological determinants of emotional states. *Psychological Review*, 69: 379–399.

Seager, W. (2002). Emotional introspection. *Consciousness and Cognition*, 11: 666–687.

Shoemaker, S. (1990). Qualities and qualia: What's in the mind? *Philosophy and Phenomenological Research Supplement*, 50(Supplement): 109–131.

Stampe, D. (1977). Towards a causal theory of linguistic representation. *Midwest Studies in Philosophy*, 2(1): 42–63.

Tye, M. (1995). *Ten Problems of Consciousness: A Representational Theory of the Phenomenal Mind*. Cambridge, MA: MIT Press.

Tye, M. (2000). *Consciousness, Color, and Content*. Cambridge, MA: MIT Press.

Tye, M. (2008). The experience of emotion: An intentionalist theory. *Revue Internationale de Philosophie*, 62: 25–50.

Tye, M. (2009). *Consciousness Revisited: Materialism without Phenomenal Concepts*. Cambridge, MA: MIT Press.

Suggestions for Further Reading

Crane, Tim. 1998. "Intentionality as the Mark of the Mental." In *Contemporary Issues in the Philosophy of Mind*, ed. Anthony O'Hear, 229-252. Cambridge: Cambridge University Press.
This paper argues that all mental phenomena are intentional, in the sense of being directed at something other than themselves; in the process, it offers an account of moods as intentionally directed at features of the whole world.
Harman, Gilbert. 1990. "The Intrinsic Quality of Experience." *Philosophical Perspectives* 4: 31–52.
This extraordinarily influential article argues that the only introspectively accessible aspect of conscious experience is its representational aspect—the fact that some experience represents this or that external object or feature.
James, William. 1884. "What Is an Emotion?" *Mind* 19:188–204.
This seminal article argues that emotions do not cause us to feel characteristic physiological sensations, but on the contrary, feeling those sensations causes, and in fact exhausts, the emotions.
Montague, Michelle. 2009. "The Logic, Intentionality, and Phenomenology of Emotion." *Philosophical Studies* 145: 171–192.
This paper argues, among other things, that emotional experiences have a sui generis qualitative character unlike that of any other type of experience (including bodily sensations).

PART IV

Mental Representation
The Project of Naturalization

CHAPTER 7

Two Notions of Mental Representation

URIAH KRIEGEL

Chapter Overview

The main thesis of this chapter is twofold. In the first three sections of the chapter, I argue that there are two notions of mental representation, which I call *objective* and *subjective*. In the fourth through eighth sections, I argue that this casts familiar tracking theories of mental representation as incomplete: while it is clear how they might account for objective representation, they at least require supplementation to account for subjective representation.

A Parable

There is a possible world where, just as I was born, a brain neuroanatomically and neurophysiologically indistinguishable from mine was placed in a vat and fed random sensory stimulations by a machine suitably hooked to the vat. In fact, there are many, many such worlds. In one of them, the influx of sensory stimulation happens to be indistinguishable from the one my actual brain has enjoyed. Consequently, let us suppose, it is impossible to rule out from the inside that I am in fact such an envatted brain: the envatted brain's stream of consciousness is subjectively indistinguishable from mine. Thus, whenever the stimulating machine is in state S1, the envatted brain undergoes an experience subjectively indistinguishable from the experience I normally undergo when I see an apple; when the machine is in state S2, it undergoes an experience indistinguishable from mine when I see a banana; when the machine is in state S3, it undergoes an experience like mine when seeing a cherry; and so on and so forth.

An interesting question concerns what the envatted brain's S1-caused apple-ish experience represents. There are two conflicting views on this. A traditional view is that it represents exactly what my subjectively indistinguishable experience does: an apple. But following Putnam's (1981, chap. 1) ingenious discussion, many philosophers have come to hold that it represents S1, the machine's state responsible for the apple-ish stimulation. The idea is, very roughly, that since the condition of the external world that stably covaries with and/or causes the brain's apple-ish experiences is S1, S1 is what experiences of that type represent in the envatted brain.

Which view is right? Does the brain's experience represent an apple or S1? My starting point is that this is really quite a silly question. There are two notions of representation, one on which the envatted brain's experience represents an apple and one on which it represents S1. In other words, the term *representation* is ambiguous and expresses two different concepts or notions. Accordingly, the term can be used in two different ways, to mean two different things. Both, however, are legitimate uses of the term *representation*: on the one hand, there is certainly a sense in which the experience represents S1, namely, the sense that the experience tracks the presence of S1; on the other hand, there is also a sense in which the experience represents an apple, namely, the sense that what the experience presents to the subject is apple-ish.

Thus, the true moral of the brain-in-vat thought experiment, it seems to me, is that a distinction must be drawn between two notions of mental representation—two different senses in which a mental state may be said to represent. The experiment is needed because in ordinary circumstances it is hard to distinguish the two notions. In my own experience of the apple, for example, what the experience presents to me and what it tracks are the same: an apple. It is only in the fantastic circumstances of the thought experiment that an experience can be envisaged that presents to the subject one thing but tracks another.

A Distinction

There are no good terminological options for drawing the distinction brought out intuitively in the brain-in-vat thought experiment. I will use the labels "the objective notion of representation" and "the subjective notion of representation," or *objective representation* and *subjective representation* for short. These terms are in many ways suboptimal, but they will have to do.[1]

How to characterize the distinction in a more theoretically involved manner is, in a way, what this chapter is about. For this reason, it would be unwise to prejudge certain issues by building commitments into the *definitions* of objective and subjective representation. Admittedly, we do need some way to fix our ideas regarding these two notions. But we can do so without unnecessary commitments through ostension of paradigmatic instances. One way to think of this is as offering an initial model of the two notions not as necessary-and-sufficient-conditions notions, but as *prototype* or *exemplar* notions. We designate prototypical or exemplary objective and subjective representations—for example, the envatted brain's—and consider a given mental representation objective or subjective if it is sufficiently relevantly similar to the prototype or exemplar.[2]

The distinction between objective and subjective representation is closely related to other, more familiar ones. Distinctions between personal and sub-personal representations, narrow and wide representations, phenomenal and psychological representations, may all turn out to be coextensive with the subjective/objective distinction.[3] Even if they do, however, this should not be, and is not here, taken to be *definitionally* true. It is not *definitional* of subjective representation that it is personal, narrow, and phenomenal—nor of objective representation that it is subpersonal, wide, and psychological. My view is that the distinction between objective and subjective representation is deeper than all these, and underlies them, but I will not argue for this here.

Instead of arguing that the distinction is deep, I now argue that it is *thorough*. I want to suggest a four-way conceptual separability of objective and subjective representation: there are (a) conceptually possible scenarios where representation varies in the objective sense but remains invariant in the subjective sense; (b) conceptually possible scenarios where representation varies in the subjective but not objective sense; (c) ones where representation occurs *at all* in the objective sense but not in the subjective sense; and (d) ones where it occurs in the subjective but not objective sense.[4] This is what I mean by the distinction being "thorough."

The brain-in-vat thought experiment exemplifies (a): in the objective sense, the envatted brain's experience represents something my experience does not—namely, S1—but in the subjective sense, the two represent the same thing—namely, an apple. It might be objected that being an apple is a natural-kind property, whose underlying nature involves imperceptible biochemical features, so nothing makes it the case that the envatted brain's experience (subjectively) represents an *apple*—rather than, say, a twin apple (i.e., a fruit superficially akin to apple but with a completely different underlying biochemical nature). In response, I would concede that it is probably more accurate to say that the envatted brain's experience represents an apple-looking thing, rather than an apple. It does not denote the *natural kind* property of being an apple, but rather the *manifest kind* property of being "apple-y" (or perhaps that of playing the apple role).[5] However, the same is true of *my* apple-ish experiences: in truth they only represent things as being apple-y, not as being apples.[6] So it is still the case that my experience and my envatted duplicate's are representationally type-identical in the subjective sense but not in the objective sense.

The following inverted-spectrum thought experiment exemplifies (b). Imagine a world just like ours except for the following detail: your—or your counterpart's—color spectrum is inverted. As a result, during snowstorms your counterpart has an experience as of a black soft substance falling from the sky, while on sunny days s/he has an experience as of peacefully yellow skies. These experiences track the same surface features of objects but present to your counterpart very different features. Thus they are representationally type-identical to your experiences in the objective sense but representationally type-different in the subjective sense.

There are familiar examples of (c)—representation in the objective sense in the absence of representation in the subjective sense. The number of rings on a tree trunk tracks the tree's age but does not present the age *to* the tree; thermometers' internal states track the ambient temperature but do not present the temperature *to* the thermometers; and so on.

There are no familiar examples of (d), but consider the following thought experiment. We can envisage a world where the only concrete particular is a disembodied soul "floating about" in otherwise empty space, undergoing a random string of conscious experiences. In fact, we can envisage many, many such worlds. In one of them, the space soul's sequence of experiences is subjectively indistinguishable from yours. In a sense, it is impossible to rule out from the inside that you *are* in fact that space soul.[7] The space soul's experiences present to it exactly what yours present to you, but unlike your experiences, the soul's do not track anything.[8] Therefore, the space soul's experiences represent in the subjective sense but not in the objective sense.

This thought experiment is similar to the brain-in-vat one, in that it too dissociates what an experience presents to its subject from what it tracks in the environment. But while in the brain-in-vat scenario the experiences still track *something*, in the space-soul scenario there is nothing for them to track. In a way, while the brain-in-vat thought experiment shows that the *identity conditions* of subjective representation are independent from those of objective representation, the space-soul thought experiment shows that their *existence conditions* are too.

Thesis

There are, in fact, many different notions of representation. We say of a reflection in a mirror or a puddle that it is an *imagistic representation* of some object or surface; we say of a graph or diagram that it provides a *mathematical representation* of some pattern; we say of a rainbow metaphor that it constitutes a *literary representation* of hope; and so on and so forth. There may well be a feature common and peculiar to all these kinds of representation, in virtue of which they all deserve the appellation "representation." But there are deep differences among them as well.[9] Most importantly, the nature of the representation relation implicated in each is very different. It is not as though literary and mathematical representations bear the same representation relation to their subject matters, with the former qualifying as literary simply because their subject matter is literary and the latter as mathematical because their subject matter is mathematical.[10] No, the very representation relation they bear to their subject matters is different.

My contention is that even within the realm of *mental* representation, we can distinguish two different senses in which mental items may be said to represent. For what makes a mental state track what it does, and track at all, is very different from what makes it present to its subject what it does, and at all. The feature in virtue of which mental states represent in one sense is completely different from that in virtue of which they represent in the other—and this is not a matter of different subject matters, since the subject matter can and often is actually the same.

If this is right, then seeking "a theory of mental representation," in the sense of a unified framework that accounts for a single relation that determines what, and that, mental states represent, may be as misguided as seeking a unified theory of literary and mathematical representation. What invites this misguide, it seems to me, is the fact that in this case the two fundamentally different kinds of representation are exhibited by the same vehicles: mental states. Ultimately, however, each notion requires its own account.[11]

The problem is that the theories of mental representation we have pursued most vigorously over the past forty years—those that fall under the rubric of "naturalistic semantics" or "psychosemantics"—seem geared to account for the objective notion of representation exclusively, disregarding the subjective notion. I will now illustrate this by going through some of the most prominent options. I will then lay out three possible reactions and consider each.

Familiar Theories of Mental Representation

Theories of mental representation familiar from the "naturalizing intentionality research program" tend to fall into two groups: causal-covariational theories and teleological theories. In its simplest manifestation, the causal-covariational approach claims that a mental state M represents a property F just in case Fs cause Ms under the right conditions (Stampe 1977). This kind of causal relation is most natural to appeal to in accounting for the tracking of external conditions. Observe, however, that the envatted brain's apple experiences do not have apples as their causes *ever*—that is, under *any* conditions. Yet in the subjective sense what they represent are apples. So this approach seems wrongheaded as an account of subjective representation. Note well: my present point is not quite that the causal-covariational approach lacks in principle the resources to account for subjective representation; rather that it is not geared to doing so, and appears to target instead (and quite plausibly) objective representation.

The best-known version of the causal-covariational approach is probably Fodor's (1990) "asymmetric dependence" account: a mental state M represents a property F iff (i) it is a law of nature that Fs cause Ms; (ii) some Fs actually cause Ms; and (iii) if any non-Fs cause Ms, the fact that they do is asymmetrically dependent on the fact that Fs cause Ms.[12] Again, this may be a promising account of representation in the objective sense, but not so much in the subjective sense. At the very least, condition (ii) is flagrantly violated by the envatted brain's apple experiences: none are caused by apples.[13]

A different account in the same spirit is Dretske's (1981) early informational semantics. According to it, M represents F iff M is nomically dependent on F—that is, iff the laws of nature are such that M is not tokened unless F is instantiated. This comes very close to the standard account of tracking in reliabilist theories of epistemic justification (indeed, see Dretske 1971) and is thus a good candidate for a theory of representation in the objective sense. But as a theory of representation in the subjective sense it seems utterly inadequate: the envatted brain has experiences as of apples even when the property of being an apple is not instantiated. So it is false that they are not tokened unless the properties they (subjectively) represent are instantiated.[14]

The other familiar approach to mental representation is so-called teleosemantics. The idea, roughly speaking, is that a mental state represents in virtue of conferring the right kind of adaptive or reproductive advantage on the subject, or more accurately, in virtue of its "correspondence" with external conditions conferring this kind of advantage.[15] Here again, there may well be much to recommend evolutionarily grounded tracking as an account of objective representation, but the prospects for such an account of subjective representation are on the face of it bleak. After all, if the envatted brain reproduces at all, it is certainly not in virtue of any correspondence between its apple experiences and apples, since there is none.[16] Note well: here again, I am not presently concerned to argue that teleosemantics is in principle incapable of accounting for the subjective notion of representation; merely that clearly it is designed to account for the objective notion.

Consider Dretske's (1988) mature theory, which augments his original informational theory with a teleological component. According to the augmented theory, M represents F not iff M nomically depends on F, but iff M is *supposed* to nomically depend on F, where this means that (i) there is a motor response R, such that M has been recruited (through a process of "discrimination learning") to have its present tokens cause R, (ii) past tokens of M nomically depended on F, and (iii) it is the case that (i) because it is the case that (ii). This fails to accommodate the envatted brain's apple experiences in several ways. First, the envatted brain does not *have* motor responses (at least if motor responses are construed as bodily states), though it may seem to itself to have them. Secondly, past tokens of the envatted brain's apple experiences did *not* nomically depend on any past instances of applehood, since there were no such instances. Finally, condition (iii) could certainly not be met, since there is no *reason* why the envatted brain has present token apple experiences—it is a pure accident.[17]

Another version of teleosemantics is Millikan's (1984, 1993) "biosemantics." Millikan's account is quite complex and not easily summarizable in a single cognitively surveyable biconditional, but a central *necessary condition* in the account appears to be this: M represents F only if there is a system S, such that (i) S consumes present tokens of M, (ii) past tokens of M occurred mostly when instances of F occurred, and (iii) S can perform its biological proper function because (i) and (ii) are the case. This necessary condition is quite obviously not met by the envatted brain's apple experiences. For starters, it is unclear how we might attribute a biological proper function to the brain's consumer system, since the brain faces no selection pressures. But more obviously, the envatted brain's past token apple experiences did *not* occur mostly when instances of applehood did.

There are other versions of teleosemantics (McGinn 1989; Papineau 1993, chap. 3), but I will not consider them here; I suspect they succumb to similar considerations. I conclude that both causal-covariational and teleological approaches to mental representation are geared toward its objective notion. The teleo-informational materials they employ are perfectly suited to account for the tracking of external conditions. (For this reason, I will often refer to them in what follows as "tracking accounts.") But to the extent that mental states can sometimes present to their subjects something they do not track, it is not clear that these materials are well suited to capture what mental states present to their subjects. To repeat, my present point is *not* that no broadly teleo-informational story could ever accommodate subjective representation. It is rather that the familiar theories in that genre are so unnatural as accounts of subjective representation that it is most reasonable, and most charitable, to interpret them as not even *concerned* with subjective representation. This is doubly plausible given how genuinely promising they look as accounts of *objective* representation.

Notions and Properties

Agreeing that the familiar theories of mental representation in the teleo-informational genre are geared toward objective representation, but wishing to maintain that they fully account for all the relevant phenomena without need of supplementation, one might exploit the gap between notions and properties. After all, so far I have only argued for a *conceptual* distinction between two kinds of *notion*. I have not argued for a *real* distinction between two kinds of *property*.

At the same time, there is a trivial sense in which a conceptual distinction creates a prima facie presumption in favor of a real distinction. Consider again the envatted brain's apple-ish S1-caused experience. Suppose that, closely studying the vat's wiring, one person claims that the brain's mental state represents S1, while another, less talented for vat engineering, claims that it represents S27. It is natural to say that the first interpreter's ascription is true, whereas the second's is false.[18] Likewise, suppose that, upon studying the neural correlates of consciousness in my brain and the envatted duplicate's, one person concludes that the brain's experience represents an apple, while another, less neurologically talented, claims that it represents an elephant. Again it is natural to endorse the first interpreter's ascription and not the second's. Thus, we have here two different true ascriptions and two different false ones. However, if two *different* ascriptions are true, then there are two different kinds of representational property picked out by those ascriptions, each a constituent of a different truthmaker.[19] In this way, the conceptual distinction between notions creates a defeasible presumption in favor of a real distinction between properties.

Given a presumptive distinction between two putative properties, several views on the ultimate relationship between them are possible. Three stand out: eliminativist, reductivist, and nonreductivist. On the eliminativist view, ultimately there is no such property as subjective representation—the presumption is simply false. The subjective concept of representation may be useful in some way, but nothing in reality matches it. Accordingly, subjective-representational ascriptions are forsooth never strictly true, except at most in a minimalist sense.[20] On the reductivist view, there *is* such a property as subjective representation, but ultimately it reduces to objective representation, or some complex objective-representational structure.[21] Accordingly, subjective representation is an "ontological free lunch," fully grounded in objective representation. On the nonreductivist view, subjective representation is a real and genuine ontological addition over and above objective representation. (This is not to say, of course, that it does not reduce to *physical* properties; merely that if it does, it is not by reducing first to objective representation.) The choice can be appreciated by considering the following inconsistent triad:

1) There exists subjective representation.
2) Subjective representation is something over and above objective representation.
3) A theory of objective representation accounts for all the phenomena of mental representation.

Each of these is individually attractive, but they cannot all be true. Accordingly, any stable position on the matter must reject one of them. The eliminativist rejects 1, the reductivist 2, and the nonreductivist 3. I will now consider each of these options, arguing that any plausible accommodation of subjective representation would involve *something* importantly *un*familiar.[22]

Eliminativism

Eliminative positions are typically motivated by considerations of explanatory dispensability. Thus, our eliminativist may argue that subjective representation would not explain anything, so there is no need to posit it.[23]

This eliminativist tack may be resisted by denying the explanatory impotence of subjective representation.[24] But more deeply, argumentation from explanatory dispensability presupposes a description of what needs to be explained. And the very description of the explananda is typically ontologically committal. Thus *explanatory* dispensability can support eliminativism about x only when combined with *descriptive* dispensability—the claim that there is no need to invoke x in describing what needs explaining. Eliminating subjective representation would thus require such a claim. Yet it is unclear how we can *describe* the scenario presented in the opening parable without mentioning a kind of representation shared by subjective duplicates. What needs to be explained in that scenario is precisely how an envatted brain stimulated identically to me is experientially presented with an apple. The very description of the explanandum thus invokes the subjective notion of representation.

The eliminativist may suggest that the apparent need to cite subjective representation in describing the scenario is an illusion, perhaps even an illusion that can be predicted from within the tracking framework of familiar theories of representation. According to Rupert (this volume, Chapter 8), for example, when we have second-order internal states that track our first-order representations, they can track only the presence of the state doing the representing, not the entity being represented. Accordingly, the second-order representation provides no genuine insight into what is being represented by the first-order representation, hence provides no support for the description of the brain-in-vat scenario as involving a representation of an apple.

However, when we consider introspectively our conscious experiences, they often (indeed typically) present themselves to introspection as directed at something outside the mind. Arguably, this is precisely the lesson of the so-called transparency of experience (Harman 1990). This is significant, because when we conceive of the brain-in-vat scenario, we seem to be employing a sort of first-person imagination whereby we imagine the envatted brain's mental life "from the inside." We imagine *being* the envatted brain and introspecting our own experiences while envatted. So insofar as the brain's experiences are imagined as subjectively indistinguishable from ours, and ours are typically felt to be intentionally directed, the brain's ought to be typically imagined as seeming intentionally directed. To that extent, the natural description of the scenario involves mention not only of the brain's internal states but also of these states' *representational properties*.

In light of this consideration, the eliminativist may wish to call into question the possibility of the scenario presented in the opening parable. In conceiving the scenario, we conceive of a mental state whose representational properties in one sense are different from its representational properties in another sense. It is to describe this conceived scenario that we introduce the notion of subjective representation. But the eliminativist view about subjective representation can resist the introduction of the notion by claiming that although the scenario is conceivable, it is not genuinely possible—it is not *metaphysically* possible. The view may be that, as a matter of Kripkean a posteriori necessity, the envatted brain's S1-caused apple-ish experience represents only S1; in no sense does it represent an apple.

Regardless of whether conceivability is generally a good guide to metaphysical possibility, however, the present objection is completely implausible. For an identically stimulated envatted brain ought to be not only metaphysically but *nomologically* possible. Consider that conscious experiences are widely acknowledged to have *neural correlates*, and it is certainly possible, consistently with the actual laws of nature, to duplicate the neural correlates of my stream of consciousness by duplicating exactly (i) the neural state of my brain at the beginning of my biological life and (ii) the sensory inputs I have enjoyed since. Everything we know about brain function suggests that this is nomologically possible and would result in duplication of my conscious experience itself. The quality of the link between conceivability and metaphysical possibility is irrelevant.[25]

Conceding that the scenario from the opening parable is metaphysically and even nomologically possible, the eliminativist might insist that the property it requires us to posit nevertheless fails to qualify as representational. She may concede that one could use the word *representation* to designate whatever one wished, but insist that the phenomenon picked out by the subjective notion is not representation *in the philosophically relevant sense*. On this version of eliminativism, the envatted brain's state does present an apple to it, but it does not *re*present an apple in any philosophically significant sense.

This smacks of a verbal issue, but let us set that aside. Whether this kind of objection is plausible depends ultimately on what we require from a property to qualify as representational "in the philosophically relevant sense." If there is any substantive answer to this question, I think it would have to appeal to the traditional idea of *intentionality* (Brentano 1874).[26] The thought would be that "the philosophically relevant sense" of representation is that which involves the features definitive of intentionality. Two definitive features stand out: (i) the feature that underlies failure of truth-preserving existential generalization and (ii) the feature that underlies failure of truth-preserving substitution of coreferential terms (Chisholm 1957). It seems clear, however, that representation in the subjective sense exhibits both features. Thus, the envatted brain's apple experience presents an apple to the brain even though there is no apple, and its morning-star experiences are "presentationally different" from its evening-star experiences even though the heavenly body is one and the same.[27] Accordingly, from "the envatted brain's experience presents an apple to the brain," we cannot truth-preservingly infer "there is something that the envatted brain's experience presents to it" (this is failure of existential generalization); and from "the envatted brain's experience presents the morning star to the brain" and "the morning star is the evening star," we cannot truth-preservingly infer "the envatted brain's experience presents the evening star to it" (substitution failure). So, subjective representation does exhibit the definitive features of intentionality and thus qualifies as representation in the philosophically relevant sense. In other words, there *is* such a thing as *subjective intentionality*.[28]

I conclude that eliminativism is prima facie highly implausible. It is true that the combination of familiar tracking theories of mental representation and a compelling argument for eliminativism about subjective representation would protect these theories' status as fully adequate to the phenomena. But it is far from obvious what such an argument would look like. Arguments to the effect that subjective representation is explanatorily and descriptively dispensable, metaphysically impossible, or philosophically irrelevant do not appear to work. Another argument might, but it is the burden of the tracking theorist to produce it. Observe that this is, essentially, the burden to supplement her tracking theory with a compelling argument for eliminativism about subjective representation.

Reductivism

The reductivist gambit in this area is to develop a broadly causal-covariational or teleological account of subjective representation. In doing so, the reductivist would show that familiar tracking theories of mental representation, even if not *geared* toward subjective representation, have the *resources* to account for it.

The simplest reductivist account would identify *something* that both my and my envatted duplicate's experiences track. Thus, my apple-ish experience and my duplicate's are elicited by the same sensory stimulation. To be sure, unlike my brain, the envatted one is not "coated" with a genuine sensorium, so the relevant sensory stimulation must be construed as stimulation of entry points to the brain itself—for example, the lateral geniculate nucleus (LGN) for visual stimulation. In a way, then, both my apple-ish experiences and my duplicate's covary stably with the presence of the right kind of LGN state. A reductivist might therefore suggest that subjective apple representation is nothing but the tracking of apple-appropriate LGN states. More generally, she may attempt to account for subjective representation in terms of tracking of the right intracranial states.

This reductivist attempt is unsatisfactory as it stands. For presumably, subjective apple representations represent apples, or apple-y things, not LGN states. It is legitimate perhaps to account for subjective representation of x (partly) in terms of tracking of y, but the reductivist does owe us an account of the relation R that holds between x and y that enables a state to subjectively represent x in virtue of tracking y. Clearly, R is not some other tracking relation, since the envatted brain's relevant LGN state bears no tracking relation to apples. Some other account of R would have to be provided. This further account would effectively constitute supplementation of familiar tracking theories of mental representation.[29]

Another reductivist approach might suggest taking the best among familiar theories of objective representation and adding to it a condition of subjective accessibility. Thus, one might hold that a mental state M presents a feature F to its subject iff (i) M tracks F and (ii) M's tracking of F is somehow introspectively accessible to the subject. If this is right, then familiar theories of mental representation only need to be supplemented with an account of introspective access to accommodate subjective representation.

The trouble with this reductive account is that it is falsified by the brain-in-vat scenario: the envatted brain has a mental state that presents an apple to it, even though it is not the case that (i) it tracks an apple and (ii) its tracking of the apple is introspectively accessible to the brain. Condition (i) is not met. If we replace condition (i) with the requirement that the state track an apple-appropriate LGN state, the problem attending the previous reductive account would reemerge: we would need an account of the (nontracking) relation between the relevant LGN state and apples (or apple-y things).[30]

A third reductive option might attempt to account for what an experience E subjectively represents not in terms of anything E objectively represents but in terms of what E is objectively represented to objectively represent. Suppose E tracks F but is accompanied by a higher-order mental state that objectively represents E as tracking G. Then on this view, although E objectively represents F, it subjectively represents G. Naturally, the higher-order objective representation is itself accounted for in terms of tracking. The upshot is an account of subjective representation that secures its independence from objective representation but at the same time appeals exclusively to materials already used in familiar theories of mental representation (it combines familiar materials in an unfamiliar way).

This reductive approach to subjective representation is much more promising, but it does face two important challenges. First, the extant literature on naturalistic theories of mental representation includes, to my knowledge, no higher-order tracking account.[31] In this respect at least, such an account would effectively constitute *supplementation* of existing familiar theories. Secondly, and more pressingly, it is far from clear how higher-order tracking could deliver the right results in brain-in-vat scenarios. To account for the brain's experience presenting an apple to it, this reductivist would have to say that the brain harbors a higher-order state that tracks an apple tracker. But it is not at all clear how the brain might *acquire* this higher-order tracker. To acquire such an apple-tracker tracker, it would have to possess a first-order apple tracker, but (plausibly) the acquisition of apple trackers depends on causal interaction with apples, and the envatted brain enjoys none.[32] As noted previously, the only apple-relevant features with which the envatted brain's apple-ish experiences causally interact are ("apple-appropriate") LGN states. But then any higher-order state that would track these would *not* be tracking apple trackers; it would be tracking LGN trackers. Here again, then, the proposed reductive account appears to require supplementation, indeed the very same supplementation discussed previously.

There may be other reductive accounts that have not occurred to me and that may succeed in casting subjective representation as an ontological free lunch (given the existence of objective representation). But as with eliminativism, it is the reductivist's burden to provide any such account. In any case, a reductivist defense of familiar tracking-based theories of mental representation would require two parts: (i) an account of objective representation in terms of tracking relations and (ii) a reductive account of subjective representation in terms of objective representation. The extant literature on mental representation contains admirable work toward (i), but virtually no work toward (ii). Supplying (ii) is the minimal supplementation that familiar theories would require.

Nonreductivism and More Radical Options

A subjective-representation enthusiast may turn the tables on the proponent of familiar tracking theories by arguing for eliminativism or reductivism about *objective* representation. Recall that one of the previous eliminativist tacks involved denying that the property shared by my envatted subjective duplicate qualifies as representational in the "philosophically interesting" sense of *intentionality*. A parallel claim could be made by the subjective-representation enthusiast. She can claim that so-called objective representation does not exhibit the features underlying failure of substitution and existential generalization.[33]

The notion that objective representation does not exhibit the feature underlying substitution failure has already been foreshadowed in the literature. Some arguments due to Searle (1991; 1992, chap. 7) and Loar (1995) could certainly be adapted in this direction. The thought is that any mental state that tracked Phosphorus would *eo ipso* be tracking Hesperus. Tracking relations, even teleologically augmented, simply cannot discriminate between coextensive entities—for reasons explored already a generation ago (see esp. Fodor 1984). In consequence, "M tracks F" and "F = G" *do* entail "M tracks G"—contrary to substitution failure.[34]

There are also arguments to the effect that objective representation does not exhibit the feature underlying failure of existential generalization (Kriegel 2011, chap. 3). Here the idea is that tracking relations, even when teleologically augmented, cannot obtain in the absence of their relata. In some worlds inhabited by my envatted duplicate there are apples, but in some there are not. Plausibly, tracking relations require the existence of the tracked. If so, in an apple-less world, my envatted duplicate's internal states could not track, and hence could not objectively represent, apples. In consequence, "M tracks F" *does* entail "There is an *x*, such that M tracks *x*"—contrary to failure of existential generalization.

Such arguments (which admittedly require more sustained development) might inspire some to go eliminativist with respect to *objective* representation. The claim would be that objective tracking relations do not qualify as representational in the philosophically interesting sense—they are not intentional.

Others may take the same considerations to suggest a *reductivist* account of objective representation. Here the idea would be that tracking relations qualify as representational (in the philosophical sense) only in virtue of bearing the right relation to subjective representation. Again following Searle's (1992, chapter 7) lead, one might suggest that M objectively represents F iff (i) M tracks F and (ii) M *potentially* subjectively represents F (or M is *disposed* to subjectively represent F). More circuitously, and now following Loar's (2003) lead, one might hold that M objectively represents F iff (i) M tracks F and (ii) M is functionally/inferentially integrated with certain subjective representations. Other reductive accounts could also be suggested.[35] What they would all have in common is the claim that tracking, however sophisticated, only qualifies as representational in the relevant (read: intentional) sense if it bears the right relation to subjective representation. Objective representations thus inherit their status as representations *from* subjective representations. In this way, objective representation is grounded in subjective representation—without the latter there could not be the former.

The most antecedently neutral approach would be nonreductivist, rejecting eliminativism and reductivism about either objective or subjective representation. On this view, the conceptual distinction between two notions of representation is paralleled by a real distinction between two mutually irreducible kinds of representational property. Importantly, such two-way nonreductivism does constitute a departure from familiar tracking theories of mental representation, as it invites supplementation of such theories by some account of subjective representation.[36]

Such an account would tell us what it is in virtue of which a mental state M subjectively represents a feature F. Just as certain tracking relations are designated by familiar theories as underlying objective representation, so some other relations (or perhaps monadic properties) would have to be designated as underlying subjective representation. One way to understand the recent flurry of work surrounding the so-called phenomenal intentionality research program (Kriegel 2013) is in this context: mental states represent subjectively in virtue of their phenomenal character. This is not the place to discuss work within this research program.[37] But note that insofar as the notion of subjective representation is motivated by consideration of environmentally insulated phenomenal duplicates such as brains in vats, it is prima facie plausible that phenomenal character would be crucial to subjective representation. Within a nonreductive framework, this is not taken to be due to the fact that tracking relations underlie phenomenal character (as in Dretske 1995); rather, tracking and phenomenology are taken to be two different sources of two different kinds of representation.

Conclusion and Future Work

It has not been my goal, in this chapter, to make a case for this sort of non-reductivism, casting objective and subjective representation as mutually irreducible.[38] My goal has been more modest and may be described as follows. Once we draw a *conceptual* distinction between objective and subjective representation, and rule out eliminativism about the latter, a certain structure emerges for a *general* theory of mental representation—a theory that accounts for *all* phenomena of mental representation. Such a general theory would comprise three chapters: (a) a theory of objective representation, (b) a theory of subjective representation, and (c) an account of the relationship between them. My goal in this chapter has been to argue that familiar theories of mental representation in terms of tracking relations are inadequate as *general* theories. For they offer us only (a) and are silent on (b) and (c). They thus fail to account for all the phenomena of mental representation. To do so, they would have to add either (i) a reductive account of subjective representation in terms of objective representation or (ii) an independent account of subjective representation. To repeat, I am open to the possibility that a reductive account of subjective representation in terms of objective representation might turn out to be right. Such an account would effectively constitute an approach to (c) and would pave the way to (b). Still, none of the familiar tracking theories of mental representation in the extant literature actually offers such a reductive account of subjective representation. It remains an outstanding intellectual debt on the part of tracking theories. My contention is that the phenomena of subjective representation cannot be dealt with simply through disregard; some positive account of them—if only a reductive account—is called for.[39]

Notes

1. We could, of course, use "representation-as-tracking" and "representation-as-presentation." But while these terms applied intuitively in the brain-in-vat scenario, words undergo subtle changes in connotative profile across contexts, and so these terms may not apply intuitively in other scenarios, even though there are no important substantial differences. (This is especially true of the "presentation.") In addition, the expressions "representation-as-tracking" and "representation-as-presentation" are clumsy.
2. What makes similarity relevant or sufficient is of course a complicated matter. If we had a full account of this, we could offer something like necessary and sufficient conditions for objective and subjective representation. Objective representation: "x is an objective representation iff x is similar to the envatted brain's state of tracking S1 in respect R and to degree D." Subjective representation: "x is a subjective representation iff x is similar to the envatted brain's state of presenting an apple to the brain in respect R^* and to degree D^*." For an initial grasp of the two notions, however, we can rely on intuitive takes on relevance and sufficiency.
3. Dennett (1969) distinguishes between personal and subpersonal mental states: the former are states of us, the latter are not. This distinction applies to representational states: sometimes we do the representing; sometimes subsystems within us do it. The distinction between wide and narrow representations is due to Putnam (1975): the former are not shared by intrinsic

duplicates; the latter are. And Chalmers (1996, chap. 1) distinguishes between psychological and phenomenal conceptions of mental phenomena: the former characterizes mental phenomena in terms of their causal relations to each other and to the environment (their "long-armed functional role"), and the latter characterizes them in terms of their experiential feel (their "phenomenal character"). This *conceptual* distinction, too, applies to mental representations as well (see Kriegel 2010).

4. Note that at this stage no claim is made about metaphysical possibility, only about conceptual possibility. The reason is that at this stage I am only interested in the two concepts of representation.

5. For the notion of a manifest kind, see Johnston (1997).

6. This view is defended by Brogaard (2013), among others.

7. Here too, it may well be possible to justifiably believe, and know, that you are not the space soul, but again this would be nondemonstrative knowledge, and being nondemonstrative, it would not *rule out* possible alternatives.

8. It is worth stressing that it matters not whether the situation the thought experiment enjoins us to envisage is genuinely possible or merely conceivable. For our distinction is in the first instance between two *notions*, not two *properties*. I will address the issue of whether there is a different property corresponding to each notion later on.

9. It was pointed out to me, in this connection, that the *Oxford English Dictionary*'s entry on representation is parceled out into seven different meanings, each subdivided into distinct usages, in a way that suggests a heterogeneous domain of phenomena. Although the entry's authors' taxonomy and organization of the domain leaves much to be desired, the multitude and variation of meaning seems to be a genuine phenomenon.

10. Likewise, it is not as though literary and mathematical representations represent due to the same representation relation, with the former qualifying as literary simply because they employ literary vehicles of representation and the latter as mathematical because they employ mathematical vehicles. We can imagine a single item functioning as a diagram in one context and a metaphor in another.

11. It is important to note, however, that there is also an intimate relation between the two notions, inasmuch as the following nontrivial connection holds: whenever I have a conscious experience that represents veridically in both the objective sense and the subjective sense, what it tracks and what it presents to me are one and the same. This congruence can hardly be an accident. There is thus a nonaccidental tie between what an experience represents in the objective and subjective senses when everything goes the way it should. So while we need separate theories for mental representation in each sense, there needs to be sufficient contact or overlap between them to explain this nonaccidental tie.

12. This last condition requires that the non-Fs cause Ms because Fs cause Ms, whereas the Fs cause Ms not because non-Fs cause Ms.

13. Arguably, conditions (i) and (iii) are not satisfied either, but we do not have to worry about that, as the dissatisfaction of (ii) is sufficient to generate the problem.

14. Moreover, in most cases (though not quite all), the nomic dependence conditions mean that Fs are the only lawful causes of Ms. It is clear that this more specific condition will not be satisfied by the envatted brain's apple experiences, since they have no apples as causes, lawful or not.

15. The term *correspondence* is Millikan's (1984, 1993) and is left unexplained. One would be warranted to suspect that the relevant correspondence relation is ultimately to be accounted for in terms of the sort of tracking relation appealed to by causal-covariational theories. If so, teleosemantics is in fact just a teleological augmentation of causal-covariational theories.

16. This line of argumentation against teleosemantics parallels closely Strawson's (2008), and is in fact adapted from it. Strawson argues that teleosemantics cannot accommodate the possibility of *pure observers*, because such observers are incapable of adaptive behavior. As example of pure observers, he cites the "weather watchers": intelligent creatures stuck to the ground and unable to move but sensitive to and intensely interested in the weather. These

creatures do not behave at all, let alone adaptively, but clearly have mental representations, argues Strawson. We can stipulate that something very similar is true of the envatted brain: it does not genuinely interact with its environment, though it seems to itself to do so.

17. Recall that in our version of the tale the machine stimulates the brain randomly; it is not controlled by an intelligent and purposeful "evil scientist."

18. The term *interpreter* is used somewhat technically here, to designate any agent engaged in ascription of representational states.

19. We can think of it this way: if objective and subjective representation were one and the same property, given that S1 is not an apple, one of the two ascriptions would have to be false. Conversely, since both ascriptions are true, objective and subjective representation must be two different properties.

20. What I mean by "true in the minimalist sense" is something like: true in the sense of satisfying the platitudes used to formulate the so-called truth schema in minimalist or deflationary theories of truth, such as Horwich's (1998).

21. We may also define a looser version of reductivism, allowing for reduction of subjective representation to objective representation plus other familiar and recognizably "kosher" materials, such as functional role or other causal/mechanistic notions. I will ignore this possibility in what follows because everything I say about the more rigorous type of reductivism should apply mutatis mutandis to this looser variety as well.

22. Clearly, the proponent of familiar tracking theories of mental representation must argue for the eliminative or reductive view. If either turns out plausible, the familiar theories may be in good shape. The nonreductive view is the least conservative of the three options and would straightforwardly require that familiar theories be supplemented with a distinct account of subjective representation. However, I will argue that even reductive views, at least in their plausible versions, would require meaningful supplementation of familiar theories of mental representation, in a sense to be duly explained. (Importantly, there are also more radical epistemic possibilities in the area. One is eliminative in the opposite direction, denying the existence of a property of objective representation. Another is reductive in that opposite direction, claiming that objective representation ultimately reduces to, or is somehow grounded in, subjective representation. If either of these more radical options prevails, familiar tracking theories of mental representation would be cast as not just inadequate but wrongheaded.)

23. In particular, since the overt behavior of subjects can be fully explained by citing internal states' tracking of the environment, there is no need to cite any other properties of such internal states.

24. Thus, there are ways of construing action so that the envatted brain acts in a way that calls for positing an experience that represents an apple. Suppose we can read off the monitor that controls the vat that our envatted brain initiates motion of "its" apparent arm in the direction of the apparent apple, performs an apparent grasping motion, and brings the apple to "its" apparent mouth. This pattern of information that we see on the monitor invites an explanation that includes the claim that the brain has a representation as of an apple.

25. In addition, even if conceivability does not under any circumstances entail metaphysical possibility, surely it provides defeasible evidence of metaphysical possibility. If so, in the absence of defeaters we would be epistemically obliged to adopt the hypothesis that the brain-in-vat scenario is metaphysically possible.

26. Interestingly, if we require historical continuity with Brentano's notion of intentionality, the subjective notion of representation is surely the more relevant one, as Brentano (1874, book II, chaps. 1 and 7) conceives of intentionality in terms of what presentation (*vorstellungen*) presents to the subject, not in terms of any tracking relations to the environment. In fact, for most sensible properties, Brentano appears to take a Kantian approach, taking them to be in some sense projected by the mind rather than inherent in the objective order of things.

27. In saying that the experiences are "presentationally different," I mean to suggest that—at least for an envatted brain unaware of the identity of Phosphorus and Hesperus—what is

presented in the case of one experience feels different from what is presented in the case of the other. I say more about this in Kriegel (2011, chap. 3).

28. Loar (1987) uses the term *subjective intentionality* to pick out something that ends up being more or less the same as *our* subjective intentionality. But my own way of introducing the notion is much more theoretically neutral: as a label for one sense of representation we find in contemplating brain-in-vat scenarios.

29. Furthermore, nothing about this reductivist account captures the subjective dimension of subjective apple representations, the fact that they present apples *to the subject*.

30. Furthermore, for either version of this reductivist gambit to succeed, an account of introspective access that did not appeal to subjective representation would have to be devised; this may not be straightforward. In particular, it is not obviously easier to describe introspective access without citing subjective representation than it is to describe the brain-in-vat scenario without doing so.

31. I develop an account of this sort in Kriegel (2011, chap. 2), but naturally I disregard it here.

32. Or, at least, familiar stories about tracker acquisition appear to require this—an alternative story would have to be devised if the idea is to get around such a causal-interactive requirement.

33. A claim in the general vicinity is made by Strawson (2008).

34. Indeed, one might reasonably suggest that even the combination of "M tracks F" and "F coextends with G" entails "M tracks G."

35. See Kriegel (2011, chap. 4) for relevant discussion.

36. It is worth noting that avoiding reduction of subjective representation to objective representation, while it institutes a kind of dualism about representation, does not constitute the sort of dualism that challenges physicalism. It is perfectly consistent with subjective representation being irreducible to objective representation that it is reducible to, say, 32 Hz oscillations in the hypothalamus.

37. For relevant work, see Loar (1987, 2003), McGinn (1988), Searle (1991, 1992), Siewert (1998), Horgan and Tienson (2002), Strawson (2008), and Kriegel (2003, 2007, 2011) inter alia.

38. One problem with this view is that it is does not deliver naturalization of mental representation and may even be in tension with such naturalization (see Kriegel 2003; 2011, chap. 3).

39. For useful comments on a previous draft, I would like to thank Stephen Biggs, Davide Bordini, David Chalmers, Allan Hazlett, and Farid Masrour. I have also benefited from presenting an earlier version of the paper at the University of Wisconsin and at conferences in Bled and Geneva. I am grateful to audiences there, in particular Gregory Bochner, Juan Comesaña, Manuel García-Carpintero, Jens Kipper, Matthew Kopec, Jack Lyons, Neil Mehta, Graham Peebles, Larry Shapiro, Allan Sidelle, and Peter Vranas.

References

Brentano, F. 1874. *Psychology from an Empirical Standpoint*. Trans. A. C. Rancurello, D. B. Terrell, and L. L. McAlister. London: Routledge and Kegan Paul, 1973.
Brogaard, B. 2013. "Do We Perceive Natural Kind Properties?" *Philosophical Studies* 162: 35–42.
Chalmers, D. J. 1996. *The Conscious Mind*. New York: Oxford University Press.
Chisholm, R. 1957. *Perceiving: A Philosophical Study*. Ithaca, NY: Cornell University Press.
Dennett, D. C. 1969. *Content and Consciousness*. London: Routledge.
Dretske, F. I. 1971. "Conclusive Reasons." *Australasian Journal of Philosophy* 49: 1–22.
Dretske, F. I. 1981. *Knowledge and the Flow of Information*. Oxford: Clarendon.
Dretske, F. I. 1988. *Explaining Behavior*. Cambridge ,MA: MIT Press.
Dretske, F. I. 1995. *Naturalizing the Mind*. Cambridge, MA: MIT Press.
Fodor, J. A. 1984. "Semantics, Wisconsin Style." *Synthese* 59: 231–250.
Fodor, J. A. 1990. *A Theory of Content and Other Essays*. Cambridge, MA: MIT Press.
Harman, G. 1990. "The Intrinsic Quality of Experience." *Philosophical Perspectives* 4: 31-52.

Horgan, T., and J. Tienson 2002. "The Intentionality of Phenomenology and the Phenomenology of Intentionality." In D. J. Chalmers (ed.), *Philosophy of Mind: Classical and Contemporary Readings* (pp. 520-533). Oxford: Oxford University Press.

Horwich, P. 1998. *Truth*. Oxford: Oxford University Press.

Johnston, M. 1997. "Manifest Kinds." *Journal of Philosophy* 94: 564–583.

Kriegel, U. 2003. "Is Intentionality Dependent upon Consciousness?" *Philosophical Studies* 116: 271–307.

Kriegel, U. 2010. "Intentionality and Normativity." *Philosophical Issues* 20: 185–208.

Kriegel, U. 2011. *The Sources of Intentionality*. Oxford: Oxford University Press.

Kriegel, U. 2013. "The Phenomenal Intentionality Research Program." In U. Kriegel (ed.), *Phenomenal Intentionality: New Essays*. Oxford: Oxford University Press.

Loar, B. 1987. "Subjective Intentionality." *Philosophical Topics* 15: 89–124.

Loar, B. 1995. "Reference from the First-Person Perspective." *Philosophical Issues* 6: 53–72.

Loar, B. 2003. "Phenomenal Intentionality as the Basis for Mental Content." In M. Hahn and B. Ramberg (eds.), *Reflections and Replies: Essays on the Philosophy of Tyler Burge*. Cambridge, MA: MIT Press.

McGinn, C. 1988. "Consciousness and Content." In *Proceedings of the British Academy* 76: 219–239.

McGinn, C. 1989. *Mental Content*. Oxford: Blackwell.

Millikan, R. G. 1984. *Language, Thought, and Other Biological Categories*. Cambridge, MA: MIT Press.

Millikan, R. G. 1993. *White Queen Psychology and Other Essays for Alice*. Cambridge, MA: MIT Press.

Papineau, D. 1993. *Philosophical Naturalism*. Oxford: Blackwell.

Putnam, H. 1975. "The Meaning of "Meaning"." In *Mind, Language, and Reality*. Cambridge: Cambridge University Press.

Putnam, H. 1981. *Reason, Truth, and History*. Cambridge: Cambridge University Press.

Searle, J. R. 1991. "Consciousness, Unconsciousness, and Intentionality." *Philosophical Issues* 1: 45–66.

Searle, J. R. 1992. *The Rediscovery of Mind*. Cambridge, MA: MIT Press.

Siewert, C. P. 1998. *The Significance of Consciousness*. Princeton, NJ: Princeton University Press.

Stampe, D. 1977. "Towards a Causal Theory of Linguistic Representation." *Midwest Studies in Philosophy* 2: 42–63.

Strawson, G. 2008. "Real Intentionality 3: Why Intentionality Entails Consciousness." In *Real Materialism and Other Essays*. Oxford: Oxford University Press.

CHAPTER 8

The Sufficiency of Objective Representation

ROBERT D. RUPERT

Chapter Overview

This chapter makes a case against subjective content, by arguing for the sufficiency of a third-person, or objective, notion of content. It is maintained that objective content, as it is typically understood, constitutes one component of a standard theoretical package that includes other constructs: conceptions, basic operations, and architectural structure. Commitment to this standard package is independently motivated, and by appealing to it, we explain away the intuitions—about, for instance, brains in vats and color-inverted worlds—that seem to demand the introduction of subjective content into our models of human thought and experience.

Introduction and Methodology

Over the past half century, prevailing views about mental representation have undergone a series of drastic changes. Wittgensteinians and behaviorist psychologists made denial respectable, deriding the idea of mental representations as confusion borne of a category mistake or as unverifiable nonsense. The cognitivist revolution ushered in a realism about mental representations, eventually giving rise to dogged and ballyhooed attempts to "naturalize" the semantics of mental representations (by explicating the representation-determining relation between psychologically—and physically—real internal entities and the properties, kinds, or individuals in the environment represented by those entities) (see Dretske, 1981, 1988; Fodor, 1987, 1990; Millikan

1984). Over the past two decades, discussion of a subjective, fully internal form of representation has blossomed, driven by the assumption that we should take at face value direct introspective awareness of something that seems like meaning, content, or representation.

This whirlwind history runs roughshod over many distinctions, one of which is particularly relevant to the position laid out in what follows. Mid-century philosophers tended to dismiss talk of psychologically real mental representations on conceptual grounds: mental representations have meaning, meaning is partly constituted by normative constraints, and normative constraints are public; so, assuming that mental representations are internal by definition, there are no mental representations (Wittgenstein, 1953). In contrast, behaviorist psychologists avoided talk of mental representation on methodological grounds; by their lights, there was no empirically legitimate way to study internal mental entities, and, much more importantly, they thought they had a way of accounting for the data without invoking mental representations (Skinner, 1957). A simple application of Ockham's razor cut mental representations out of the behaviorist tool kit. The cognitivist revolution rose on similarly contrasting motivations. Some philosophers abandoned behaviorism because it did not countenance the first-person perspective (recall Putnam's super-Spartans). Others, however, put no special emphasis on the first-person perspective; they argued that one could not do justice to the empirical data—about language acquisition, for example—without positing internal representational units (Chomsky, 1959; Fodor, 1975).

Recent developments have a different flavor, however. The proliferation of books and articles about consciousness—about Mary the superscientist (Jackson, 1982), the explanatory gap (Levine, 1983), phenomenal consciousness (Block, 1995), and the zombie-inspired hard problem (Chalmers, 1996)—aroused dissatisfaction with the cognitivist compromise; functionally defined mental representations, and their relations to external entities they tracked, left cold those who were impressed by the apparently rich experiential contents of their own inner, mental lives. This most recent transition—to consciousness-based discussions of mental representation—lacks naturalistic motivation,[1] though, and, in my opinion, this is telling.

The behaviorist rejection of introspectionism in psychology was meant to express a scientific urge, as was the introduction of internal mental representations by nativist linguists and memory scientists (e.g., Miller, 1956). The cognitivists embraced Ockham's razor no less than the behaviorists; they disagreed with behaviorists regarding what theoretical posits were necessary to account for the empirical data. This seems to me to be the right strategy, one that I pursue in the remainder. Ockham's razor—together with the long history of successful naturalistic theorizing—recommends that we make a serious attempt to account for the data that drive the subjective turn without positing any new form of mental representation. These data (which I refer to as the 'relevant data' or the 'data in question' in what follows) consist primarily of the ways that philosophers express their conviction that there is a distinctive category of representation or meaning: subjective or internalist content. I shall insist, however, that accounting for these reports is decidedly not the burden of an objective notion of mental content alone. In order to account, for example, for the judgments about possibility philosophers issue in response to thought experiments, one must advert to theories of cognitive processing, broadly speaking; but this is no strike against the sufficiency of objective content, for, historically, theories of processing have been part of the theoretical package that includes mental representations with objective mental content. Appeals to objective content alone do not account for the relevant data, but they were never meant to. Objective theories of representational content attribute content to units that play a role in cognitive or mental processes, and the characteristics of these processes explain much of the relevant data: the reports of introspective access to states with a special sort of subjective content or reports of intuitions (or judgments)—about thought experiments, for instance—that would seem to support a notion of internalist, subjective content. So, theories of objective content, as theories of content for mental representations, needn't be supplemented at all, they need only be placed in a package with the kinds of theoretical elements that normally accompany them in psychological modeling; a package that contains only this one kind of content.

Mental Representation and Objective Content

As noted, the cognitivist revolution ushered in a new era of realism about mental representations, and it did so in conjunction with an emerging computer science. As a result, mental representations were frequently referred to using the language of 'data structures', 'symbol strings', 'information-bearing states', and 'machine tables'. Many of those who had functionalist leanings in philosophy of mind were inspired by computational cognitive science (Fodor, 1975), and, as a result, this language appeared in philosophical as well as scientific discourse. What would render such a structure a representation, though? What makes it specifically representational? How, for example, should we understand the idea that it has content?

Think of this partly as a methodological puzzle (Stich, 1983; Fodor, 1987). Scientific procedure seems to speak in favor of a so-called narrow methodology, one that focuses solely on the causal processes that eventuate in intelligent behavior. Given a generally localist assumption about causation, one should expect the content of mental representations to be determined fully by internal processes, at least if such content is to play a causal role. After all, the proximal cause of behavior had better be inside the organism doing the behaving!

An inferential- or conceptual-role semantics offers one objective notion of representational content for internal states, objective in the sense that the content of a given mental representation is determined entirely by causal and structural relations that can be specified fully and can, in principle, be measured determinately, from the third-person, scientific perspective. On this view, the content of a mental representation is constituted entirely by some subset of the causal interactions it enters into (Block, 1986). So far as I can tell, the many shortcomings of such a view (Fodor, 1998) outweigh whatever benefits might accrue to the placement of content in a location that makes it a candidate causal contributor to the production of behavior.

Two such shortcomings strike me as particularly problematic. First, if part of what constitutes a given conceptual- or inferential-role content is that the vehicle bearing such content participates in certain, privileged inferences, then that vehicle's having that content cannot explain, causally, why those inferences occur, on pain of circularity; one should not hold that the unit has its given content because the unit causes certain transitions *and* that it causes those transitions because it has the content in question (Fodor, 1998, chap. 1). Second, the inferential-role view seems to rob mental representations of the sort of intentionality we take them to have. If their content supervenes only on the internal structure, then content isn't a matter of being related to the objects represented, the *actual things* that we think about—Sandy Koufax, zebras, charge, and so on—at least on the assumption that the internal states do not determine what's in the environment.

Moreover, many of the arguments taken to speak in favor of a competing externalist semantics for natural-language terms—Kripke's (1980) arguments from error and ignorance, for example—seem naturally to apply to mental representations, particularly if one adopts the view that linguistic units have the content they do partly because they express the content of the mental representations that produce them. Consider, too, certain realist intuitions in philosophy of science that seem best accommodated by a framework that includes external content: we tend to think that different scientists holding very different theories of, for instance, electricity are thinking about the same phenomenon—the one the nature of which they disagree about—and this thought might seem even more compelling as regards one scientist whose thinking evolves from one stage in her career to the next.

More scientifically oriented considerations seem to reinforce the need for externally oriented representational content. Psychology discovers laws stated in terms of content (Pylyshyn, 1984; Fodor, 1998; Burge, 1986), but inferential- or conceptual-role content varies radically from subject to subject. It would seem that only external content can consistently provide a common aspect to various subjects' water thoughts, for example; regardless of what idiosyncratic beliefs various subjects might have about water, they can all be about the same stuff in the environment—H_2O. Moreover, regardless of what one thinks about intentional laws, cognitive science seems rife with explanations that presuppose externalist content; it is presupposed that stimuli activate internal units that control behavior distinctively oriented toward the kind of stimuli that those internal units track (cf. Ramsey [2007], who worries that tracking is garden-variety causal mediation). And, returning to a metascientific perspective, we might wonder how we could possibly make sense of the scientific endeavor itself if scientists weren't thinking *about* the subjects in the lab, the lab equipment, their coauthors, editors at the journals to which their results are to be sent, the NSF director who facilitates review of their grant applications, and so forth.

Here, then, is this section's takeaway message. The most promising version of an objective, or third-person, view of content takes the form of a semantic externalism, not an inferential- or conceptual-role theory. But, in the event of overreaching, let me fall back to a watered-down line: since there seem to be good reasons to posit an objective, externalist (or tracking) notion of cognitive content, we should ask whether that content suffices to account for data that might suggest the need for additional forms of content, either conceptual- or inferential-role or some form of subjective content.

Concepts, Conceptions, and Architecture

In this section, I sketch the elements of a model of human cognition. The picture presented draws primarily on traditional computational modeling practices, although it can be adapted more or less easily to accommodate other approaches in cognitive science (e.g., dynamicist [Port & van Gelder, 1995] or connectionist [Rumelhart, McClelland, & the PDP Research Group, 1986] approaches). Although it is only a sketch, I hope it provides the reader with sufficient background to see how, in the section that follows, I mean to deploy this package of resources in order to account for the relevant data.

Concepts (or Mental Representations), Atomic and Otherwise

The bearers of mental content—the things filling at least one slot in the representation relation—are often referred to as 'concepts'. In what follows, I use the more neutral term 'mental representation' so as to avoid theoretical disputes over the requirements that a mental representation must meet in order to qualify as a concept. As bearers of content, mental representations can fruitfully be thought of as vehicles. Such vehicles should be individuated independently of their content—that is, nonsemantically (Rupert, 1998)—which jibes nicely with computational theories of processing (Fodor, 1994, chap. 1), as well as with other forms of mechanistic models in the cognitive sciences.

Mental representations can be either atomic or compound. Atomic mental representations, conceived of nonsemantically, are the smallest units that affect cognitive processing. Given a stock of atomic mental representations, cognitive operations can compound such units into strings or organized collections of other sorts. (I presuppose that, in our mechanistic models of cognition, cognitive operations are sensitive only to nonsemantic properties; this does not preclude a story according to which semantics also plays a role, but it will not be in the nuts and bolts of processing.) Atomic representations are thus the minimal content-bearing units—minimal relative to processing.[2] The content of a compound representation is a function of the content of its atomic components, where that function may take the form, for example, of a typed grammar.

This view of mental representation provides at least three kinds of non-semantic material to the causal-explanatory enterprise: nonsemantically individuated atomic units, processing operations that compound and otherwise operate on (by, e.g., writing, rewriting, decomposing, or transforming) strings of those atomic units, and rules that determine the content of a compound string as a function of the content of component atoms. Bear in mind that these materials appear in standard theories concerning the role of content-laden units in psychological explanation (Pylyshyn, 1984; Fodor, 1994). As such, to invoke these when accounting for the relevant data is neither to supplement theories of objective content, qua theories of content, nor is it to supplement the theoretical framework that serves as the standard home for theories of objective content.

Conceptions

The notion of a conception builds on the idea of a compound mental representation. Atomic mental representations are the building blocks for individual compound strings, which might be thought of, in the first instance, as analogous to simple sentences (e.g., "Cows are mammals"). Individually, such strings represent the world as being a certain way (by, e.g., having satisfaction conditions). Often it is thought that certain groups of such compound representations play privileged cognitive roles. Take a specific atomic mental representation in a given subject. Typically, this appears as a component of numerous stored or standing strings. So, we might characterize a subject's conception of x (or x's) as the entire collection of stored strings such that each string in the collection contains at least one instance of X. Typically there are *very* many of these, and, thus, to stand a chance of being theoretically useful, conceptions are typically limited to some proper subset of the collection—what is thought to be the subject's core knowledge concerning the individual, kind, or property represented by the atomic representation in question. An atomic mental representation might be COW, and the conception of cows might be a set of mental structures such as {COWS ARE MAMMALS, COWS ARE ALIVE, HUMANS KEEP COWS ON DAIRY FARMS, COWS ARE BIG, COWS ARE ANIMALS}; this set might be larger and contain much of what the subject represents about cows, but it does not consist in everything the subject believes about cows. Various forms of conceptions of have been proposed, among them file folders (Forbes, 1989), knowledge structures (Cummins,

1996), and frames (Minsky, 1974). It is a matter of some dispute what should go into this set. Putting too little into it creates versions of the frame problem,[3] but putting too much into it creates the problem that no two people share the same conception of a given kind, property, or individual; more generally, the issue gives rise to much hand-wringing about the analytic-synthetic distinction (Fodor & LePore, 1992) (among those who are inclined to think of conceptions as word meanings, which I am not).

For present purposes, I need not give a full account of conceptions. In fact, I'm inclined to think they play no role, as distinctive theoretical constructs, in the causal-explanatory enterprise. I discuss them here partly to warn against the conflating of intuitions about conceptions (of some grain or another) with intuitions about the content of atomic mental representations. To be sure, there could be some sort of content that attaches distinctively to conceptions (inferential-role semantics seems to offer an obvious possibility). We should bear clearly in mind, however, the possibility that content attaches, in the first instance, to atomic mental representations only, and that contributions of other factors—such as intuitions about conceptions—account for erroneous intuitions about mental representations. Perhaps more to the point, interactions among strings of mental representations may account for the relevant data, regardless of whether there is, for any x, a privileged theoretical construct—the subject's conception of x. Thus, we should keep in mind the possibility that interactions among compound representations play a causal-explanatory role even if conceptions—as a kind of meaning, in particular—play no such role.

Architecture

Models of cognition typically include an architecture. Cognitive architectures take many forms—classical, connectionist, dynamicist, subsumption, and associationist—but, essentially, the architecture is the collection of basic elements and operations that constitute the cognitive system, together with any fixed structure or structure-related constraints on the execution of those operations; it is the collection of tools available to play a causal-explanatory role at the level of cognition. In the case of computational models, the cognitive architecture includes the stock of atomic mental representations and a description of their processing-related properties, the operations available (including such things as parameter settings relevant to the performing of those operations—say, decay rates in a short-term memory buffer—and rules for compounding those operations into more complex operations), and also the various components that play specialized roles in the overall functioning of the cognitive system—what is distinctive of them and how they're connected to each other. For example, face recognition in humans might proceed by a series of operations that is relatively independent of the processing of the incoming speech stream, and it may be left to a third, downstream component to localize the source of the speech (thereby binding it to a face, if one is available). If so, these are architectural facts—about which components of the cognitive system transfer information to which others, to what extent they do, what limitations there are on such communication, and what forms of behavior they control as a result.

The preceding provides a sketch of the tools available for the construction of specific models of human cognition processing. Modeling that employs such tools has been productive (see, e.g., various incarnations and applications of the ACT-R and SOAR architectures), although there is vigorous debate among cognitive scientists as to whether this kind of modeling is on the right track or whether alternatives should be pursued more intensely (cf. Chemero, 2009).

Consider, now, the dual role that modeling might play in the current context. On the one hand, modeling permeates the sciences. So, in describing the tools for modeling human cognition, I am providing no more or less than one would provide in connection with any other science. But, this is a model of human thought, and thus should, in principle, model the very cognitive processes involved in the formulation and use of models, including the formulation and use of cognitive models. This requirement might seem most pressing if one has a certain general view about human cognition. I contend that modeling manifests our fundamental cognitive urge: we model everything from the motions of objects in the heavenly bodies to the minds and behaviors of our conspecifics. We are, cognitively speaking, modelers in the first instance (and I am inclined to think that language use is itself an act of model application, which accounts for much of the context specificity of language use). Everyday thought models everyday data and the systems giving rise to it; scientific thought models more carefully data systematically collected or experimentally produced. But, all human understanding is essentially an exercise in modeling, and this includes the understanding of how we formulate and use models in cognitive science or philosophy.

The preceding sketch of the tools available for the modeling of cognition also provides the materials for self-reflective modeling, for modeling the cognitive act of modeling. We are modelers, and thus, when we turn to understanding ourselves, we construct models of human cognition itself, models of how we model the world. Such modeling is vindicated by the results. (Presumably, the world is the sort of thing subject to modeling; the success of our various modeling enterprises itself is best explained by the assumption that the world is the sort of things with recurring elements and standing relations among them and is thus amenable to modeling.) In what follows, I will try to explain away the relevant data concerning mental representations by applying the roughly computational model sketched previously to show how we naturally model our own experiences and, to some extent our own thinking, erroneously; I will attempt to model how we naturally construct a model that includes a property of intrinsic, subjective internalist representation, in the absence of anything having that property. Furthermore, the model I suggest of the process of constructing an erroneous model includes only objective, tracking representation, at least so far as representation or content goes. In effect, then, I argue that there is only objective, tracking mental representation by invoking a model that includes only this one form of representation (together with other elements of the standard package) to explain why we produce the data that would seem to support the existence of subjective representation, by explaining how humans construct models of their own psychological processing that contain representations with empty reference, representations that nevertheless help to produce reports that include such terms as 'subjective representation.'

Explaining the Cases

In Uriah Kriegel's complementary piece (this volume, Chapter 7), he lays out a range of kinds of intuition (or conceptual judgment) that seem to entail the existence of a distinctive form of subjective content. He expresses the first of these as follows: "There are conceptually possible scenarios where representation varies in the objective sense but remains invariant in the subjective sense" (this volume, Chapter 7). As an example of such a scenario, Kriegel describes a color-inverted world—that is, a world in which human subjects have the same color experiences, but in which the colors in the world have been systematically swapped (for instance, subjects employ the actual-earth internal color experience of red to track what are now blue things—e.g., 'red delicious' apples—in the environment).

In my view, we can, and should, account for the judgment in question without invoking a kind of subjective representation that remains constant across subjects in the color-inverted and actual worlds. Insofar as the judgment itself involves a concept of such constant representation, the task in what follows is to model this erroneous application of the concept of representation. But, first, two preliminaries: Notice an element missing from the package described in section "Concepts, Conceptions, and Architecture"—a self, beyond the architecture (see Rupert, [2009] for further discussion). Among the enduring commitments of philosophy of mind is that there exists an entity, a person, to whom subjective, personal-level content is presented (McDowell, 1994). I find such a view unmotivated, however. It is true that subjects learn to use such pronouns as 'I', and a valence of conviction colors many uses of them (in such sentences as "*I* am the one who sees; my visual cortex doesn't see!").[4] Moreover, it might be, for example, that certain forms of executive control work more efficiently if there is a set of compound mental representations (recall the discussion of conceptions) that is specially rigged to motor output and such that all of the compound strings in the set share a common atomic representational element that we would naturally describe as a way to refer to oneself. But none of this entails the existence of an entity or distinctive construct, the self, intuitions about which ground claims about subjective representation.

Of course, the fact that some of us make the judgments in question (that, for example, the *person* sees, not the cortex) must be accounted for somehow. If the standard package can do so, however, without presupposing a distinctive person who, for instance, makes reliable judgments about what contents are presented to it, judgments that might be used to argue in favor of the existence of a distinctive form of subjective content, this may support an eliminativism about the self. I will not pursue this project in any detail, but the following discussion of the causal efficacy of vehicles and of the illusion of internal content should provide the reader with a further sense of how I think one best accounts for intuitions about a distinctively personal level.

Second, I propose to muddy the distinction made earlier between inferential- or conceptual-role theories of content, on the one hand, and externalist theories of content, on the other. From my perspective, what is essential to externalist theories are their tracking nature—the fact that some kind of causal, covariational, or informational relation holds between the representing vehicle and the individual, property, or kind represented. When conceived of as purely a matter of tracking, though, the issue of location becomes irrelevant; the thing being tracked can just as well be internal as it can be external to the human organism in which the tracking vehicle appears. There's nothing unusual about this idea from the standpoint of cognitive modeling; it's common enough to include "pointers"—that is, units that function to represent other units (e.g., the units stored at an address to which the pointer points [Newell & Simon, 1997/1976])—in computational models. Additionally, the complex pattern of neural connections one finds in the humans suggests an abundance of within-brain tracking relations (Goldman-Rakic, 1987). To further muddy the waters, I hold that externalist contents in the cognitive system frequently piggyback, exhibiting the kinds of relation found in cases of linguistic deference. For instance, one internal vehicle might borrow organismically external content from another internal vehicle by externalistically representing that second vehicle. (In general, philosophers have, I think, tended to ignore such possibilities because of their privileging of a personal level at which genuine content can be content only of a state of a complete subject, which is identified [roughly] with the organism. On such a view, the idea that there could be a vehicle with internal-externalist tracking content—which content is not self-revealing at the locus of that vehicle—doesn't make sense; any content is content of the entire organismically oriented subject, so any tracking relation between vehicles both of which are internal to the subject will determine a kind of content that must be accessible, or self-revealing, to the subject as a whole. On my view, all of this talk of entire subjects is misleading or at least puts the cart before the horse. Let's first model the data—intelligent behavior and the like—then see what sort of self that modeling yields and whether it makes sense within that framework to talk about internal representational vehicles the content of which might be, in the first instance, no more than another internal, tracked vehicle.)

Preliminaries out of the way, we can ask why philosophers would have the intuition that color-inverted earth is possible, if all representational content is externalist. The judgment in question involves the application of the concept of representation or of intentionality. Whether the judgment is correct depends on whether the property represented—that is, the property (or relation) of representing or being about—could be instantiated in a world that satisfies the description of color-inverted earth (or whether, say, given the nature of the intentional relation, there simply can't be sameness in internal intentionality when there is difference in external intentionality, and so no world satisfies the description in question).

How do we acquire the concept of intentionality? Elsewhere (Rupert, 2008), I propose that the acquisition of REPRESENTS SOMETHING (as a one-placed representational vehicle) proceeds by the application of that vehicle to other internal vehicles, such as COW, DOG, MAMA, HOUSE in contrast to its nonapplication to such vehicles as UNICORN, BOOGIE MAN, and SNIPE.[5] Grouping alone—using a method of samples and foils (Stanford & Kitcher, 2000)—homes in on a tracking relation, although I suspect it does not do so without some feedback provided by interactions with the environment that help to guide the classification of different internal vehicles into samples and foils; some terms initially treated as samples may come to be treated as foils when the child's executive systems fail to discover the robust causal connections to, say, sensory experiences that executive systems detect in standard samples.

This thought brings two essential elements to the fore: vehicles and their interconnections. When we think about our own thoughts, we activate vehicles that track other vehicles. We don't know this a priori because the vehicles tracking other internal vehicles do so via a causal relation; thus, what's on one side of the relation, the tracking vehicle, may quite successfully track what's on the other side of the relation, without the tracking vehicle's controlling accurate reports on the various properties of the thing tracked—that is, the represented vehicle.[6] It is possible, then, that when we have the intuition that subjects in color-inverted earth share subjective representations with earthly subjects, the things actually shared are vehicles. I say to myself, "I could be in *that* same state, even if colors were inverted," which is true, but what I may not be able to report on or reason about very accurately is the nature of "*that* state"; I claim that what is demonstrated by the vehicle controlling judgments and reports is a vehicle, not a content. (Thus, this yields a very thin notion of sameness of subjective representation: to have the same vehicles active across contexts.)[7]

What role is played by the interconnectedness of vehicles? As suggested previously, such interconnections play a role in the acquisition of the notion of intentionality or representation, even if these represent a pure tracking relation; patterns of interconnections (for instance, DOG's being activated in a variety of contexts in which sensory representations—such as FURRY FELLING ON MY BODILY SURFACE—are also active) help to determine which vehicles activate the further vehicle REPRESENTS SOMETHING. Such patterns of activation help the subject to home in on vehicles that represent; moreover, because of their tight connection to the application of REPRESENTS, these associations create an illusion of inferential-role content: INTENTIONAL and REPRESENTS are the ur-semantic mental representations (their activation tracked by SEMANTIC), and as a consequence, things closely associated with their application—such as causally interconnected sets of vehicles—get treated as semantic as well, even when they are not of the same natural kind or do not instantiate the same natural properties as those represented by the other terms to which SEMANTIC applies. So, subjects treat these interconnections as somehow content constitutive, even though they are mere causal contributors to content determination (Rupert, 2008). When we consider color-inverted earth, then, we are inclined to think that such networks of interconnected vehicles remain in place (although we couldn't produce this description on simple reflection), and this contributes to the judgment that subjects on earth and on color-inverted earth share representations; and this generates the illusion that there is some kind of content that is nontracking. It generates the illusion that even though objective, externalist content (e.g., the color being thought about when viewing red delicious apples) has changed, something semantic has remained the same.

Notice that this deflating explanation is not built from materials assembled ad hoc. Two of the most influential tracking theories (Fodor, 1987; Dretske, 1988) propose, for independent reasons, that the content-fixing, tracking relation can be causally mediated by other representations.

What about "conceptually possible scenarios in which representation varies in the subjective but not objective sense" (Kriegel, this volume, Chapter 7), an illustration of which is the traditional inverted-spectrum case? A straightforward explaining away of this intuition—that an inverted internal spectrum is possible—runs as follows: one can imagine that a very different network of internally tracked and internally tracking vehicles gets attached to the environment in just the way that one's current network is—at least, this is how one should articulate what one is imagining if the conceptual possibility is a genuine metaphysical possibility. Such appeals to difference in vehicle across sameness in external content help to explain other phenomena as well (including substitution failures—see Fodor, 1990, chap. 4).

The third case is "representation in the objective sense in the absence of representation in the subjective sense." Kriegel offers the example of tree rings, and there are many others that have been discussed in the literature, from thermostats and fuel gauges to magnetosomes used by certain bacteria. Take the example of tree rings. Depending on one's theory of content, a number of tree rings may not qualify as a representation; it is one thing to label a theory 'tracking' to get across a core element of it, but theories of the tracking variety generally involve a complex set of necessary and sufficient conditions; no serious theory in the field holds that x represents y if x naturally means (in Grice's sense) y or x was simply caused by y. For the sake of argument, though, let us pursue the matter further, as if tree rings do represent the age of the tree, in keeping with our best tracking theory. Here it's important to distinguish between cognition and representation. Representations are part of the cognitive scientist's tool kit, but no one in the field thinks that the activation of representations alone accounts for intelligent behavior (the *explananda* that the standard package was assembled to explain). Trees don't use language, plan, remember, build buildings, construct scientific theories, and so forth, and they don't partly because they have only (objective) representations and none of the other components that contribute to the explanation of intelligent behavior. Recall, too, the contribution of interacting components to the creation of the illusion of subjective content. In this case, we judge that something is missing, relative to the human case, but it is a mistake to take that something to be a form of content (subjective content); it's everything else (architecture, interaction between representations, etc.) that's missing.

The fourth case involves subjective representation in the absence of objective representation. The clearest case would be that of a conscious being in a universe containing nothing else (Kriegel, this volume, Chapter 7). Again, I think an account of the possibility intuition falls out of my framework. In this world, the subject has within her all of the standard elements—including cognitive vehicles and their causal interrelations.

Epilogue

Have I eliminated subjective content, or rather provided a (perhaps boring) reduction of it? Readers might suspect that it's the latter, for why not take SUBJECTIVE CONTENT itself to represent—that is, to internal-externalistically track—a natural kind or property, the property had by collections of appropriately interrelated strings of mental representations (roughly, those related by inferential roles in the way the elements of a conception are supposed to be—perhaps with a special emphasis on diagnostic roles of certain connections relative to the determination that a given vehicle actually represents something)?

Although this seems like a reasonable reading of the situation, matters are not so straightforward. In the section "Mental Representation and Objective Content," I reviewed various reasons to be skeptical about the value of inferential- or conceptual-role content. If my concerns about such content are well founded, it plays no role in the causal-explanatory enterprise. By some lights, then, although interactions between various vehicles might be genuine aspects of reality—ones that supervene on natural processes that are part of the causal order or are covered by natural laws—they nevertheless fail to provide an appropriate target for tracking (cf. Kriegel, 2011, 96). At least on one conception of the naturalization of content, content-determining relations should hold between natural kinds or properties (Rupert, 1999); that would seem to be what it amounts to for intentionality or content to "really be something else" (Fodor, 1990), where that something else is part of the natural, causal order. If conceptions aren't natural kinds or properties, how can they enter into the causal relations that they must in order to be tracked, and thus represented?

Perhaps, though, I'm mining an excessively narrow-minded vein here, with regard to the relata of the tracking relation. Perhaps SUBJECTIVE CONTENT does genuinely track something along the lines of conceptions. In that case, I have offered a reduction of sorts, but one that vindicates only a very thin notion of subjective content, relative to how subjective content is often understood. This reduction provides no support, for example, for the view that the perceptual states of which we're immediately aware have intrinsic qualitative character or that the mind has immediate awareness of a rich sort of content that makes its theoretically interesting properties available directly to the cognitive processes that generate responses to thought experiments or produce verbal reports of philosophical intuitions. Moreover, on this view, the reduced notion of subjective content is a structured collection of interrelated vehicle strings, not something that attaches to an individual mental representation, atomic or compound (of the form of a simple sentence). It may be something real—there to be picked out by tracking vehicles—but may play no role in cognition or the production of behavior, beyond their of the activation of the vehicles doing the tracking.

Notes

1. Naturalism is not equivalent to empiricism. The former holds that the theoretical, analytical, and experimental methods employed by our most successful sciences provide the best method for finding the truth or acquiring knowledge (or justified beliefs), but naturalism makes no commitment—quite the contrary—to the view that all concepts are constructs from observations, impressions, or sensory experiences or that all justification rests solely on empirical observation; in other words, any sensible naturalist should reject empiricism.
2. The characterization of a representation's being minimal with respect to content is a tricky matter. If content is purely externalist, then one might think the only semantically minimal representations are representations of fundamental particles, forces, or relations; in all other cases, the thing represented is physically (or metaphysically) compound and thus, as a semantic value, not atomic.
3. Conceptions promise to play a useful role from the perspective of cognitive engineering: the conception of x's contains information particularly relevant to reasoning or problem solving vis-à-vis x's; when an x-related problem arises, executive processes access the conception of x—a computationally manageable collection of information—and, voila, the tools for a solution are at hand. At least one version of the frame problem arises, however, when we realize that almost any bit of a subject's knowledge, no matter how far removed from x's it seems at first blush, might be relevant to the solution of an x-related problem, depending on the context. If

our x-conception is to remain manageable, we seem bound to exclude much of this potentially relevant information, at significant cost: our model of cognition cannot explain how people quickly and fluidly access all manner of contextually relevant information.

4. Dualist philosophers sometimes reject the idea of an entity to which subjective content is presented and instead take the relevant relation to be something more like constitution; on the latter view, subjective content partly constitutes the states of the subject. This may be a promising path to pursue (whether within a dualist framework or not), but such pursuit should comprise the development of an adequate theory of processing—that is, an account of how something that constitutes one part of the self interacts with other things so as to give the erroneous intuition that the constitutive part is being presented to the whole. So far as I understand what it is for x to be presented to y, its holding entails that x is wholly distinct from y. I suspect that such a story, once told, will make reference to elements and relations structurally similar to those of the objective account. In doing so, it may lend itself to an eliminativist account (in the terms used by Kriegel) of subjective content, of the sort to be developed below.

5. The use of, for example, 'UNICORN' refers to a certain vehicle individuated nonsemantically—say, in terms of its computational role or some of its neural characteristics. Which vehicle? It is easiest to designate it as the one that systematically controls utterances of 'unicorn'.

6. The treatment of the attempt at a priori knowledge in this case does not place it on par with other attempts at a priori knowledge. We may be able to achieve more reliable a priori mathematical knowledge by applying structural operations to vehicles that represent number properties (in my view, via a causal semantics: TWO tracks *two-ness* in the environment, so far as I can tell). It is one thing to track structural relations and perform structurally sensitive operations that preserve truth; this ability may be built into the architecture and may facilitate the acquisition of mathematical knowledge. It is another thing to think that when one vehicle tracks the activation of another vehicle, the former thereby can produce accurate reports about the various properties of the tracked vehicle; thus, there's plenty of room for, and reason for, skepticism in the case of supposed a priori reasoning about the workings of our own minds that does not automatically bleed over to other domains in which we think we have a priori knowledge. Thanks to David Chalmers for pressing me on this issue.

7. This thought can be extended to the case of phenomenal experience: my thinking about what it's like for me to see red is just to think about the sensory vehicle that plays the red-detection role in my actual life!

References

Block, N. (1986). Advertisement for a semantics for psychology. In P. French, T. Uehling, and H. Wettstein (eds.), *Midwest studies in philosophy: Studies in the philosophy of mind*, vol. 10 (pp. 615–78). Minneapolis: University of Minnesota Press.

Block, N. (1995). On a confusion about a function of consciousness. *Behavioral and Brain Sciences* 18, 227–287.

Burge, T. (1986). Individualism and psychology. *Philosophical Review* 95, 3–45.

Chalmers, D. (1996). *The conscious mind: In search of a fundamental theory.* Oxford: Oxford University Press.

Chemero, A. (2009). *Radical embodied cognitive science.* Cambridge, MA: MIT Press.

Chomsky, N. (1959). A review of B. F. Skinner's *Verbal Behavior. Language* 35, 26–58.

Cummins, R. (1996). *Representations, targets, and attitudes.* Cambridge, MA: MIT Press, 1996.

Dretske, F. (1981). *Knowledge and the flow of information.* Cambridge, MA: MIT Press.

Dretske, F. (1988). *Explaining behavior: Reasons in a world of causes.* Cambridge, MA: MIT Press.

Fodor, J. (1975). *The language of thought.* Cambridge, MA: Harvard University Press.

Fodor, J. (1987). *Psychosemantics: The problem of meaning in the philosophy of mind.* Cambridge, MA: MIT Press.

Fodor, J. (1990). *A theory of content and other essays.* Cambridge, MA: MIT Press.

Fodor J. (1994). *The elm and the expert: Mentalese and its semantics*. Cambridge, MA: MIT Press.

Fodor, J. (1998). *Concepts: Where cognitive science went wrong*. Oxford: Oxford University Press.

Fodor, J., and LePore, E. (1992). *Holism: A shopper's guide*. Oxford: Blackwell.

Forbes, G. (1989). Cognitive architecture and the semantics of belief. In P. French, T. Uehling, and H. Wettstein (eds.), *Midwest studies in philosophy*, vol. 14 (pp. 84–100). Notre Dame: Notre Dame University Press.

Goldman-Rakic, P. (1987). Circuitry of primate prefrontal cortex and regulation of behavior by representational memory. In F. Plum and V. Mountcastle (eds.), *Handbook of physiology*, vol. 5 (pp. 373–417). Bethesda, MD: American Physiological Society.

Jackson, F. (1982). Epiphenomenal qualia. *Philosophical Quarterly* 32, 127–136.

Kriegel, U. (2011). *The sources of intentionality*. Oxford: Oxford University Press.

Kripke, S. (1980). *Naming and necessity*. Cambridge, MA: Harvard University Press.

Levine, J. (1983). Materialism and qualia: The explanatory gap. *Pacific Philosophical Quarterly* 64, 354–61.

McDowell, J. (1994). The content of perceptual experience. *Philosophical Quarterly* 44, 190–205.

Miller, G.A. (1956). The magical number seven, plus or minus two: Some limits on our capacity for processing information. *Psychological Review* 63, 81–97.

Millikan, R.G. (1984). *Language, thought, and other biological categories*. Cambridge, MA: MIT Press.

Minsky, M. (1974). A framework for representing knowledge. MIT-AI Laboratory Memo 306.

Newell, A., and Simon, H. (1997). Computer science as empirical inquiry: Symbols and search. In J. Haugeland (ed.), *Mind design II: Philosophy, psychology, and artificial intelligence* (pp. 81–110). Cambridge, MA: MIT Press. Reprinted from the *Communication of the association for computing machinery*, 19 (March 1976), 113–26.

Port, R., and van Gelder, T. (Eds.). (1995). *Mind as motion*. Cambridge, MA: MIT Press.

Pylyshyn, Z. (1984). *Computation and cognition: Toward a foundation for cognitive science*. Cambridge, MA: MIT Press.

Ramsey, W. (2007). *Representation reconsidered*. Cambridge: Cambridge University Press.

Rumelhart, D., McClelland, J., and the PDP Research Group. (1986). *Parallel distributed processing: Explorations in the microstructure of cognition*. Vol. 1, *Foundations*. Cambridge, MA: MIT Press.

Rupert, R. (1998). On the relationship between naturalistic semantics and individuation criteria for terms in a language of thought. *Synthese* 117, 95–131.

Rupert, R. (1999). The best test theory of extension: First principle(s). *Mind & Language* 14, 321–55.

Rupert, R. (2008). Frege's puzzle and Frege cases: Defending a quasi-syntactic solution. *Cognitive Systems Research* 9, 76–91.

Rupert, R. (2009). *Cognitive systems and the extended mind*. Oxford: Oxford University Press.

Skinner, B.F. (1957). *Verbal behavior*. Acton, MA: Copley Publishing Group.

Stanford, P.K., and Kitcher, P. (2000). Refining the causal theory of reference for natural kind terms. *Philosophical Studies* 97, 99–129.

Stich, S. (1983). *From folk psychology to cognitive science: The case against belief*. Cambridge, MA: MIT Press.

Wittgenstein, L. (1953). *Philosophical investigations*. G.E.M. Anscombe and R. Rhees (eds.), G.E.M. Anscombe (trans.). Oxford: Blackwell.

Suggestions for Further Reading

Dretske, Fred. 1981. *Knowledge and the Flow of Information*. Cambridge, MA: MIT Press.
This book offers an information-theoretic account of the nature of mental representation, according to which mental states carry information about the world in virtue of bearing certain counterfactual-dependence relations on it.
Fodor, Jerry. 1975. *The Language of Thought*. Cambridge, MA: Harvard University Press.
This agenda-setting book argues that the medium of thought is language-like, and therefore representational, in that it involves internal states with semantic value and syntactic structure.
Loar, Brian. 2003. "Phenomenal Intentionality as the Basis for Mental Content." In *Reflections and Replies: Essays on the Philosophy of Tyler Burge*, ed. M. Hahn and B. Ramberg, 229–257. Cambridge, MA: MIT Press.
This seminal paper sketches an overarching outlook on mental representation as fully derived from the primitive power of conscious experience to present the world outside it.
McGinn, Colin. 1988. "Consciousness and Content." In *Proceedings of the British Academy* 76: 219–239.
This is an early exploration of the idea that the mind's representational powers may be grounded in consciousness; it is argued that conscious experience is not just an accidental medium of representation but entails its own distinctive type of representation.

PART V

The Nature of Mind
The Importance of Consciousness

CHAPTER 9

Speaking Up for Consciousness

CHARLES SIEWERT

Chapter Overview

This chapter begins by explaining what is meant by 'phenomenally conscious' in a way that unites and develops three ideas commonly used to introduce this notion: that conscious states are none other than *experiences*; that there is *something it's like* for one to be in them; and that in the case of vision they stand out by contrast with their absence in blindsight. On the basis of the resulting conception of consciousness, a case for its importance is made along the following lines. Conscious experience gives us warrant for judgments about both the things it reveals and experience itself. Moreover, consciousness underlies our grasp of language and is arguably essential to our having minds at all. Finally, it has enormous ethical significance, since it lies at the heart of our concern for ourselves and for others.

Introduction

Is consciousness important? "Well, isn't it obvious? I mean, if we were *uncon-scious*, and just *slept* through everything, we'd miss a lot." This would be an understandable response to what is, after all, a fairly strange thing to ask. But to learn something from the question we need to hear it in a way that makes the answer less evident.

We could begin by saying that we're not asking specifically about the importance of *being awake*. For one thing, consciousness in the sense at issue may be reasonably thought to occur in both waking and sleeping. When, in waking life, someone you see *looks* a certain way to you, and when asleep, you *dream someone looks* that way to you—these might both be counted as "states of consciousness," "subjective experiences," episodes in your "stream of consciousness." Secondly (more provocatively), some conscious states—experiences—can go missing even when someone is awake and visually responsive. Most people are familiar with the idea that we may respond to visual stimuli that we at most only *unconsciously* perceive. What does it matter then that we have *conscious* states—experiences? What does consciousness do for us? Answering these questions is far from straightforward.

Partly this is because it is difficult to explain just what should be understood by 'consciousness' in the relevant sense. It is unclear (to say the least) that we share some prephilosophical, "folk," or "commonsense" interpretation of the word sufficiently discerning and stable to merit our trust. In any case, when authors try to explain their understanding of this term, perplexities soon arise—along with large disagreements regarding what sort of states or activities are conscious in the sense at issue, and how (if at all) consciousness is involved in the exercise of intellect and character. These problems—concerning the "scope" of consciousness—bear significantly on our main question.

Here is how I want to grapple with this complex of issues. I will first explain how to understand consciousness in the sense gestured at with talk of "subjective experience"—what has lately been called *phenomenal* consciousness—while initially remaining neutral on certain basic controversies. I will then summarize my stance on these questions, saying why I think that consciousness is pervasively involved in both perception and thought. Finally, against this background, I will argue that consciousness is that through which we know what's around us, what's on our minds, and what we mean; it is that by which we have minds at all; and it lies at the heart of our concern for ourselves and for others. And if that doesn't make it important, what would?

Let me make a couple of disclaimers up front. First, I will not address the question of what causal impact consciousness has or doesn't have on the world. Though this issue often dominates philosophical attention, I believe the dimensions of importance I wish to examine here have priority. Second, I recognize that doing the relevant matters full justice requires much more than is possible in this essay.

Phenomenality: What It Is

'Consciousness' is a treacherous word. We must try to make as clear as we can what we are talking about. And much depends on how we start. For one thing, it is crucial to preempt the influence of certain questionable assumptions about the scope of phenomenal consciousness. Recall my query about how consciousness is involved in the "exercise of intellect and character." I lifted this phrase from Gilbert Ryle's *Concept of Mind* (1949/2009), a book whose influence did so much to create the academic subfield *Philosophy of Mind*.

The phrase occurs in the context of an implicit dismissal of the importance of consciousness, where he suggests that the "stream of consciousness" (if it comes to anything) contains nothing but a series of *sensations*—insufficient for the exercise of intellect and character, doing little to differentiate the minds of human beings from those of other animals, geniuses from idiots, the sane from the insane (ibid., 183–185).

This perspective had an enduring impact on the canon that took shape in philosophy of mind anthologies and introductory discussions. Ryle helped implant a lasting tendency either to quarantine consciousness (in the "stream" sense) off in some theoretical ghetto of "sensations" or "feels," where it could be segregated from intelligence and understanding, or else at least to narrow it to a subclass of distinctively sensory, cognitively primitive mental representations. As part of this tendency, many philosophers of the past sixty years or so have premised their discussions of mind on a contrast between "qualia"—the "qualitative character" or "feel" of, for example, sensations of color or pain—and "propositional attitudes" (e.g., a belief that something is the case). Consciousness in the sense lately termed *phenomenal*—what I will call "phenomenality"—has frequently been assumed to amount simply to the former—these sensory "qualia" or "feels."

We should take none of this picture for granted. It commands no pre-Rylean professional consensus, and if it attained orthodox status in certain circles, we ought to question the legitimacy with which it did so. To assume from the start that phenomenality is confined to a narrow sensory range is unnecessary and prejudicial. For this reason too I avoid the term 'qualia.'[1]

But then just how *are* we to begin? We need to explain how to interpret 'phenomenal consciousness' in a manner substantive enough to get us started and neutral enough to leave open questions that shouldn't be begged. To this end, I have proposed an account that lays out three distinct but mutually supportive ways of understanding what phenomenality is. These I label the "subjective experience," "subjective contrast," and "subjective knowledge" conceptions.[2] Each needs an airing here, because each introduces ideas critical to the way I assess the importance of consciousness. I will explain each in turn.

Subjective Experience. I indicated earlier that a state conscious in the phenomenal sense is what is otherwise known as "an experience." And an experience—as it may seem innocuous to say—is something one experiences. But this is ambiguous. Consider first that I experienced a feeling (of anger, amusement, anxiety, etc.)—and *what was experienced* (the feeling) was *an experience*. Now also, I experienced Hurricane Sandy, and that—the hurricane—was *quite an experience*. These seem to be "experiences" in two rather different senses. In the first, "feeling" case (but not the second, "hurricane" case) *what is experienced*, the *experience*, is none other than—it simply coincides with—the *experiencing* of it.

This point gives us a first foothold in elucidating the notion of consciousness. Something is "an experience" in the sense in which all and only conscious states are, just when it *coincides with someone's experiencing it.* So a hurricane is *not*, but a feeling of anxiety *is* (or at least can be) in this sense "an experience," hence a conscious state. For an experienced *hurricane* does not coincide with anyone's experiencing it, while there is a sense in which an experienced *feeling* does.

The next step is to move beyond "feeling." To experience a feeling is to feel it. And one feels one's own feelings in a "coincident" or "internal accusative" sense. (The feeling felt is none other than the feeling of it.) But instances in which one *feels a feeling* are only members of a species of the broader class we're interested in: *experiencing an experience.* For example, normally, when you see something somehow colored and shaped, its color and shape *look* somehow to you. We don't normally speak of *looking* as a kind of *feeling*, nor do we say that something's looking red *feels* somehow to us. But in the same sense in which you experience your feelings, you can *experience* something's looking to you as it does; in that sense *you experience its visual appearance* (i.e., its appearing visually to you). Its looking to you as it does is thus an experience in the sense at issue—and so, a (phenomenally) conscious state.

The final move is to introduce talk about *differences in how* one experiences an experience. In the case of feelings, these will be differences in how some feeling feels to you—for example, the difference between how a pain feels and how an itch feels, or the difference between how two distinct pains feel to you. And this point too can be carried over even where we do not speak of "how a feeling feels." So, for example, something may look to you a certain color and shape. And how you experience its looking to you colored and shaped may change—say, as lighting, orientation, and focus of attention alter. We may also say, when this happens, that *how* it looks colored and shaped to you changes, as long as we recognize that this does not entail that something then *appears to you to change shape or color.* In fact, during this change in how you experience the appearance of a certain shape and color, it may nonetheless *appear or look the same* in shape and color.

We will return to this important point (about phenomenal constancy). For the moment just note this. In the same ("internal accusative") sense in which you may experience a feeling, you may also experience something's looking to you somehow colored and shaped. And just as we may speak of differences in *how your feeling feels* to you, we may speak of differences in *how you experience something's looking blue and circular* to you. And we may take these latter also to determine differences in how something looks to you. But all this is compatible with saying that what looks blue and circular to you is not the experience, the visual appearance of color and shape. For even as the experience *changes*, what looks blue and circular may also both *look* and *be constant* in color and shape.

Pulling all these remarks together, a state of S is *phenomenally conscious* just in case it is an experience S experiences in the *coincident* sense and differs from other experiences with respect to *how it is in this sense experienced.* Differences in how experiences are experienced are differences in their *phenomenal character*. And differences in phenomenal character of your experience are differences in what *phenomenal features* you have. To the aforementioned examples of looking and feeling, I would immediately add sensory appearances generally. Instances of something's sounding, tasting, smelling, or (tactually) feeling somehow to someone are phenomenal—provided they are experienced in this internal accusative sense. But how rich the variations are in how one experiences appearances (whether they would distinguish geniuses from idiots, for example), and whether experiences are all merely sensory in nature, or whether occurrent *conceptual thought* is *also* experienced in the coincident sense—these "scope" questions—we may initially leave open. I call this the "subjective experience" conception of phenomenality. For experience in this sense coincides with the subject's experience of it and differs in kind whenever the subject experiences it differently.[3]

Subjective Contrast. Let's move now to a second way of understanding phenomenality. Here we cast consciousness into relief by considering—from the subject's point of view—the difference between *having* and *lacking* it (or more precisely, the difference between having and lacking certain varieties of it). To this end it is helpful to consider how we might interpret the clinical phenomenon of "blindsight." As is now well-known, this is a condition in which subjects suffering damage to the visual cortex deny seeing types of visual stimuli in circumstances where—pretrauma—they would have readily affirmed it, even though now (when "forced" to select from a list of set options) they show the ability to successfully identify these types of stimulus they deny they see. On one interpretation of the condition, to say that such subjects have "blindsight" is to say that in *one* sense they *do see* the relevant stimulus (they have sight), and in *another* they *do not* (they're blind). To identify the relevant sense in which they *don't* see, first, consider a specifically visual sense of 'look' in which no object in a pitch dark room *looks* any way at all to a person. Now, interpret 'see' in such a way that a person cannot be rightly said to *see* something that *looks* to her no way at all. Then, regarding blindsight, we say that in this sense, the blindsighter correctly denies *seeing* the stimulus, even though she correctly discriminates it (in verbal judgments, in movement) because retinal stimulation from it triggers activity in what's left of her visual system. So in a sense she's blind to the stimulus, she doesn't see it—for it doesn't look anyhow to her. But in another she does see it: the sort of discrimination of visual stimuli she retains could also be regarded as a kind of "seeing." Once we have this conception of blindsight, we can consider the prospect of forms apparently more removed from actual cases. For example, we may conceive of the blindsight judgments arising *spontaneously*—without forced choice prompting—though the judged stimuli still don't look any way to you.

Yet further refinements on the conceptual exercise are possible.[4] But without drilling any deeper, we can use what we now have to elucidate what phenomenality is. It is that feature exemplified in cases of something's looking somehow to you, as it would not be in blindsight. Similar reflections could be conducted using other "appearance" words—'sound,' 'smell,' 'taste,' and 'feel'—yielding analogous contrasts between phenomenal perception, and a kind of "blind" discriminatory capacity vis-à-vis sensory stimuli. Necessarily, any instance of its looking somehow to you (sounding somehow, etc.) in the sense conspicuous in our imagined subjective contrast is a *phenomenally conscious state*, and an instance of such a feature is a *phenomenal* feature. We might then define the notion of phenomenal differences among these features—and of variations in "phenomenal character"—by saying that these are differences such as may obtain only among phenomenally conscious states, and which are (in at least some contexts) subjectively discernible (discernible to first-person reflection). While this "subjective contrast" conception picks out the phenomenal sense with reference to sensory paradigms, nothing inherent to it implies that differences in phenomenal character cannot go beyond the merely sensory. And perhaps we can analogously give content to some notion of "blindthought" to contrast with cases where things are "cognitively apparent" to us. Again at this stage, we simply note this "scope" issue and leave it in suspense.

Subjective Knowledge. We come now to the third conception. We might also call this the "what it's like" conception. It has become common to train attention on phenomenal consciousness by use of this locution—saying something along the lines of: phenomenally conscious states, experiences, are states that there is *something it's like for one to be in* (something it's like for the experiencer).[5] But the locution is puzzling. Moreover, it seems that it makes good sense to speak of "what it's like for someone" in many cases where we would not want to assume we are identifying a state that is conscious in the targeted sense.

Consider, for example, the daring feat of Felix Baumgartner. On October 14, 2012, he ascended in a tiny capsule suspended from a helium balloon to a height of 24 miles above the earth. Then he jumped. Hurtling back down at more than 800 miles an hour, he finally opened his parachute to make a safe landing. It seemed natural to many of us to wonder, "What was that like for him?" But while our question assumes, plausibly, that there was something it was like for him to fall as he did, it seems doubtful that we should regard his *falling* as phenomenally conscious, in just the sense in which things *looking* to him as they did during the fall or his then *feeling* as he did could be said to be conscious. His fall was not "an *experience*" in the sense that would require it *coincide* with his experience of it. For we should probably want to say that it could have occurred *unexperienced* by him—as presumably it would have if (unhappily) he had passed out the moment he leapt. And in that case, we should say that *for him* there would have been *nothing* it was like to fall to earth—nothing of this sort we could sensibly be curious about—any more than we suppose there is in the case of a falling meteor. This suggests that where some types of states are concerned (like falling), there is something that it is like for one to be in them only *nonessentially*—due to the contingent presence of other types of states.

We might add that even when there *is* essentially something it's like for one to be in a certain type of state, still there might only *derivatively* be something that's like—if knowledge of what it's like arises only from knowing what it's like to be in *other* types of states that could be found without it.[6]

These reflections lead to the following strategy for homing in on consciousness. With some types of states, there is *essentially and nonderivatively something it's like for one* to be in them. These types constitute the genuine phenomenal features; the states that instance them are the bona fide phenomenally conscious states. So, for example, even if there was nothing essentially and nonderivatively that it was like for Felix to *fall*, there *is* something it's like for one to *feel* the way it felt to him to fall. There is *essentially* something this was like for him, because one couldn't possibly feel this same way when there was just *nothing* that was like for one. There is *nonderivatively* something this was like for him, because there is no *further* feature, to which feeling this way is inessential, such that what it was like for him to feel this way derived entirely from the presence of *that* feature.[7] So feeling this way (that *type*) is a phenomenal feature, and this particular occasion of feeling (that *instance*) is a conscious state.

But how should we interpret this "something/what it's like" locution to which I have made appeal? I propose the following. Knowledge of what it's like to have some feature is a certain kind of "subjective knowledge" of it. In part, and more specifically, it is knowledge *of what feature it is*, which requires either *having the feature oneself or being able to imagine having it*. And this is a certain *nontheoretical* knowledge. That is to say, a knowledge of what feature it is that does not require one can give a theoretically satisfying account or explanation of that feature. (Contrast this with what we would expect of someone who claimed to know what mass or velocity is.) Notice that on this account, again, it is perfectly alright to say that there is something it was like for Felix to fall. However, falling of this sort is not a phenomenal feature (and an instance of falling is not a conscious state), if this feature is not *essentially* suited for one to claim or desire knowledge of what it's like to have it. For—and this is the basic proposal—a phenomenal feature is a feature essentially suited for one to claim or desire a nontheoretical and not just derivative, subjective knowledge regarding what feature it is. And a phenomenally conscious state is an instance of a phenomenal feature. Such instances differ in "phenomenal character" just when the features in question differ phenomenally—that is, they differ in some way that makes them essentially suitable for one to claim or desire a subjective, nontheoretical, nonderivative knowledge of what that difference is.

I offer this third and final, "subjective knowledge," "what it's like" conception of phenomenality as a complement to the previous two. The three, I maintain, harmoniously converge. Bringing the third together with the first, we may see that *differences in what it's like* (essentially and nonderivatively) for one to have phenomenal features are *differences in how an experience is experienced* by a subject. Bringing the third together with the second "subjective contrast" conception, in the sense in which something may *look chartreuse* to you—a kind of "look" that we have supposed must be missing in a blindsight case—there is, essentially and nonderivatively, *something it's like for it to look that way to you*. Finally, bringing the second together with the first, for something to look (sound, smell, etc.) some way to you is for you to experience (in the internal accusative sense) its looking (sounding, smelling, etc.) to you as it does: its looking (etc.) to you these ways are experiences that coincide with your experiencing them.

The union of these three conceptions constitutes my basic explanation of what I mean by '(phenomenally) conscious state,' 'phenomenality,' 'phenomenal character,' and 'phenomenal feature.'

The Scope of Phenomenality

I need now to show how to move beyond this initial "base" conception to a view more committed with respect to the controversies—especially those relating to the "scope" of consciousness—first held in suspense. For this is essential to addressing the question of importance. So let me lay out the rudiments of my view.[8]

On the basis of my understanding of sensory appearances (ways of looking, feeling, etc.), and the phenomenology of object constancy (derived from my "subjective experience" and "subjective contrast" conceptions), I find that the phenomenal character of sense experience brings with it a kind of object-directedness—it makes experience "objectual," we might say. And if, in large measure through the exercise of sensorimotor skills, you can make spatial objects stably apparent, and exercise an ability to "get a better look" at things so as to improve or correct appearances—of shape, color, location, movement, texture, and so forth—then you've got all you need to have phenomenal features assessable as accurate or correct, inaccurate or illusory. Since what it's like for you to sense suffices for such objectuality and assessibility, it suffices for the kind of intentionality involved in perceiving the location, shape, and movement of things, and where certain colors, sounds, flavors, and scents occur.

On my view, the phenomenal character of sense experience is yet still richer in the way it makes objects "significant" to us than this alone suggests. Here I draw on my *subjective knowledge* conception of consciousness. There is essentially something it's like for us to *recognize*, sensorily, things as of given kinds when we perceive them, and what it's like is not entirely derivative from what it's like for things to appear to us merely spatially distributed in a certain way. There is irreducibly something it's like for that orange thing to look to you *recognizable as a pumpkin* (it looks "pumpkin-ish") and something it's like for the "face" carved in it to look to you "surprised" or "sinister."[9] Someone may ask whether this means sense experience has "conceptual content."[10] But the question is not, I believe, entirely well formed. What I would say is that insofar as capacities for perceptual recognition are *part* of what is involved in concept possession, and these capacities are arguably not—where at least *some* concepts are concerned—entirely detachable from *full* concept possession (involving relevant inferential abilities), conceptual understanding is implicated in the phenomenal character of adult human sense experience. Furthermore, even when—outside the context of perceptual recognition—we enjoy varying occurrent conceptual thought and linguistic understanding, what this is like for us is not discernibly just the same as what it's like for us to have sense and imagery experience of the sort one could have in the complete *absence* of conceptual understanding. Thus there are "cognitive" as well as sensory phenomenal features. (Or as some like to say, there is "cognitive phenomenology."[11]) We experience conceptual thought and understanding just as surely as we experience tickles and tastes.

Although the view just summarized makes intentionality or "content" internal to phenomenal character of the sort we typically enjoy, it commits to no "reductive representationalist" theory of consciousness—whether "first-order"[12] or "higher-order."[13] And in fact, I use my account to argue against such views.[14] The key point here is just that there is a defensible conception on which the phenomenal character of experience embraces object perception and recognition together with occurrent linguistic understanding and conceptual thought. Only in light of such an inclusive (not "stingy") conception of consciousness, I believe, do we judge its importance fairly.

Perceptual Knowledge and Introspection

I now will discuss two aspects of what I call the *epistemic* import of consciousness. Consider first how we confirm or disconfirm ordinary perceptual judgments about what is in our surroundings. Here is one I confirm just about every morning: *There's a pair of socks*—clean and of the right size and (matching) color.

How do I manage this? I do it by getting a *good enough look at* something to make such judgments. And how good a look I get at something is a matter of *how it looks to me*. I need something to look to me—to visually appear to me—clearly and in enough detail, close enough, for long enough, in good enough light, with adequate constancy in its color, shape, size, and location appearance, for me to have warrant to judge: *these are clean, matching socks.* And getting a good enough look allows me to confirm as well as I do such ordinary judgments because of how I coordinate looking with other sensorimotor activity: I touch and feel my socks. Perhaps I (cautiously!) sniff and smell them.

Making things in this way apparent to myself (and thereby warranting what I think about them) is typically a spontaneous, effortless, and nondeliberative activity. And it need involve no conscious "higher-order" thoughts about my experience. To confirm or disconfirm judgments in the way I've suggested does not require that I think about myself as doing such things or that I form an intention to do them for such and such reasons: for example, I don't necessarily *decide* to look harder at what's before me *in order to* confirm or test a judgment. And warranting judgments does not necessarily involve justifying beliefs by inferring their truth from other beliefs held. By getting a good enough look at something, you can confirm (and thus warrant) a judgment about it, just as surely as you can by inferring its truth from what you believe.

This view is rooted in my conception of the experience of sensory constancy. Visual experience can enable us to identify public spatial objects, and to make judgments about their location, size, color, and shape, only if it exhibits the forms of stability that allow us to track objects constant with respect to these features through variations in their appearance. We are able to rely on appearances to make, confirm, and correct the judgments of location, shape, color, and size, just because experiencing something's visual appearance *varies* as it does when one experiences an appearance of something *constant* in location, shape, color, and size.

Once we grant this basic picture, we have reason to think that consciousness has considerable *epistemic* significance—it is enormously important with respect to perceptual knowledge and warrant. Its looking to me in ways that constitute my getting a good look at something (and its otherwise sensorily appearing to me well enough for me to get a "good feel," "hear," "taste," or "smell" of something) is for me to have phenomenally conscious experience. And it is ordinarily through making things thus apparent to myself that I can make warranted judgments about perceived things. Therefore, the possession of common sensory phenomenal features plays a pervasive role in warranting common judgments about what I find around me. And without warrant for making *such* judgments, I would arguably have none for *any* I make about the world in which I move and live.

Now let's look at a second dimension of epistemic import—relating to introspection. There are various ways of arguing that consciousness is crucial to the distinctive right with which we judge of our own minds. Here is how I make the connection.[15]

To start, consider forms of thought expressible with phrases such as "The way this feels to me . . ."; "The way this tastes to me . . ."; "The color this looks to me . . ." We can use complex phrases like these combining demonstratives or indexicals[16] and "appearance" words to identify phenomenal features. These can express ways of thinking—in one blow—both about *features of surrounding objects* (color, shape, etc.) and *our own (phenomenal) features* (things looking, tasting, feeling, etc., to us as they do). Let us call these "phenomenal-indexical thoughts." Now notice that in some such phenomenal-indexical thought you can identify *what* phenomenal feature you are thinking of in a way that enables you to *recognize further characterizations of it as correct or incorrect.*

For example, I might think of a given color merely as "The color this looks to me . . ." (thereby thinking also of its looking to me as it does), prior to classifying it using general color vocabulary, such as 'green,' 'purple,' or 'fuschia.' (That is, I understand which color I mean when thinking of it as *the color this looks to me*, and there is no general nonindexical classification C, such that, had I not thought of the color this looks to me *as C*, I wouldn't be thinking of that specific color at all.) So I understand in this preclassificatory way what color *and what way of looking* I am thinking of, so as to be able to go on to complete the phrase with some recognizably correct (or incorrect) classification: "The color this looks to me . . . is *maroon*." Similarly: "The way this [wine] tastes to me . . . is *flinty*." "The way this feels to me . . . is *viscous*." In any case, we can in this way identify what phenomenal feature we're thinking of and recognize how to classify it. I will put this by saying that this form of thought sometimes constitutes "identification for recognition" of phenomenal features.

From the sheer fact that I know what feature I'm thinking of when I say "The color this looks to me," we can't infer straightaway that I do in fact have the phenomenal feature of which I am thinking (i.e., that this thing does look that way to me). Consider that I may well know just what feature I am thinking of when I say "The color this looks to *you*," even though it does not look to you as I thought it did. But the first-person case is different. There is reason to hold that, whenever I identify for recognition some phenomenal feature in *first-person* thought, *I myself actually have the very feature identified*. For recall what phenomenal features *are* (on my "subjective knowledge" conception): these are features essentially suited for one to claim or desire a subjective, nontheoretical knowledge regarding what features they are, not entirely derived from other such knowledge. If that's indeed what they are, then at least some of these features will be such that *you and I* do sometimes know what features they are by having them ourselves. For if we're entitled to think such features are instantiated at all, we know what at least some of them are in this way (by having them). We would have no right to think there even *are* features essentially suited to be known firsthand if *we* had absolutely no such knowledge of them. But then, just when *do* we know what these features are by having them? We would *never* know what such features are in this way, if we didn't have such features whenever we identified them for recognition in first-person thought. For there is just no better candidate occasion for us, no more favorable condition, in which to have this sort of knowledge. This yields the result that whenever you successfully identify *phenomenal* features for recognition in *first-person* thoughts, you actually have them.

Now, I sometimes do take myself to understand *which* feature I am thinking and speaking of, when I say something like, "The color that looks to me" or "The way this feels to me." And in the absence of reasons to doubt this, I am in a particular case entitled to presume I *do* understand what I am speaking of. (That I understand/know what I mean when I speak is, I take it, a defeasible but warranted presumption of rational discourse generally.) So lacking reasons to think I don't understand what I mean, I am entitled to think I do identify phenomenal features for recognition in first-person thoughts. And then—based on the principle that when I do this, I actually have the features identified—it follows that I am entitled to believe I do have specific phenomenal features: those of which I would be thinking/speaking. Thus I have warrant for certain (admittedly as yet meager!) first-person judgments—judgments such as *The color this looks to me is apparent to me* and *I feel this way now*.

But we can add to this meager kernel. For I would not understand 'looks' and 'feels' (and other appearance words) if I were not generally competent in correctly *further* qualifying them *somehow*—by, for example, attaching color terms to 'looks' or terms like *itchy* and *painful* to 'feels.' If I am to understand 'looks' as it figures in an expression of phenomenal-indexical thought, I need competence in saying things like: 'The color this looks to me is…green.' 'This way I now feel is…itchy.'[17] So, provided there is no reason to doubt my competence with basic color and "feeling" vocabulary, if I have warrant for *the meager* first-person judgments, I also have warrant for slightly less meager—let's call them "rudimentary"—judgments, such as *This looks green to me* and *I feel an itch now*. Similar remarks, I suggest, would apply to many first-person judgments about sensory appearances.

We can expand this beyond the "rudimentary," to account for the warrant with which we can make somewhat more "nuanced" judgments about our experience—including the sort that figure in the phenomenological arguments I've been giving—such as the judgment that the ways something's shape appears to me can differ, even as it does not appear to me to change shape. And, I would venture, once we recognize that there are (not just sensory) but *cognitive* phenomenal features, we can construct a similar story there. I can attend to what I am (or *was* just) *thinking*, by noticing the way it (cognitively, phenomenally) *seems* (just *seemed*) to me. I thereby identify what it's like for me to think/understand as I do on a given occasion (as *the way it seems to me*). I identify that (cognitive) phenomenal feature—one which, when I thus succeed in thinking of it, I inevitably *actually have*. And, in trying to *articulate* how it (cognitively) seems to me (as I must be able to do, if I am to think verbally at all), I can recognize the aptness (or inaptness) of my expression.

It would certainly be fair to ask for more details about all this. But if this account of introspection (or one relevantly similar[18]) is correct, there is a second dimension of epistemic significance to acknowledge. For we have a warrant for judgments about things appearing to us as they do, and about our thinking of them as we do, which derives from (i) the fact that we can identify for recognition a phenomenal feature in first-person thought, and that when we do, we actually *have* the very feature we identify, together with (ii) a (defeasible) presumption that we understand what we're talking about. Since the sort of warrant provided is distinctively first personal, and since it essentially depends on the phenomenality of our sensory and cognitive states, in recognizing it, we see that consciousness bears a second major kind of epistemic import. In addition to providing a distinctive kind of warrant to our perceptual judgments about what's around us, it furnishes a special sort of warrant to "introspective" claims.

Mind and Meaning

The next dimension of importance I propose concerns linguistic understanding. Think again of a case where you understand 'the shape this looks to me' in virtue of something's visual appearance to you. Now compare this with a hypothetical blindsight case, in which (necessarily) the visual stimulus does *not* look any way to you. Since you have blindsight, you have some kind of *visual* capacity with respect to the stimuli you discriminate. Further, it is commonly thought that there can be nonphenomenal visual representation. So we can suppose that, in a case where you "blindsee" something, if you were to speak of 'the shape I *visually represent* this to be,' there would be something for your words to pick out. Now let your overt discriminatory behavior toward the stimulus be as spontaneous as you please. The issue is this. In the phenomenal case, you understand what you mean by 'the shape this *looks* to me,' prior to classifying it in general terms (as, e.g., a 'circle'). But what about in the blindsight case, where the stimulus does not look any way to you—would you understand, in this preclassificatory way, *which* shape you spoke of as 'the shape I *visually represent* this to be'?

Imagining myself in this scenario, it seems to me I would not understand which shape it was (if any) that I "visually represented" *this shape* to be—except insofar as I classified that shape in general, nonindexical terms (as a circle, triangle, or whatever). My nonconscious vision just would not put me in a position to have a preclassificatory knowledge or understanding of *which* shape that was. (Much as I am in no position to know which shape I'm speaking of, if I say 'the shape of the most frequently inscribed Etruscan letter.' I just have no idea which one that is.) I would seem to lack such understanding in the scenario, as long as I am forbidden to draw on *other phenomenal perception*—for example, tactual/proprioceptive—of the stimulus, or perhaps some experience of *imagination* (visualizing a shape), to supply myself with an interpretation.

Suppose you share my judgment about the hypothetical case. Let us also assume that if you did understand such demonstrative phrases to pick out a specific feature on their occasion of utterance, then you should be able to tell that you did. The lesson then is this. Nonphenomenal visual representation would not enable you to understand a phrase like 'the shape I visually represent this to be' to pick out a specific shape—it wouldn't afford you a preclassificatory knowledge of *which* shape *that* was by perceiving it. Thus, allowing for a moment a use of 'see' that could apply to either phenomenal or nonphenomenal vision, we might also say that blindsight could not furnish us the same wherewithal as conscious vision to interpret the phrase 'the I shape I see this to be,' so as to understand which shape was meant.

Let's consider now a phrase where we leave out the "appearance" (e.g., 'looks') talk and simply combine a demonstrative with a generic term to form a "type demonstrative"—like 'this shape.' Relying only on some form of *non-conscious* vision, could I be furnished with a preclassificatory understanding of *which* shape was meant by 'this shape' on an occasion of its utterance? Here nothing *looks* to me shaped anyhow at all; I cannot identify, prior to classification, which shape (if any) I (nonconsciously) see something to be; and I cannot rely on nonvisual modalities to perceive the shape. In such circumstances, it seems to me I would also lack a preclassificatory, identification-for-recognition, perceptual understanding of just which shape *this shape* is.

This seems to show that to secure the relevant understanding I need *phe-nomenal* perception. Similar considerations would, I believe, yield similar results regarding understanding "type demonstratives" for color ('this color'), and the argument could be extended to other modalities and the sensibles associated with them ('this sound,' 'this flavor,' etc.). In sum, I cannot get a basic, perception-based understanding of type demonstratives without reliance on appearances.[19]

Now, to return specifically to the case of shape, this also seems correct: to be able to *learn general shape terms* ('trapezoid' and 'rhombus') by perception, I need to have the sort of perception that would put me in a position to understand 'this shape' and 'that shape' as referring to different specific shapes, prior to classifying them in general nonindexical terms. I need the kind of perception that would enable me to know things of the form: *this* shape is the same as *that* shape, and different from *this other* one. If I had no perception of this kind, I would have none through which I could *learn* to understand general terms for shape. It follows that, had I lacked phenomenality, I would have been in no position to learn shape classifications perceptually.

This point surely is not specific to *shape* but applies to *size* ('this big') and *location* ('this far from here') as well. If so, then we can conclude that I could not have perceptually acquired the capacity for spatial thought with only *nonphenomenal* perception on which to rely. Could I then engage in general spatial thought at all? Perhaps it will seem I could, if I imagine that, without a capacity for perceptual learning, I may still be engaged in symbolically expressed *phenomenal thought*—so that what it's like for me is what it's like to be immersed in some silent soliloquy about geometry. I'm not sure that it is possible to have such an experiential understanding of shape concepts utterly ungrounded in perception. But if we suppose it is, we would still be making thought and understanding dependent on *phenomenality* of a (cognitive) sort. What if we remove even this? If we remove from my history any perception and learning capacities of the sort required for understanding, as well as experiential thought, what would be left that might possibly suffice to give me an understanding of general spatial terms? The only relevant activity it seems we can suppose still present when all this is taken away is the interpretable production of symbols: I manipulate symbols in a way that can be taken by an interpreter as, say, the construction of geometrical proofs. Here we might seem to have a cognitive analogue of blindsight—instead of a visual performance without visual appearance, a *cognitive* performance without *cognitive* appearance. However, if this kind of interpretable symbol production were *all* I were capable of, it wouldn't suffice for understanding. For one might follow rules for manipulating strings of symbols in a way that *accords* with a (geometrical) interpretation, without so understanding them oneself. One might move the symbols around in this manner while regarding them as only so many uninterpreted concatentations of shapes—not as symbols that *refer* to shapes.[20]

The moral seems to be that without phenomenality, I wouldn't understand words to express spatial concepts. But if I cannot understand spatial concepts, then plausibly, I cannot understand *any* ordinary concepts. For if 'circle' and 'square' are beyond me, and I can conceptualize no recognizable spatial features, how am I to grasp 'dog' or 'chair'? If this line of thought is correct, phenomenal features play essential epistemic roles in warranting thought about one's surroundings and one's own mind. Had we no phenomenality, we would not understand our own utterances—they would mean nothing to us.

Insofar as *understanding* is an epistemic notion, this gives us a third epistemic aspect of phenomenality's importance. But it leads further. For if we understood nothing by our utterances, we would *say* nothing with them and *express* nothing—no judgments, no desires, no commitments, no joy, regret, or respect. If what remained in the face of an utter lack of experiential understanding and perception would not enable us to have linguistically expressed attitudes, it would not enable us to have the very same types of attitudes *without* language. (If it did, we would have to say, incredibly, that the role of consciousness is just to supply the means for verbal articulation of attitudes we can have just fine speechlessly.) But now, if all this is right, and absent consciousness, we would have no perception of the sort adequate to play a role in concept acquisition and judgment formation, should we wish to call what might still remain "perception"? If so, we might say this would only be perception of a distinctively *mindless* sort. For there is an important difference between having and lacking the sort of perception that can support conceptual understanding, and (if the foregoing is correct) phenomenality is essential to having it. Assuming then that a lack of concept-supporting perception and experiential understanding would leave us without the resources for conceptual activity, and in that sense would make us "mindless," we can conclude that without consciousness we would have no minds.

Here you may say, "Still, isn't it at least conceivable that we could, through changes in our brains, *lose* consciousness entirely, but—perhaps because they have been 're-wired' and 'retrofitted'—continue to move around and produce sounds that would make our activities interpretable and predictable through mental state attributions?" (We would still be "intentional systems," in Daniel Dennett's terms.) So we can intelligibly envision becoming "zombies" in the philosophers' sense. Would we not still have minds?" No. For even if I concede the conceivability of my "zombification," such a scenario would entail that I had no perception that could give me a preclassificatory understanding of 'this shape.' So I would be unable to perceptually recognize that, for example, *this shape is a square*. And if I am unable to do this, and also incapable of *experiencing thought* about squares, I would no longer understand what 'square' means. At most I would have capacities for relevant interpretable symbol manipulation—which, again, doesn't suffice for understanding. The point remains that without consciousness nothing would mean anything to us, and we would, in a nontrivial sense, be literally mindless.[21]

From here we can argue that *nothing* could have a mind without consciousness. For will we say that maybe *other* types of creatures (extraterrestrials and computerized robots) *could* have totally nonconscious minds? If so, they would need to differ from us in some way *relevant* to giving them the minds we would lack without consciousness. But what are we to suppose they would have, which we *don't* have, that would give them genuine (albeit "zombie") minds, where we need consciousness? Perhaps they are supposed to be internally physically very different from us, or have a different computational architecture. But why in the world would *that* give them an alternative, *nonphenomenal* means to mental reality? Unless you can put your finger on a difference between us and whatever sort of zombies (if any) you wish to countenance, and explain why *that* difference should be relevant to giving *them* minds *we* can't have without consciousness—why *this* should give *them* what only *consciousness* can give *us*—then you should, I think, conclude that phenomenality is generally essential to mind. If this is right, then consciousness has not only epistemic but also a sort of *ontological* importance. That something has a mind is an important fact about *what it is*. It is presumably essential, for example, to being a *person*. This bears on the topic of the next section.

Ethical Significance

I turn finally to the *ethical* role of phenomenality. I take this as my point of departure. Individual persons (and perhaps at least some individual animals that aren't persons—your beloved pet, say) have an *irreplaceable value*, which sets us (them) apart from things that have the merely functional (hence replaceable) value of tools. Roughly speaking, tools, valued only as tools, are discardable and replaceable without loss of value as long as the new ones do the same job: any old corkscrew will do as long as its value is exhausted by the job of getting the bottle open. Not so with individual human persons. (For simplicity I will here leave aside other animals.) While your parents or your children may have—to put it chillingly—some "functional value" for you, that does not mean you are ready to concede that the situation would be no worse if they were to be destroyed and replaced with duplicates that "functioned just as well"—parentally or filially—provided this involved no lamentable waste of resources. I assume we will be content to distinguish the sort of irreplaceable value persons have, not only from the functional value of "replaceables," but also from the "aesthetic" value of natural and artificial entities (which might also give them irreplaceability), as well as from the irreplaceable value that something might have in virtue of occupying a unique *historical niche* (the guitar your daddy gave you or the original Declaration of Independence).

With this in place, I can come to recognize that my life has an irreplaceable *personal* value for me, only insofar as it is phenomenal. First, I compare (i) a future in which I survive in the more or less ordinary way I expect and hope with (ii) a future in which I am destroyed and replaced by a duplicate. (Let us stipulate in (ii) whatever lack of continuity with my body and psychology would make this "Twin Charles" not *me*, but a mere *copy*.) Faced with these two futures, I frankly admit that I strongly prefer (i) survival over (ii) replacement by a duplicate. Grant me that this preference is rational.

Now here's a further scenario: some change occurs to my body that utterly destroys my consciousness. Ordinarily, I would imagine this as a case where I fall into a permanent coma and become a "vegetable." But again, recall the specter of "zombification" earlier raised. If I find that intelligible, I might, instead of imagining myself comatose, much more fancifully suppose that I become "zombified"—able to move about and make sounds much as before, though utterly bereft of consciousness. The question then arises, if I envision becoming either a *vegetable* or a *zombie*, would the evaluative preference I had for survival over duplication remain? Set aside whatever *aesthetic* or *historical* value I might award myself that would incline me to value survival. (Anyway, there is none!) I would say that, once consciousness leaves me forever, survival is no better than duplication. And that is still true, even if I suppose that it is open to me to survive as a zombie.[22]

Maybe, in imagining analogous futures for *yourself*, you discover a similar attitude. Maybe not. But if you do, you show that you accord consciousness an immense ethical value: without it you lose your irreplaceable value as a person. Perhaps, in eliciting these intuitions, we evince values that rest on nothing deeper that could justify them. But that wouldn't show we are irrational to hold them. And we *can* say something to justify them, in fact. For given our earlier argument, there are no minds without phenomenality. Now clearly, there are no persons without minds. So it is no wonder that my irreplaceable value as a person depends on consciousness.[23]

The point here does not seem to reflect an essentially *egocentric* concern. Just as you may take yourself to be irreplaceably valuable as a person, so you might take another. And so *you* might take *me* to be valuable in this way. Now, if you find your irreplaceable value as a person hinges on your consciousness, how about your regard for me? Should you think that whereas you find you have no irreplaceable value as a person left when consciousness is irrevocably stolen from you, there is reasonably some such value to be found in me? Not unless there is some difference between us that would make sense of this. And I don't see that there is. I conclude that phenomenality is essential to someone's irreplaceable value as a person—whether this be oneself or another.

Consider this final, additional way to see the ethical significance of consciousness. You may not find *anything* is truly of irreplaceable value. And you may not agree with me that nonphenomenal beings are inevitably mindless. Still, you can agree to this: how it is right or good for you to treat someone or something depends very much on whether they are *suitable recipients of empathy*. Where empathy is appropriate, you should treat whom or what you encounter with a special kind of care.

Now what is the sense of 'empathy' that makes this seem a truism? I would propose that you *empathize* in the relevant sense only if you *recognize what condition someone else is in, based on knowledge of what it's like for someone to be in that condition*. And (drawing on my earlier account) that is to say, your recognition is based on knowledge of what that type of condition is, which requires either having been in it oneself or being able to imagine being in it. It follows from this that someone or something is a suitable focus of empathy, only if there is something it's like for them to be in the condition that they are in. But that will be so only if they have some feature that there is *essentially and nonderivatively* something it's like for them to have. And a feature of this type is none other than a *phenomenal* feature. It follows from all this then, that having phenomenal features is a precondition of being a suitable recipient of empathetic concern—which, as we said, makes a huge difference to what constitutes good ethical treatment.

"So you're telling me that how I should treat something depends on whether it's conscious. Thanks, but that was already pretty *obvious*." Well, I am not just saying this. For I am tying the concern for conscious beings specifically to the *phenomenal* sense of consciousness *as it is explained here*. This is worth bringing out since it is not clear that other ways of understanding what consciousness is will provide an adequate rationale for granting it moral import.[24]

Conclusion

Once we understand sufficiently what consciousness is, we can see that because of consciousness, we have warrant for perceptual judgments about what's around us and for introspective judgments about our own minds; without it, we would not understand anything we say, and we would be, in a sense, literally mindless. Further, consciousness underlies empathy and a regard for the irreplaceable value of persons. Thus, consciousness is enormously important.

It may be helpful, in closing, to sketch a response to Geoffrey Lee's thoughtful case for its *unimportance* (this volume, Chapter 10)—at least as expressed in an earlier draft of his contribution. This I took to be its gist. If consciousness does have strong epistemic significance, *and* reductive materialism is true, then the difference between conscious and nonconscious states should make a big "natural" difference. Any such differences would have to be evident to objective ("Martian") observers, through considering the (reduced) physical natures of conscious states. But the Martians would find no big difference. For it would be evident to them that, whatever epistemic role conscious states actually play in us, states of totally nonconscious ("zombie") beings could play *very similar* roles. Zombie beliefs would be as justified by zombie perception and introspection as our beliefs are by *phenomenal* states. Thus, from the objective point of view, consciousness has no great epistemic significance—and likely no moral importance.

I cannot here do justice to the details, but hopefully my reply will help clarify the issues. Lee's view seems to assume that totally unconscious beings would understand their utterances and express attitudes. But this should not be granted. For if my earlier reasoning is correct, they would not. (And, in a sense, they would not even have *minds*.) Hence, these imaginary beings would have no mental states epistemically like ours and no irreplaceable value as persons. So consciousness remains important. Second, even putting aside this objection, I might still rationally find that my irreplaceable value as a person lies in my phenomenality. Nor is my empathy argument for ethical import undone by the possibility of zombie minds. Moreover, even if that possibility were conceded—and with it the possibility of a zombie *epistemology* bearing analogies to our own—consciousness would still be highly epistemically important *in us*. Consider, by comparison, how the practical importance of *feeling pain* is so dramatically revealed in (real, if fortunately rare) cases of congenital insensitivity to pain. A child born with this condition feels no pain—even when holding her hands on a burning hot surface or after breaking her ankle in a fall. It seems clear that, in missing these feelings, such children miss something important—since they are so heedless of danger. Do we then erase this apparent importance of feeling merely by contemplating some conceptually possible world in which *unfeeling* creatures reliably escape damage and destruction? It would be a mistake to use inconsequential absences of consciousness that are *merely imagined* to eliminate its *real-world* importance. Analogously, such imaginings bear little on real-world *epistemic* importance: the importance that appearances actually have in warranting our judgments about our surroundings and ourselves.

Perhaps a Martian mind that refused to address these matters through serious first-person reflection would find no importance in consciousness. But must my judgments of importance be validated by some postulated intellect's "view from nowhere"? Maybe there is a reductionist theory that says some such vindication is required—though the connection between physicalism and this normative demand is a bit unclear to me. In any event, it needs to be shown that the case for such a thesis is so powerful that I should forsake the value of my own experience, rather than conclude that our imagined Martians' "objectivity" would simply blind them to it.[25]

Notes

1. It seems to me that the association of "qualia" with the traditional idea of "sensible qualities" encourages us to assume that only somewhat cognitively low-grade sensory functions should be deemed conscious. Also, we may reasonably doubt the reality of the sensory "quale"—where this is conceived of as something atomistic, determinate and modality specific that fixes the character of experience. But that shouldn't make us doubt that *consciousness* is real.
2. I explain these three a little differently, in somewhat more detail in Siewert (2012b).
3. The conception proposed here offers one way of interpreting John Searle's (1992) claim that experience in the sense relevant here (and hence consciousness) is "ontologically subjective"—that is, it is something that exists only when it is experienced by a subject. But notice: nothing in my account implies that experiences occur entirely "within the subject" (or her head) and cannot be "world involving." Nor am I saying that the nature of an experience is entirely exhausted by how the subject experiences it.
4. I discuss elaborations on the notion of blindsight as a means to clarifying our understanding of consciousness in Siewert (1998, chaps. 3–4). I work out a shorter and somewhat revised version of these ideas in Siewert (2010).
5. Nagel (1974); Block (2002).
6. Consider, for example, this type of state: a sequence of shapes "(9_9)" *looks to you recognizable as a "tired face" emoticon,* or else just as a *"nine dash nine."* That this is described as a *"looking"* means that there is essentially something it's like for one to be in a state of this type. But someone (not me) might allege that knowing what it's like for this array of figures to look recognizable as of a type derives just from knowing what it's like for this to look to you *as it might to someone to whom it did not look recognizable as of any type,* plus some other background (non–"what it's like") knowledge—the knowledge that one is then *judging* this to be a "tired face" emoticon, say.
7. As I understand this: what it's like to have some feature F *derives entirely* from what it's like to have some other feature G just when what it's like to have F is only derivatively knowable. This means: one can know what it's like to have F, *if and only if* one knows what it's like to have some *other* feature or features, to which having F is inessential—with the addition of certain other conditions that don't consist in further knowledge of what it's like to have some feature.
8. I explain and argue for this view in Siewert (2006, 2011, 2012a, 2012b, 2013).
9. However, I wouldn't put this, in the manner of Susanna Siegel (2006), by saying that these "properties are represented" in the content of visual experience. For I don't want to say that the experience or visual appearance must be *inaccurate* or *illusory* if the item is not (biologically) a pumpkin, or if it's not surprised or sinister. Even then, it *accurately* appears "pumpkin-ish" and as having a surprised or sinister "look"—I would say.
10. I'm thinking here of the debate between "conceptualists" like John McDowell and nonconceptualists like Christopher Peacocke and Michael Tye. For this controversy see the papers collected in Gunther (2002).
11. For detailed argument, see Siewert (2011).
12. For example: Dretske (1995) and Tye (2002).
13. For example: Carruthers (2000, 2004), Lycan (2004), and Rosenthal (2002).

14. I believe we cannot reduce phenomenal character to a special form of "first-order" sensory representation, partly because of arguments rooted in my "subjective contrast" (blindsight) conception of phenomenality, and partly on the grounds that what it's like to enjoy occurrent thought is irreducible to the phenomenal character of sense experience (and imagery) of a sort we could have in the complete absence of understanding. And I reject higher-order and self-representationalist reductionist strategies partly on the grounds that—depending on what kind of representation is at issue (i.e., what kinds of thoughts, perceptions, and self-representings)—often or always we simply have no warrant to ascribe to ourselves the relevant extra layer or curlicue of intentionality that the reductionists wish to posit, even when we are right to think our lives are rich in "first-order" phenomenal appearances (see Siewert 1998, chaps. 4–6, 8; 2010; 2011; 2012a).

15. The view here is a condensed and slightly revised version of the account I explain and defend in more detail in Siewert (2012a).

16. Sometimes a distinction is drawn between *indexicals* (like 'I' and 'you') and *proper demonstratives* (like 'this' and 'that'). For my purposes here, this distinction is not important, and I will classify both forms of systematically context-dependent referential expressions together, under the "indexical" label.

17. Even so, there is no specific classification C (such as *green*) such that, had I not thought of the color this looks to me *as C*, I wouldn't be thinking of just that color appearance at all. Moreover, there still may be no way I have of completing the ellipsis in these cases that captures the manner of looking (feeling, etc.) in all its cognized specificity.

18. These would include accounts that endorse the first component of what Brie Gertler (2012) calls "the acquaintance approach"—which says that some first-person judgments about experience enjoy a distinctive epistemic status in virtue of the fact that they are essentially bound up with the occurrence of their truth makers. Falling in this group are not only Gertler's own view, but also Terry Horgan's (2012), as well as Dave Chalmers's (2003) account of phenomenal concepts.

19. Though I cannot engage in a detailed comparison here, it should be noted that my argument bears complex similarities and differences with those of John Campbell (2002) and Declan Smithies (2011, 2012) linking consciousness and demonstrative reference. Part of what distinguishes my view is its focus on "preclassifcatory understanding" of demonstrative/indexical identification of (not particulars but) *features*.

20. One can take away *this* much from John Searle's (1980) famous "Chinese Room" thought experiment, even if one does not accept all his conclusions. (The point I want here could be granted even by someone attracted to what Searle calls the "systems" and "robot" replies to his argument.)

21. The notion of "nonconscious zombie" suggested here ties an envisaged absence of consciousness to a difference in internal physical structure and composition and, for this reason, is broader than the notion that figures in Chalmers's (1994) argument for property dualism: his zombies are possible beings *microphysically type identical* to phenomenally conscious ones like us. For Dennett (1991), it would be a mistake to contrast ourselves in thought even with zombies in the broader sense, because there is just nothing more to being conscious *or* to having a mind than being an intentional system of a certain kind. On my view though, Dennett's philosophy implicitly denies the reality of consciousness (Siewert 1998, 2010). But once you *recognize* its reality, you can require more for genuine mentality than just being interpretable and predictable via the "intentional stance." (Crudely put: because of consciousness, there can be more to having a mind than just acting as if you do.) Thus, I can hold there is room for a position, like John Searle's (1992), Uriah Kriegel's (2011), and the one proposed here, that makes mind dependent on consciousness. I have not here addressed the question (answered very differently by Searle and Kriegel) of what relationship between conscious and nonconscious states makes some of the latter count as genuinely mental. Perhaps: the postulation of nonexperiential states of mind is warranted just to the extent that it can explain why one's experience has the character it has—but if a creature has no experience at all to account for, it has no mind.

22. In the background of these thoughts are the influential discussions of personal identity in Parfit (1984), Lewis (1983), and Nozick (1981). My point here does not, I believe, require I commit to a specific view of just what forms of bodily or psychological continuity will carry my identity into the future. And I could make much the same point as I want here, even if I conceded that in either the "permanent coma" or the "zombie" scenario I would cease to exist, strictly speaking. The essential thing is just that there is a contrast to be made between survival and duplication, and "survival value" (so to speak) vanishes when consciousness does.
23. I make a (partly overlapping) argument to the conclusion that consciousness is intrinsically valuable in Siewert (1998, chap. 9).
24. Indeed on some of them, it is becomes puzzling that the presence or absence of consciousness (and of specific forms of it) has the significance one might have thought. Sometimes this is because of the way the theory seems to overintellectualize consciousness. (Consider "higher-order thought" theories. Why in the world should the fact that a creature *thinks* that it is in a certain sort of sensory state transform this state into a suitable focus of empathetic concern, when it was not before?) Sometimes, on the other hand, the problem seems to be that one's theory *deintellectualizes* consciousness. (Consider "first-order" theories that confine consciousness to the sensory domain. We surely would feel empathy for parents of children that have disappeared. But how could what calls to our concern here be merely what *sensations* they feel, and nothing at all of what *thoughts* are preying on their minds?)
25. I would like to thank Michael Barkasi, Steve Crowell, Casey O'Callaghan, Uriah Kriegel, David Pitt, and Declan Smithies for helpful feedback on drafts of this chapter.

References

Block, N. (2002). "Concepts of Consciousness." In D. Chalmers (ed.), *Philosophy of Mind: Classical and Contemporary Readings*, 206-218. Oxford: Oxford University Press.
Campbell, J. (2002). *Reference and Consciousness*. Oxford: Oxford University Press.
Carruthers P. (2000). *Phenomenal Consciousness*. Cambridge: Cambridge University Press.
Carruthers, P. (2004). "HOP over FOR, HOT Theory." In R. Gennaro (ed.), *Higher-Order Theories of Consciousness*, 115-135. Philadelphia, PA: John Benjamins.
Chalmers, D. (1994). *The Conscious Mind*. Oxford: Oxford University Press.
Chalmers, D. (2003). "The Content and Epistemology of Phenomenal Belief." In Q. Smith and A. Jokic (eds.), *Consciousness: New Philosophical Perspectives*, 220-271. Oxford: Oxford University Press.
Dennett, D. (1991). *Consciousness Explained*. Boston, MA: Little, Brown.
Dretske, F. (1995). *Naturalizing the Mind*. Cambridge, MA: MIT Press.
Gertler, B. (2012). "Renewed Acquaintance." In D. Smithies and D. Stoljar (eds.), *Introspection and Consciousness*, 93-127. Oxford: Oxford University Press.
Gunther, Y., ed. (2002). *Essays on Nonconceptual Content*. Cambridge, MA: MIT Press.
Horgan. T. (2012). "Introspection about Phenomenal Consciousness: Running the Gamut from Infallibility to Impotence." In D. Smithies and D. Stoljar (eds.), *Introspection and Consciousness*, 405-412. Oxford: Oxford University Press.
Kriegel, U. (2011). *The Sources of Intentionality*. Oxford: Oxford University Press.
Lewis, D. (1983). "Survival and Identity." In *Philosophical Papers,* vol. 1, 189-229. Oxford: Oxford University Press.
Lycan, W. (2004). "The Superiority of HOP to HOT." In R. Gennaro (ed.), *Higher- Order Theories of Consciousness*, 93-113. Philadelphia, PA: John Benjamins.
Nagel, T. (1974). "What Is It Like to Be a Bat?" *Philosophical Review* 4: 435–450.
Nozick, R. (1981). *Philosophical Explanations*. Cambridge, MA: Harvard University Press.
Parfit, D. (1984). *Reasons and Persons*. Oxford: Oxford University Press.
Rosenthal, D. (2002). "Explaining Consciousness." In D. Chalmers (ed.), *Philosophy of Mind: Classical and Contemporary Readings*, 406-421. Oxford: Oxford University Press.
Ryle, G. (1949/2009). *The Concept of Mind*. London: Routledge.

Searle, J. (1980). "Minds, Brains and Programs." *Behavioral and Brain Sciences* 3: 417–458.

Searle, J. (1992). *The Rediscovery of the Mind*. Cambridge, MA: MIT Press.

Siegel, S. (2006). "Which Properties Are Represented in Perception?" In T. Gendler Szabo and J. Hawthorne (eds.), *Perceptual Experience*, 481-503. Oxford: Oxford University Press.

Siewert, C. (1998). *The Significance of Consciousness*. Princeton, NJ: Princeton University Press.

Siewert, C. (2006). "Is the Appearance of Shape Protean?" *Psyche* 12 (3).

Siewert, C. (2010). "Saving Appearances: A Dilemma for Physicalists." In George Bealer and Robert Koons (eds.), *The Waning of Materialism: New Essays*, 67-87. Oxford: Oxford University Press.

Siewert, C. (2011). "Phenomenal Thought." In T. Bayne and M. Montague (eds.), *Cognitive Phenomenology*, 236-267. Oxford: Oxford University Press.

Siewert, C. (2012a). "On the Phenomenology of Introspection." In D. Smithies and D.

Stoljar (eds.), *Consciousness and Introspection*, 129-167. Oxford: Oxford University Press.

Siewert, C. (2012b). "Respecting Appearances." In Dan Zahavi (ed.), *The Oxford Handbook of Contemporary Phenomenology*, 48-69. Oxford: Oxford University Press.

Siewert, C. (2013). "Intellectualism, Experience, and Motor Understanding." In J. Schear (ed.), *Mind, Reason, and Being-in-the-World: The McDowell/Dreyfus Debate*, 194–226. London: Routledge Press.

Smithies, D. (2011). "What Is the Role of Consciousness in Demonstrative Thought?" *The Journal of Philosophy* 108.1: 5–34.

Smithies, D. (2012). "The Mental Lives of Zombies." *Philosophical Perspectives* 26: 343–72

Tye, M. 2002. *Consciousness, Color, and Content*. Cambridge, MA: MIT Press.

CHAPTER **10**

Materialism and the Epistemic Significance of Consciousness

GEOFFREY LEE

Chapter Overview

Conscious experiences are commonly thought to have special epistemic properties: for example, they are thought to acquaint us with themselves and with external objects and events and enable us to form justified beliefs about ourselves and about the world. This chapter argues that if reductive materialism is true, this gives us reason to doubt that consciousness is unique in having these special epistemic properties. We tend to think that it *is* unique: for example, we tend to think that if we were turned into functional zombies by having our biological neurons replaced by artificial silicon components, this would put us in a massively impoverished epistemic state. I argue that this belief is grounded in a belief that there is a deep natural divide between beings that have consciousness and beings that lack it. But if reductive materialism is true, then it is wrong to think that there is any such deep natural divide, suggesting we should revise our belief in the unique epistemic significance of consciousness. I consider several strategies someone could adopt to resist this conditional conclusion. For example, they could hold that what it *is* to be conscious is to have states with this special significance. I argue that these strategies fail. If reductive materialism is true, then being a zombie can be just as good as having consciousness (at least epistemically).

Introduction

Conscious states are often thought to have great significance as a source of knowledge, both of the environment around the conscious subject and of the subject's own mind. Conscious perception is thought of as an interface between belief states and the environment, presenting us with the local world in a way that allows us to form knowledgeable judgments about it. And conscious states themselves seem known to us in a peculiarly direct way—they are self-illuminating or self-revealing, the intimate epicenter of everything that is known to us. The special kinds of epistemic significance that attach to consciousness will be my subject here. More specifically, I am interested in whether conscious states are *unique* in the kind of epistemic role they play, or whether something other than consciousness could do the same work. Could a completely unconscious being have internal states with much the same epistemic significance as our conscious states?

We certainly have intuitions that suggest otherwise (Siewert, in Chapter 9 of this volume, does a good job of making these vivid). For example, it seems plausible that a blindsighted subject who is able to reliably guess what is in the "blind" part of her visual field without consciously perceiving it, does not know about this part of the environment in anything like the way that conscious experience would allow. One explanation for this is that conscious experience is *necessary* for a certain kind of epistemic relationship to the environment. Despite such intuitions, I will argue that if materialism is true, we have reasons to doubt the idea that consciousness is unique in its epistemic properties. On the materialist view consciousness is a high-level physical or functional feature of the brain (or some larger system). A being with a quite different cognitive architecture might lack this (seemingly) special property but have internal states that play a similar role, including in the provision of reliable mental representations of the environment and their own mind. I will argue that despite lacking conscious awareness, such a being might be in an epistemic situation just as good as ours.

By contrast, Siewert argues that consciousness is unique in its epistemic significance, grounding the justification of perceptual and introspective beliefs, and our understanding of perceptual and introspective concepts. He claims that a philosophical zombie could *not* have internal states that play the same epistemic role, and even goes as far as to claim that consciousness is necessary for having any mental states at all. He rejects reductive materialism, so perhaps his overall view is not incompatible with my conclusions here. However, the arguments he offers do not seem to depend on rejecting reductive materialism: so if I am correct, these arguments are inadequate, even if his view remains a live possibility.

I will discuss the following three kinds of epistemic significance that seem to attach to conscious states: *doxastic significance, intrinsic epistemic significance*, and *concept-grounding significance. Doxastic significance* has to do with the ways conscious states are able to confer justification (or other positive epistemic status) on beliefs. For example, it is often held that conscious perceptual states can contribute to justifying perceptual beliefs, as when an experience of the color of a surface helps to justify you in judging what color it has. *Intrinsic*

224 • Geoffrey Lee

epistemic significance has to do with the ways in which conscious states are in themselves epistemically valuable. The idea is that conscious states intrinsically involve a kind of epistemic relation either to the environment or your own mind, independently of what you believe. Some theorists elaborate in terms of the idea of *acquaintance*—an experiential relation that directly confronts you with something and enables you to know it in a special direct way. Intuitively, even if you lacked the capacity for belief, conscious acquaintance would still provide a form of epistemic contact with the world. Finally, *concept-grounding significance* has to do with the role of conscious states in enabling a subject to grasp concepts that refer to internal or external items, such as the objects or events one is acquainted with in having a perceptual experience. For example, a conscious perceptual experience of the color of a surface may be part of what enables you to think of the color as "that color." I will focus particularly on doxastic significance, arguing that if materialism is true, consciousness is not unique in its ability to have this kind of significance: there is a family of states that an unconscious being could enjoy, which have the same doxastic significance as if they were conscious. Intrinsic and concept-grounding significance will play a role though, because it might be claimed by an opponent that they explain why consciousness is unique in its doxastic significance. I will return to this idea subsequently.

Epistemic significance is not the only kind of significance thought to attach to consciousness, and it is worth briefly discussing the other varieties before proceeding. One of them is moral or practical significance. If we believe that certain entities have intrinsic value, one plausible candidate would be experiences like pleasures and pains (and even if we don't believe in intrinsic value, it is certainly true that we *care* about pleasure and pain). More strongly, it might be held that conscious experience is necessary part of the ground for *all* value in the world—that without conscious experience nothing would matter. Despite its obvious importance, this kind of significance won't be my focus here (although I suspect many of the points here about epistemic normativity have analogues in the practical case).

A third kind of significance, whose connections to the epistemic significance of consciousness will be explored here, is what might be called "natural significance." Consciousness (or specific kinds of consciousness) is naturally significant if it is a highly "natural" property, or if there is a deep natural divide between the beings that have consciousness and those that do not (this being one reason why consciousness might be thought to have special scientific interest). Following Armstrong and Lewis (see Armstrong, 1978; Lewis, 1983), many philosophers, including myself, believe that properties are distinguished by some objective measure of naturalness, and that one goal of science is to articulate what these natural "joints" in the world are. For example, we want to say that two electrons are objectively more similar than an electron and a proton, even though there are ways of understanding what a "property" is on which all particles share equally many properties (e.g., they are equally many sets of possible objects to which they belong). It seems that some of these "thin" properties count more toward objective resemblance than others, and this gives an important role for the concept of "naturalness."[1] Being conscious seems to be a particularly striking objective resemblance between objects, and for this reason, it might be supposed that consciousness is a highly natural property.

Although the natural significance of consciousness won't be my main focus in this chapter (it is the focus of Lee [forthcoming]), it will play an important role in the argument; in particular, my discussion will be organized around an argument to the effect that *if* consciousness lacks special natural significance, then it lacks special epistemic significance (in certain sense).

I am going to challenge the epistemic significance of consciousness, but it is important to be clear on the strength of the challenge I am offering. For any kind of significance that allegedly attaches to consciousness (epistemic, practical, or natural), I would distinguish three grades of challenge to it. First, one could deny that *anything* is significant in the relevant respect. For example, one might be skeptical about whether there is any objective distinction of naturalness between properties (e.g., Goodman, 1983; Taylor, 1993) or be a nihilist, denying that anything is intrinsically valuable, or be skeptical about whether there is any objective sense in which some cognitive states are epistemically significant—(e.g., more "rational," "justified," or epistemically valuable) than others (e.g., Field, 2009). Second, one could think that although some things are significant in the relevant respect, consciousness does not have the relevant significance, or at any rate is *less* significant in the relevant respect than other entities—for example, one might think that only beliefs can have epistemic value, and conscious experiences only have derivative epistemic value, for example, as their reliable causes (Davidson, 1986). These are not the challenges I will be primarily concerned with here. Instead, I am concerned to deny the idea that consciousness has *unique* significance, in the sense that there are no similar properties—properties that an unconscious being could have that are *equally* significant (in some given respect perhaps). Consciousness does not "stand out from the crowd."

To get a sense of this view, imagine you are faced with the following dilemma (a similar case is given by Dainton [2008, p. 181]): You are suffering from a degenerative neural condition. If it is left untreated, you can expect only another year of relatively normal cognitive functioning, and you will be dead in two years. Scientists offer you a treatment that will not only extend your lifespan but also enhance most of your cognitive processing (your ability to access stored information, reason with it, etc.) while leaving most of your current mental states (your personality, beliefs, desires, intentions, etc.) intact. Your friends will meet a brighter, sharper, version of your former self. There is one large catch, however—the treatment involves gradually replacing your neural circuitry with a functionally equivalent silicon proxy, the result being that you will completely lose your capacity for conscious experience (it is not specified how it is *known* that this will be the result—we just stipulate that it is known). You will still "perceive" the world in some sense, but your perception will completely lack the characteristic subjective feel that makes mental states "conscious" in the sense that we seem to care about (often referred to by philosophers as "phenomenal consciousness").

Should you accept the treatment? I think most people would not accept it. Having conscious experience seems to be necessary for having the kind of life we care about, and being without it—having the "light inside" permanently extinguished—seems pretty much as bad as ordinary death. Notice, however, that this reasoning is only sound if the silicon zombie states aren't as *good* as conscious states in some sense. Suppose, however, that the zombie states have the same moral, epistemic, and natural significance as our conscious states do. Then it is hard to see how they are less desirable, and it looks like we ought to accept the operation. My claim will be that if materialism is true, then there are zombie states that have the same natural and epistemic significance as conscious states, and to that extent at least, are just as good. I call this view "deflationary pluralism."

Some terminology is helpful in order to define the view more precisely. Let us say that a state is "consciousness-like" if the functional constraints it puts on the cognitive architecture of an organism at least superficially resemble those associated with consciousness. We can say that a being is *pseudo-conscious* if they are in an internal state that is consciousness-like but are not conscious. More specifically, we can distinguish between internal states that are *folk*-consciousness-like and *empirically* consciousness-like.[2] A being is *folk-pseudo-conscious* if she is in an internal state that satisfies the functional criteria that ordinary people associate with consciousness (e.g., the ability to report the relevant states), but is not conscious. A being is *empirically pseudo-conscious* if she is in an internal state that satisfies many of the architectural details that have been found empirically to be associated with consciousness (e.g., having perceptual modules feeding into a central pool of information used to reason and initiate high-level motor plans) but is not conscious. We can make the same distinctions for determinate kinds of conscious states. For example, we can talk about pseudo-pain, folk-pseudo-pain, empirical pseudo-pain, and so on.

Let us further distinguish *quasi-consciousness* and pseudo-consciousness. A being is quasi-conscious just if she is pseudo-conscious and her form of pseudo-consciousness is equally significant as consciousness. We may want to distinguish different kinds of significance here: we can talk about epistemic quasi-consciousness and practical quasi-consciousness, and we could make more fine-grained distinctions. The distinctive claim of the deflationary pluralist is that, as well as consciousness, there is a whole family of ways of being quasi-conscious. The claim I am interested in here is that *epistemic*

quasi-consciousness is possible: an unconscious being that superficially dupli-
cated us could be equally justified in her beliefs and equally well "acquainted"
with her environment as us.

The deflationist's claim that forms of pseudo-consciousness can have the
same significance (natural, epistemic, or practical) as real conscious experience
can be made vivid by considering disputes about problematic cases such as lobsters or aliens, where it is unclear whether a being has conscious experience. The
deflationist may regard these as empty questions, in the sense that even if these
being aren't conscious, they may have a consciousness-like internal state that
is equally significant as consciousness, and so the dispute about whether they
are conscious does not concern where some special deep boundary between us
and other creatures lies. Another way of looking at it is that even if our concept
of "consciousness" does not include lobsters, perhaps a variant on our concept
that did include them would be no worse than our concept, in the sense that it
would not miss a deep boundary that our concept *does* mark. (See Sider [2011]
for a development of the notion of an empty question along exactly these lines.)

Deflationary pluralism implies, and so depends on, the weaker claim that a
being might superficially duplicate us without being conscious. Some theorists,
superficial functionalists (Block, 2002), might deny this, holding that having a
functional organization superficially like that of a conscious human is sufficient
for being conscious. It is worth noting, however, that a quite radical version
of superficial functionalism is required to imply that no form of pseudo-
consciousness is possible. The problem is that there is more than one way to
superficially functionally resemble a conscious system, and they could only *all* be
sufficient for consciousness if consciousness is an extremely abstract property
that is determined by every such mode of resemblance (or it is highly disjunctive).
For example, a human baby and an android might both have consciousness-
like internal states but resemble conscious beings in very different ways, and
as a result, they have very little in common with each other (see McLaughlin,
2003). For this reason, I believe superficial functionalism—or at least the radical
kind that would undermine deflationary pluralism—to be an implausible view,
which I will set aside here, acknowledging that it warrants more discussion. I will
assume that at least *some* forms of pseudo-consciousness are possible.

The Grounding Argument for Deflationary Pluralism

I will organize my discussion around an argument that links together the natural significance and epistemic significance of consciousness (or normative
forms of significance more generally, including practical and epistemic significance). I call it the natural-normative grounding argument, or the "grounding
argument" for short. Let us say that consciousness has "strong epistemic significance" if epistemic quasi-consciousness is impossible (and let us define
"strong natural significance" similarly). The argument looks like this:

(1) Consciousness has strong epistemic significance only if it has strong natural significance.
(2) If reductive materialism is true, consciousness does not have strong natural significance.
(3) Conclusion: if reductive materialism is true, then consciousness does not have strong epistemic significance.

To get a feel for the argument, it is helpful to first consider the analogous argument for the moral or practical significance of consciousness. Consider conscious pain compared with a zombie analogue of conscious pain—an unconscious state with a superficially similar functional role. Intuitively, there is a massive difference between these two things. One is a mere functional simulacrum of a kind of state that is very special in virtue of having "phenomenality" or "subjective feel." Moreover, although conscious pain would be judged by many to be an inherently bad thing, many would think that the zombie analogue is not at all bad in the same way. What is the relation between this apparent normative fact and the apparent fact that there is a "deep" difference between pain and zombie pain? On one view (an epistemic version of which is discussed in detail subsequently), the deep difference just *consists* in the fact that pain is bad and zombie pain isn't. However, I don't think this is the intuitive view—intuitively, pain is bad and zombie pain isn't in part *because* they are massively different kinds of things. This massive difference can't therefore *consist* in the normative difference, but must rather be something else that (at least partly) *grounds* it. The obvious candidate is that there is a deep *natural* difference between pain and zombie pain.

But *is* there a deep natural difference between pain and zombie pain? Arguably, if reductive materialism is true, then there is not.

Reductive materialism (as I understand it) is the view that consciousness is identical to a high-level functional or physical property of the brain or some larger system (ditto for more determinate kinds of consciousness). Thus, consciousness and its determinates have "real definitions" (specifications of what it is to have the property in terms of these other properties) in terms of more basic physical and functional properties, implying that facts about consciousness hold wholly in virtue of facts about the physical and functional properties of conscious systems.

If reductive materialism is true, it might be argued that real pain won't be in any way special from an objective perspective compared with pseudo-pain—they are both fairly similar high-level physical-functional properties of a psychological system. To make this idea vivid, imagine a Martian scientist comparing the physical-functional state that *is* pain to the analogue zombie state in, say, a silicon-based life-form. She will see very abstract high-level similarities in the mental architectures of the two life-forms, with completely different realizations of these architectures. It is implausible that the Martian

scientist will think that any great natural significance attaches to one realization over the other—it is not as if the realization that enables consciousness
will be seen as having a magical glow. In this sense, pseudo-pain might be
rather *similar* to real pain. If this is right, we may on reflection want to retract
our initially confident judgment that pseudo-pain can't be just as *bad* as real
pain, which seems to be partly based on the assumption that they are *not at
all* similar.

Compare this with the situation if reductive materialism is false. The alternatives are property dualism and "non-reductive materialism," views on which
consciousness and its determinates are primitive irreducible properties whose
instantiation does not depend in any intelligible way on lower-level facts: they
are metaphysical brutes (I think it is fair to characterize these views this way,
even if the primitivist thinks that mental properties supervene on lower-level
properties—as on a "non-reductive materialist" view—since this will be brute
supervenience of one kind of primitive property on other primitive properties.) On a primitivist view like this, the Martian scientist's knowledge of the
physical and functional differences and similarities between us and pseudo-
conscious aliens won't reveal the fact that we are distinguished in a deep way
from the aliens by enjoying primitive phenomenal properties.

In Lee (forthcoming), I unpack the Martian scientist metaphor in detail, discussing the different interpretations of "natural significance" one could have and
the inference from "the Martian won't see a big difference in natural significance
between consciousness and pseudo-consciousness" to "there *is* no big difference" (assuming reductive materialism). A thought experiment that helps one
see the point involves imagining a spectrum of cases linking a conscious being
to a pseudo-conscious being like a silicon android. Each being in the spectrum
has the same high-level architecture—they are in the same "consciousness-
like" state—but there is a small difference in realization from one case to the
next (e.g., a few neurons might be replaced by functionally equivalent silicon
components). Even though there is consciousness at one end of the spectrum,
and no consciousness at the other end, the shift from one case to the next will
seem trivial from an objective perspective—the perspective of the Martian
scientist. So there appears to be no point at which we reach a monumental
divide between cases of consciousness and cases of mere pseudo-consciousness,
supporting the view that consciousness and pseudo-consciousness have equal
natural significance. (Note: I am intending this thought experiment as more of
an aid to intuition than as an argument for deflationism.)

It is natural to object that even if the Martian scientist sees no big divide
between us and unconscious silicon beings, we can appreciate that there *is* a
big divide given the understanding of consciousness we get "from the inside."
In brief, my response to this is that if reductive materialism is true, then the
natural significance of consciousness is not best appreciated "from the inside"
but rather is optimally assessed given knowledge of what consciousness really

is—that is, given knowledge of its real definition in physical/functional terms.[3] Given reductive materialism, the objective, not the subjective, perspective is privileged for assessing the natural significance of consciousness—that is, the Martian scientist is in a better position to understand the natural significance of consciousness than we are.

For the purpose of this discussion then, I will assume that premise 2 is correct—that if reductive materialism is true, then there is no special natural significance that attaches to consciousness but not to any form of pseudo-consciousness. I am interested in what this assumption implies about the other forms of significance alleged to attach to conscious states, in particular epistemic significance.

If the grounding argument works for the practical significance of consciousness, then it is quite plausible that it works in the epistemic case as well. If you think that a conscious percept can acquaint you with the environment, enable you to think about features of the environment and form judgments about them, whereas an unconscious state can do none of these things, intuitively this difference is *grounded* in the fact that an unconscious state is a quite different type of thing from a conscious one. It is not what the difference *consists in*. I think this grounding argument may be more controversial in the epistemic case than in the moral case, but nonetheless it has force. Most of what follows will be concerned with discussing how viable it is to reject it (i.e., to reject premise 1), holding that consciousness has special epistemic significance that is *not* grounded in special natural significance.

I will now proceed by considering two different kinds views, each of which, if correct, would undermine the grounding argument. First, one could take the view that to be conscious just *is* to be in a state with a certain kind of epistemic significance; so it is in the very nature of consciousness that epistemic quasi-consciousness is impossible. I call this view *normativism*. The alternative to a normativist view is to hold that although consciousness is not defined in terms of its epistemic significance (which I interpret as implying that it is a natural property of the kind that features in causal laws and explanations of the kind found in science), it nonetheless has strong epistemic significance—for example, the norms governing belief formation in fact imply that conscious experience is required to have rational belief. I call this view *strong epistemic naturalism*. I think any attempt to defend the strong epistemic significance of consciousness will be in either one of these categories: I now consider them in turn.

First Response: Normativism—Being Conscious *Just Is* Having States with a Certain Epistemic Significance

According to the grounding argument, if consciousness has strong epistemic significance, this is partly grounded in the fact that there is a big natural divide between the conscious beings and the rest (premise 1). One way around this is to claim that consciousness is just *defined* in terms of its epistemic significance, in such a way that having states that function like conscious states, and that have the epistemic role of conscious states, is what *makes* you conscious. On this view, the big divide between conscious and unconscious beings is not a natural one that ought to be salient to a Martian scientist, but rather one defined in epistemically normative terms; it is the divide between having states with a certain kind of (normative) epistemic significance and lacking such states. As well as conflicting with the natural/normative grounding claim (premise 1), this view can be understood as directly incompatible with the existence of epistemic quasi-consciousness (i.e., the conclusion of the argument), implying that the grounding argument must be unsound. I think this rejection of grounding is counterintuitive, but the view is still worth discussing in some detail.

I will assume that the kind of epistemic significance that is supposed to define consciousness is *doxastic*; that is, it has to do with the way conscious states can contribute to justifying beliefs, such as beliefs about your environment, or beliefs about your own mind. We can think of this in terms of the existence of epistemic *norms* governing the formation of belief. Belief formation involves a transition from a prior to a posterior mental state, where the mental state involves a set of beliefs and other relevant states, such as conscious experiences. A necessary condition on a belief being justified will be that it is formed in accordance with the relevant transition norms. The normativist thinks that the conscious states a subject has are, at the very least, *relevant* to what transitions they are justified in making; that is, they are relevant to whether the subject is following the relevant transition norms.[4] For example, if I have a conscious perceptual experience as of a yellow feather, this may contribute to my being justified in forming the belief that there is a yellow feather before me, in accordance with a norm governing the formation of perceptual belief.

We can call this kind of relevance to justification *weak doxastic significance*. Consciousness having weak doxastic significance (as I understand this) is consistent with forms of pseudo-consciousness also having it. There might be alternative norms that a zombie could follow, norms that ground the rationality of transitions from pseudo-conscious states to beliefs.

We can say that consciousness has *strong doxastic significance* if there are no such analogues of consciousness-involving norms—that is, if the correct epistemic norms are *consciousness-requiring*. Normativism is supposed to imply this stronger significance because it is the view that following the norms that govern certain kinds of psychological transitions (e.g., those from perception-like states to beliefs) is *sufficient* for being conscious. We can understand this as the view that consciousness is defined by a "functional-normative" role:

Normative Functionalism: Being conscious (or having some specific type of consciousness) is the property of being in a state that plays a certain functional-normative role.

A functional-normative role is like a regular causal role, except that the mental transitions that specify the functional role are taken to have a normative aspect—they are (by definition) transitions that one *ought* to perform if one is in the relevant mental state. For example, a normativist about perceptual consciousness might define it in terms of a norm telling one to "endorse" the content of a perceptual experience one is in; for the normativist, having a conscious perceptual experience might be taken to partly *consist* in being in some state that is governed by a content-endorsement norm.

Playing a normative-functional role is a stronger requirement than playing the corresponding causal-functional role, precisely because it adds in a normative requirement. Satisfying the functional requirement might not be enough to satisfy the normative requirement: for example, it might be that to be conscious—and thereby to have states capable of grounding justified beliefs about yourself and the environment—the relevant functional property has to be realized on a certain kind of neural hardware (this is one reason why normative functionalism is compatible with the possibility of pseudo-consciousness). On the other hand, satisfying the functional requirement might be sufficient for consciousness; the view would still differ from regular functionalism in the sense that it holds that the nature of consciousness is partly normative, having to do with its role justifying belief.

What exactly are the epistemic norms that govern consciousness (and on this view define it)? It will be helpful at this point to distinguish two kinds of views of the normative role of conscious experience that a believer in strong normative significance might have. First, they might believe the following:

Strong Foundational Significance Thesis: Necessarily, if a belief is justified non-inferentially (i.e., not on the basis of other beliefs), part of the ground for this justification is the existence of a conscious state.

The picture here is one of a grand web of beliefs, most justified inferentially through a chain of other beliefs, but some providing a foundation on the periphery, where justification by inference from other beliefs gives out. These non-inferential beliefs are justified by transitions from conscious experiences (e.g., conscious perceptions), which thereby ground the whole structure. We can understand the grounding claim here as implying that if you lack conscious states, then your non-inferential beliefs are not justified: *only* consciousness can provide such a foundation. Thus a zombie's non-inferential beliefs, and any other beliefs whose justification depends on that of non-inferential beliefs, are not justified. This suggests that a zombie can't have *any* justified beliefs. Having said this, it might be plausible to restrict the view, so that only a certain class of non-inferential beliefs, such as introspective psychological judgments and non-inferential empirical judgments, are held to require conscious experiences to be justified. This would allow for the fact that some non-inferential beliefs, such as a priori beliefs about mathematics, do not seem to be justified by experience. On this restricted version, a zombie might be able to form justified beliefs about mathematics and other a priori matters, but would not be able to have justified beliefs about its environment or its own psychological states.

Phenomenal consciousness might play a more general justificatory role than injecting from the foundations, as it were. For example, *access internalists* hold that the fact (or proposition) that p can only be part of a subject's reason for believing that q if the subject has "access" to p in some sense. For example, Freudian repressed beliefs do not seem to be rational grounds for other beliefs—if I repressedly believe that Britain is not the world's greatest nation, I can't use this as a premise in reasoning. One way of understanding the relevant notion of "access" is in terms of a subject's phenomenal states:

Phenomenal Access Internalism: Necessarily, the fact that p can only be part of a subject's reason for believing that q if p is available to phenomenal awareness (a similar view is defended by Smithies [2012a]).

We can say that p is "available to phenomenal awareness" just if p is either the content of a belief that is consciously accessible, or p is the content of a perceptual experience, or is an introspectible fact about a phenomenal state (such as the fact that it is an intense pain, or a visual experience of blue). Phenomenal access internalism implies that consciousness has a more general role conferring justification than merely injecting justification at the foundations because it requires that *anything* that is part of a subject's reasons for believing something is consciously accessible, including the contents of beliefs that have been formed by inference from other beliefs.

These views combine with normativism as follows. For the foundationalist normativist, being conscious just *is* being capable of mental transitions that satisfy the relevant foundational norms. For the phenomenal access internalist normativist, being conscious will be the property of having states that are subject to the relevant access internalist norms[5] (e.g., they are available for justified self-ascription).

Is there anything that can be said to independently justify the normativist view? By way of analogy, consider the view of philosophers like Davidson (1973), McDowell (1985), and Dennett (1971), who think there is a normative aspect to the ascription of propositional attitude states. The idea is that to treat a subject as having intentional states like beliefs and desires is to treat them as rational agent with states governed by certain epistemic norms; for this reason, intentional ascription is subject to a "principle of charity," according to which subjects of belief and desire are, ceteris paribus, rational. One can understand this as the view that belief and desire states are at least partly *defined* in terms of their rational relations to each other, and so belief/desire ascriptions are at least partly normative statements (although there are other interpretations of the view[6]). One can imagine a theorist who thinks that a similar point is correct for conscious experience—that we can only make sense of it as a content-bearing state by conceiving of it as standing in certain rational relations to other mental states, rational relations that partly define what it is to have the conscious state.

In response to this, there seems to be an important disanalogy between conscious experiences and propositional attitudes. Our understanding of what consciousness is clearly does *not* depend on a holistic understanding of how it fits into a whole cognitive system, including how it is rationally related to other kinds of mental states. In particular, we know what conscious states *are* by simply *introspecting* them, a process that doesn't require any background theoretical understanding of other aspects of the mind and their rational relations to consciousness. This seems an obvious contrast with our understanding of what beliefs are, which may require a grasp of rational belief-desire psychology (even if we can introspect beliefs). If it is true that we do not conceptualize conscious states in terms of their rational relations, it would be surprising if they are in fact individuated this way; certainly, the burden of proof is on the normativist to show this.

As well as lacking clear independent support, there are direct arguments against normativism about consciousness. In particular, there are problems that arise when we look at how it plays out on different views of the metaphysics of normative facts. I will argue that however we develop the view, it is either incompatible with reductive materialism or otherwise problematic.

Normativists who are realists about norms in general, either think that there are irreducible normative facts or that normative facts can be reduced to non-normative facts somehow (e.g., they might say that for a norm to hold is for people to *accept* that it holds).[7] Normativists who believe that there are irreducible normative facts will construe facts about consciousness as holding partly in virtue of these irreducible normative facts. But this is incompatible with reductive materialism: I am thinking of reductive materialism as implying that facts about consciousness hold wholly in virtue of facts about the functional and material properties of conscious systems, and therefore not in virtue of irreducible normative facts.[8,9]

If this is right, then for realist normativism to be consistent with reductive materialism, the normativist will have to be a reductionist about normative facts. However, normative reductionism is independently very implausible: for example, if we say that normative facts are a special kind of natural fact, such as the fact that certain people *accept* certain norms—it is hard to see how they are genuinely normative, or have normative force.[10] Furthermore, whatever natural fact about us constitutes consciousness-requiring norms obtaining, it seem likely that a similar natural fact will obtain for pseudo-conscious beings; for example, even if *we* accept that consciousness-requiring norms obtain, it will also be true that *they* accept that pseudo-consciousness-requiring norms obtain. The realist reductionist normativist will therefore find it hard to maintain that there is any deep asymmetry between us and pseudo-conscious beings.

What about the combination of normativism with *anti*-realism about norms? Normative anti-realists generally either hold an error theory about normative claims (holding the view that all normative claims are false) or are expressivists (holding the view that normative claims are not really genuinely fact stating).[11] Thus the error-theoretic normativist will say that statements about consciousness are always false, because they involve normative commitments that nothing ever satisfies (because there are no normative facts), whereas expressivist normativists will say that statements about consciousness are not properly fact stating, but rather serve to express non-cognitive attitudes like desires. Are these views at all plausible? A consciousness error theory seems obviously false, and the expressivist view, although interesting and worthy of more discussion, is quite counterintuitive. It is plausible that when we talk about conscious experience we are intending to represent reality as being a certain way, and not merely emote or perform some other kind of non-descriptive act.[12] In this context however, a more fundamental objection to both anti-realist views is simply that by denying consciousness any kind of robust existence, they are also denying it any kind of robust significance.

To sum up, we can think of normativism as the view that conscious states are by definition those that play a certain role justifying beliefs; this will likely either be a foundational role justifying non-inferential beliefs or a role in providing the propositions about world to which the subject has the kind of access needed for them to provide reasons for belief. Despite being an obvious way to defend the strong epistemic significance of consciousness, we saw that it is hard to give the view independent motivation—for example, the considerations that support a normative view of propositional attitudes don't translate well to conscious states. We also saw that different views of the nature of normative facts lead to different version of normativism that each are problematic in one way or other. Let us therefore move to consider a different response to the grounding argument.

Second Response: Strong Epistemic Naturalism—Consciousness Is a Relatively Shallow Natural Property, but Nonetheless Unique in Its Epistemic Significance

The other kind of view that might allow one to defend the strong epistemic significance of consciousness by rejecting the grounding claim (premise 1) is what I'll call strong epistemic naturalism (SE naturalism). On this view, consciousness is *not* defined in normative terms—it is a completely natural phenomenon, such as a complex functional property—but nonetheless it has strong epistemic significance. Because the SE naturalist rejects the grounding claim, she denies that this epistemic significance is grounded in a deep natural divide between conscious and unconscious beings (consciousness is not an outstandingly deep natural property). Rather, the fact that the correct epistemic norms are consciousness requiring is either brute or grounded in something other than the nature of consciousness itself. The view therefore cannot explain the strong epistemic significance of consciousness in the same way that normativism can, but it has the advantage of being able to treat consciousness as a completely natural phenomenon.

I will assume here that a zombie can have propositional attitudes and other mental states (e.g., pseudo-conscious perceptual states) with contents at least analogous to the contents of our mental states (I say "at least analogous" because their beliefs about pseudo-consciousness will not have exactly the same content as our beliefs about consciousness). Siewert, following Searle (1989), rejects this assumption, although his case for it depends on a prior rejection of the epistemic significance of any zombie states. A full argument for my conditional conclusion would consider in detail the claim that consciousness is necessary for intentionality in general. Unfortunately, I do not have space to discuss this here: unsurprisingly, my view is that if there is no deep natural asymmetry between us and functional zombies (as I think is true on a materialist view), then they can at least have something extremely similar to our intentional states.

I will focus on a version of SE naturalism that involves the doxastic significance of consciousness, but the idea that it has intrinsic epistemic significance (e.g., that conscious states acquaint their subject with the environment or their own mind) or concept-grounding significance (conscious states enable subjects to form certain concepts, such as concepts of objects and properties that the experiences acquaint their subjects with) will be part of the discussion as well.

The version of SE naturalism that I'm interested in therefore involves the claim that there exists a set of norms governing the correct formation of belief, which together imply that conscious experience is *required* for certain kinds of beliefs to be justified. I'll call this the "consciousness-loving" view. As before, I will assume that the consciousness lover is either a phenomenal foundationalist or a phenomenal access internalist. I will assume that their zombie-loving opponent believes in the existence of similar norms but thinks that these norms are consciousness-neutral, so that a pseudo-conscious zombie could also follow them. For example, instead of thinking that only phenomenal states can play a foundational role, they might hold that a class of pseudo-phenomenal states can also do this.

How might the consciousness lover justify their normative view? There appear to be three possibilities: (1) To hold that consciousness-requiring norms have a ground in certain non-normative facts, such as the fact that conscious states provide "acquaintance" with themselves or with external events (the "external grounding" strategy); (2) to hold that consciousness-requiring norms are explained in terms of other epistemic norms, norms that do not themselves mention consciousness (the "normative grounding" strategy); or (3) to hold that certain consciousness-requiring norms obtain, but that this fact can't be further explained—it is one of the consciousness lover's basic commitments. I'll call this the "no grounding strategy."

Let me consider these three defensive strategies in turn, starting with the external grounding strategy. I can think of the three ways that consciousness-requiring norms might be thought to be externally grounded in non-normative facts: (1a) they are grounded in the intrinsic epistemic significance of consciousness, (1b) they are grounded in concept-grounding significance of consciousness, or (1c) they are grounded in what I will call the "introspective significance" of consciousness (a view defended by Smithies [2012a, 2012b]).

Again, to say that conscious states are "intrinsically epistemically significant" is to say that they are an epistemic good in themselves, independently of their role in conferring justification on beliefs. A likely elaboration of this idea would be that conscious states provide conscious *acquaintance* with objects and events in the environment or with the subject's own mind, where acquaintance is an epistemic relation that can be enjoyed even by creatures incapable of belief. It might be thought that it is because zombies cannot be acquainted with the world or their own minds in the way that we can, that they cannot have knowledge or justified belief about these things in the way that we can. When it comes to grounding the norms governing belief, it might be said that it is a basic goal of belief formation to form beliefs based on evidence that is phenomenally accessible, and this basic norm is grounded in the intrinsic epistemic significance of conscious acquaintance. A comparison with moral norms might be illuminating. Why should we try to prevent pain? On one view, this is because pain is intrinsically bad, and this intrinsic badness explains why a pain-prevention norm obtains. Similarly, consciousness might have intrinsic epistemic goodness in a way that explains why certain consciounsness-requiring epistemic norms obtain.

The zombie lover should counter-respond as follows: it is hard to see what this alleged "intrinsic" epistemic significance of conscious acquaintance could amount to. We are assuming that if reductive materialism is true, then conscious acquaintance does not have special *natural* significance; considered as an objective natural phenomenon, there is nothing special about conscious acquaintance over a pseudo-conscious functional analogue of acquaintance that could be enjoyed by a zombie. But the only other kind of significance we have a fairly clear understanding of is *normative* significance; conscious acquaintance might be significant because it is involved in the norms governing belief formation or epistemic enquiry more generally. But then this is not a separate, more "intrinsic," kind of significance and therefore cannot plausible *ground* or *explain* the correctness of the relevant norms. Compare with the moral case again: one might object to the story told in the last paragraph by pointing out that the "badness" of pain can only be understood in terms of the fact that we ought to prevent pain; it therefore cannot ground this normative fact.

A second external-grounding approach is try to ground consciousness-requiring norms by appealing to the role of consciousness in the possession of certain concepts. Here I have in mind an approach like the one elaborated by Peacocke (1992, 2004), which attempts to explain the correctness of certain epistemic norms in terms of the conditions for possessing concepts, in this case "observational," "perceptual," or "recognitional" concepts, concepts whose mastery requires applying them to conscious experience in various ways. For example, it might be said that possessing the concept "red" requires being disposed to use this concept in judgments based on conscious experiences of red surfaces. According to this view, the correctness of certain consciousness-requiring norms for judgments involving "red" flows from the fact that these are the norms one must follow in order to *have* the concept in the first place.

Can this approach help the consciousness lover? One might think that there is nothing to stop a zombie from possessing observational concepts analogous to ours, but whose possession involves responding to pseudo-conscious states rather than conscious states, and thus following norms that are not consciousness requiring. Prima facie then, the concept-possession approach actually supports rather than hinders the zombie lover's view. However, it might be replied that not all concepts are on a par—perhaps some concepts have possession conditions that make them in some way defective (e.g., Peacocke [1992] argues that this is the case with Prior's [1967] concept "tonk"). Perhaps zombie observational concepts are *epistemically defective* because the zombie does not know what he is thinking about in the intimate way that conscious experience allows us to.

The problem with this is that we will probably need to appeal to an independent intuition about the epistemic role of consciousness to argue that only consciousness can ground non-defective observational concepts. This is another place where the intrinsic significance of consciousness might seem to play a role. For example, one might be attracted to the idea that conscious perception acquaints you with the environment, and the function of observational judgments is to exploit this acquaintance at the level of thought. On one elaboration (see, e.g., Campbell, 2002), this amounts to the acquaintance providing you with knowledge of the semantic values of your observational concepts, knowledge that is, intuitively, required for using concepts with genuine understanding of what they refer to. For example, when I think "this flower is beautiful," I might know which flower I'm thinking about because I am enjoying a conscious visual experience of the flower. A zombie cannot think about the world in a way that is grounded in conscious acquaintance and so might lack this special kind of knowledge of what their thoughts are referring to. In short, it might be that the doxastic significance of consciousness is explained by its concept-grounding significance, which is in turn explained by the intrinsic epistemic significance of conscious acquaintance.

This assumes again, however, that there is something intrinsically epistemically special about conscious acquaintance, as opposed to the pseudo-conscious acquaintance of a functional zombie—and the problem is that it is hard to understand what this means, if it is not a matter of natural or normative significance. This suggests that the concept-possession approach cannot on its own help the consciousness lover, although it does link doxastic significance with other forms of significance in an interesting way.

A third approach that is worth briefly mentioning is due to Smithies (2012a, 2012b). Smithies thinks that only introspectively accessible mental states can provide justification for our beliefs, a kind of access internalist view. Furthermore, he thinks that only phenomenally conscious states are introspectively accessible. Thus, he thinks the existence of consciousness-requiring norms can be explained in terms of an access internalist conception of justification (which he further elaborates in terms of the idea that a justified belief is one that would survive ideal critical reflection) and what we might call the "introspective significance" of phenomenal experience.

The problem with this approach is that our functional zombies do appear to have something like introspective access to their mental states, even though they lack consciousness. Smithies needs a reason why zombie introspection isn't as good as phenomenally grounded introspection. Giving such a reason will require, in effect, adopting one of the other strategies on the list since it involves explaining why the norms governing introspective belief formation are consciousness-requiring. In fact, his view seems to really be a kind of no-grounding view (a type 3 strategy): there are consciousness-requiring norms governing introspection that can't be further explained (he motivates them with blindsight-type examples but does not attempt to ground them). So his approach, although adding some flesh to a consciousness-loving picture, does not constitute a separate approach to the others I will consider.

Having looked at the external-grounding strategy, let's now briefly consider the normative-grounding strategy. Can consciousness-requiring norms be explained in terms of other, more basic norms? It is controversial what basic norms might govern belief formation, but plausible suggestions are external norms telling us to form true beliefs, or have beliefs formed by norms that reliably produce true beliefs, or more "internalist" norms, such as a norm telling us to have coherent beliefs. It doesn't matter for my purposes exactly what norms of this kind, if any, hold, because there is a general problem with this strategy. The problem is that a functional zombie can have beliefs that exactly mirror our beliefs, standing in the same causal and inferential relations, and formed on the basis of equally reliable processes linking them with the world outside the head. So, apart from norms explicitly mentioning consciousness, it seems likely that they can satisfy *any* plausible general epistemic norms, whether they are of a more internalist or externalist variety. Thus, it is implausible that such general norms imply more specific consciousness-requiring norms. So if there *are* consciousness-requiring norms, it is more plausible to say that they are among the most basic norms than to suppose that they are grounded in other norms.

If the consciousness lover concedes that there is no deeper normative ground for consciousness-requiring norms, and also that there is no plausible external ground for them, then it looks like the only option left is a no-grounding view: consciousness-requiring norms cannot be further explained. If the consciousness lover adopts this position, can anything further be said to arbitrate in a debate between them and a zombie lover? On this option, their disagreement is analogous to a disagreement about what the basic moral norms are. Such basic normative disagreements are notoriously hard to resolve; for example, it seems plausible that they can even survive ideal rational reflection by the disputing parties. Might the disagreement about the rational role of consciousness be like this?

In fact it is not obvious that *all* disagreements about basic epistemic norms are in principle unresolvable in this way. For example, some basic epistemic norms might be knowable a priori. Or more weakly, it might be that there are constraints on what the correct epistemic norms are that are knowable a priori, which at least rule out some proposed norms. Maybe the zombie lover's normative view can be seen to be wrong after sufficient a priori reflection.

Unfortunately, there do not appear to be plausible a priori constraints to settle the dispute. What a priori constraints on epistemic norms are there? In my view, the only plausible candidates have to do with the relationship between the laws of logic (or more broadly logic and probability theory) and the rules of correct reasoning. As Harman (1986) famously emphasized, there is no really straightforward relationship between logical truths and rational norms. Nonetheless, it is plausible to think that rationality is constrained by logic. If the truths of logic are knowable a priori (and it is far from obvious that they are), then perhaps we can know a priori some constraints on the laws of rational reasoning. Even if this is true, however, these logically constrained rational norms are not the ones that are relevant to our debate. The laws of logic constrain the rules governing the rational moves *between* beliefs—what we might call "process norms." But a zombie can perfectly well reason in a rational way in this sense. We might put this by saying that the zombie is "process rational." Our dispute is over what might be called "input norms"—norms governing transitions from outside the space of beliefs (e.g., from conscious experiences to beliefs). And these norms are apparently much more remotely related to the kinds of epistemic constraints that can perhaps be known a priori, such as those given by logical rules, or mathematical facts about probability. Or at least, whether inputs into the system have to be conscious or merely pseudo-conscious appears not to be something to be settled based on such a priori considerations. If this is right, then it is implausible that there is any a priori resolution available in the dispute between consciousness lovers and zombie lovers.

Does this mean that the dispute between a no-grounding consciousness lover and the zombie lover is unresolvable? There are still some considerations remaining that we haven't looked at. In particular, even if consciousness-requiring norms can't be further explained, a case might be made that they are (or are not) *in fact* the correct norms.

On the side of positive arguments for such norms, we might consider cases designed to elicit the intuition that rationality really does require consciousness. First, there is the simple fact that *for us* it seems to be true that if we can't consciously perceive that some state of affairs obtains, then we should refrain from making a non-inferential perceptual judgment about it. For example, if I am trying to find out through perception whether there is a chair in front of me, then, intuitively, unless I have a conscious experience of a chair, any judgment I make is no more justified than a random guess. This intuition seems to hold up, even under the assumption that such "blind guesses" would in fact be reliably correct. This is the moral of blindsight cases: intuitively, if a blindsighted subject has no conscious experience corresponding to a region of space, but can nonetheless make reliable guesses about what is in that region, these guesses are not justified beliefs, unless the subject has some independent reason for thinking that the guesses are reliable. Further, as Smithies emphasizes, these intuitions hold up even if we suppose that we are dealing with a "superblindsighted" subject, for whom these judgments come naturally and do not seem like guesswork. According to Smithies, the best explanation of why this is the correct verdict about these cases is that consciousness is strictly necessary for rational judgment.

I personally do not find this conclusion as plausible when I consider a hypothetical functional zombie rather than an individual with localized super-blindsight. It is obviously possible to make sense of a functional zombie as a responsible epistemic agent, including in assessing the transitions they make from pseudo-conscious states to beliefs. This suggests that there might be an alternative explanation for why blindsighted guesswork isn't rational. One possibility is that given that we are conscious, consciousness plays a special epistemic role *for us*, so that only conscious states can ground rational belief *for us*. Nonetheless, it could be that for other creatures another kind of internal state—such as a variety of pseudo-consciousness—could play exactly the same role. We can even imagine an alien version of blindsight, in which a region of a pseudo-conscious alien's visual field, although eliciting reliable guesses, is not pseudo-conscious in the right way to allow them to be justified. An alien theorist might explain this by claiming that for aliens, only pseudo-conscious states of a particular kind can serve as reasons for belief. Thus, there might be an exact symmetry between the norms that the aliens follow and those that we follow, norms that in each case explain why blindsighted guesses, or their alien analogues, are not rational. Consciousness being locally, but not globally, significant in this way, is perfectly consistent with our intuitions about blindsight cases.

Can the zombie lover say anything to motivate this kind of picture over the consciousness lover's vision of consciousness having global epistemic significance? It is at this point that I think reductive materialism, which has not played a role so far in the discussion in this section, might give us a little traction. Suppose we accept the view that if reductionism is true, then consciousness does not mark a deep natural divide between us and the pseudo-conscious aliens. The difference between them and us is merely in how our high-level cognitive architecture is functionally and physically realized, a difference that in no way marks us out as special from the perspective of objective description of the natural facts; a Martian scientist would not find us remarkable relative to our alien counterparts. If there is nonetheless a massive normative difference between us, this is surprising for two reasons.

First, as emphasized by the grounding argument, we intuitively expect a massive normative difference between cases to be reflected in a significant natural difference. That's why if there is no big natural divide between cases of pain and cases of pseudo-pain, this tends to undermine our confidence that pseudo-pain isn't as bad as real pain. Think again about the spectrum of cases linking us with a pseudo-conscious zombie that exists if materialism is true—the trivial natural difference between one case and the next seems insufficient to ground a big normative difference, whether of a practical or epistemic kind. The grounding intuition remains powerful; given that a strong case has *not* been made *in favor* of strong epistemic naturalism, it could be argued that if reductive materialism is true, this puts a burden of proof on the consciousness-loving side.

This is supported by a second observation: if the difference between us and the pseudo-conscious aliens is merely in how our mental states are realized, it is hard to see how this is the right *kind* of difference to ground a deep epistemic divide. Intuitively, rationality or epistemic status are objective notions whose application to a mental state shouldn't depend on such idiosyncratic details, but rather on more relevant features of the context, such as whether the mental state's content stands in the right logical relations to other represented contents. For example, it would be absurd to say that the rationality of a subject's beliefs depends on the color of her hair, because this is an arbitrary characteristic of the subject that has no intelligible relationship to an objective ideal of rationality. Perhaps such a principle of non-arbitrariness could rule against consciousness-requiring norms, if the difference between consciousness and pseudo-consciousness is merely an idiosyncratic difference in the realization of high-level functional structure.

Bearing this in mind, we might describe the state of play as follows: there appear to be no uncontroversial deeper norms that can be appealed to in order to explain why consciousness-requiring norms might obtain, and attempts to externally ground these norms in the nature of observational concepts or in the intrinsic significance of consciousness do not seem to work. This suggests that such norms will have to be considered brute and inexplicable, but such inexplicable norms seem implausible if consciousness has no deep natural significance: then the difference between conscious and pseudo-conscious beings is merely an arbitrary difference in the way that their high-level architecture is physically realized. The dependence of rationality on such facts offends against the grounding intuition and is puzzling because these realizer facts have nothing to do with the kinds of facts that are paradigmatically associated with rationality, such as facts about the relations between the representational contents of different mental states. I suggest that this puts the burden of proof on those who insist that consciousness *is* necessary for rationality.

Conclusion

Conscious states appear to have very special epistemic properties. According to the grounding argument, they are not uniquely special in this way: if materialism is true, there is no deep natural divide between conscious beings and non-conscious beings, and this means that there is no deep epistemic divide either: an unconscious being could have quasi-conscious states that play much the same epistemic role as ours. We considered a few different ways that a defender of the strong epistemic significance of consciousness could respond to this, focusing on responses that accept reductive materialism, and as a result accept that consciousness lacks strong natural significance. We found these views lacking. It appears that if reductive materialism is true, conscious beings do not occupy as special place in the realm of possibilities as we might have a thought; consciousness is but one among many interesting and unusual ways of configuring physical material.[13]

Notes

1. Although the meaning and theoretical utility of "natural" is typically given by a number of different theoretical roles, not just its role in grounding objective resemblance (see Sider, 2011).
2. See Block (1978) for the related distinction between folk functionalism and empirical functionalism.
3. A qualification: if a Russellian Monist version of reductionism is true (see Chalmers, 2003; Stoljar, 2006), then there may be a sense in which knowing the real definition of consciousness in terms of physical/functional concepts won't amount to full knowledge of which property it is. A full argument for deflationism would need to consider this case.
4. Notoriously, this is a view rejected by certain theorists, like Davidson (1986), who thought that "only a belief can justify a belief." We will not consider this view here.
5. This latter view could be regarded as a kind of normative version of a dispositional higher-order thought view (e.g., Carruthers, 2003): what makes a state conscious is that it is immediately available for justified self-ascription.
6. On a weaker interpretation, the role of norms is not in individuating beliefs and desires, but only in making sense of the epistemology of belief ascription: we need to use the principle

of charity to decide between competing attitude ascriptions that are consistent with the subject's overt behavior (see Kriegel, 2011, chaps. 1 and 4).

7. See Boyd (1988) for a classic defense of normative reductionism in the case of moral norms.

8. Note that the point is not that realism about norms is incompatible with reductive materialism, as I am understanding it here. The grounding of consciousness facts in functional/material facts is compatible with primitive normative facts existing—it will just have to be that the normative facts are not part of the ground of the consciousness facts.

9. Even nonreductivists about consciousness might want to reject nonreductionist realist normativism for similar reasons. For example, most property dualists regard phenomenal properties as natural properties, at least in the sense that they might be subject to natural laws in much the way fundamental physical properties are. Presumably, this is incompatible with them being individuated in irreducibly normative terms. Related to this, the idea that there is a scientific project of figuring out what consciousness is in natural terms arguably depends on the assumption that it is a wholly natural phenomenon. If it isn't, then such a project is, arguably, misconceived in much the way that a scientific investigation into the nature of objective moral goodness would be.

10. See Parfit (2011), part 6, for a helpful discussion of the difficulties with normative reductionism in the case of practical normativity.

11. For classic statements of the error theory and expressivism, respectively, see Mackie (1977) and Hare (1952) (both focus on practical, rather than epistemic norms). Field (2009) argues for a version of expressivism about epistemic norms.

12. Despite this objection, psychological expressivism has been endorsed in various forms by a number of authors, most notably by Wittgenstein in his remarks on pain ascription (Wittgenstein, 1953). A notable recent attempt to develop the view is Hellie (manuscript).

13. Thanks to Wes Holliday, Uriah Kriegel, and Declan Smithies for helpful feedback and discussion of earlier drafts.

References

Armstrong, D. (1978). *Universals and Scientific Realism: A Theory of Universals.* Vol. 2. Cambridge: Cambridge University Press.

Block, N. (1978). Troubles with functionalism. *Minnesota Studies in the Philosophy of Science* 9: 261–325.

Block, N. (2002). The harder problem of consciousness. *Journal of Philosophy* 99 (8): 391–425.

Boyd, R. (1988). How to be a moral realist. In G. Sayre-McCord (ed.), *Moral Realism.* Ithaca, NY: Cornell University Press. pp. 181–228

Campbell, J. (2002). *Reference and Consciousness.* Oxford: Oxford University Press.

Carruthers, P. (2003). *Phenomenal consciousness: A naturalistic theory.* Cambridge: Cambridge University Press.

Chalmers, David J. (2003). Consciousness and its place in nature. In Stephen P. Stich & Ted A. Warfield (eds.), *Blackwell Guide to the Philosophy of Mind*, pp.102–143. Malden, MA: Blackwell.

Dainton, B. (2008). *The Phenomenal Self.* New York: Oxford University Press.

Davidson, D. (1973). Radical interpretation. *Dialectica* 27 (1): 314–328.

Davidson, D. (1986). A coherence theory of truth and knowledge. In Ernest LePore (ed.), *Truth and Interpretation: Perspectives on the Philosophy of Donald Davidson.* Oxford: Basil Blackwell.

Dennett, D. (1971). Intentional systems. *Journal of Philosophy* 68: 87–106.

Field, H. (2009). Epistemology without metaphysics. *Philosophical Studies* 143 (2): 249–290.

Goodman, N. (1983). *Fact, Fiction, and Forecast.* Cambridge, MA: Harvard University Press.

Hare, R. M. (1952). *The Language of Morals.* Oxford: Clarendon.

Harman, G. (1986). *Change in View: Principles of Reasoning.* Cambridge, MA: MIT Press.

Hellie, B. (unpublished manuscript). "Out of this World."

Kriegel, U. (2011). *The Sources of Intentionality.* New York: Oxford University Press.

Lee, G. (Forthcoming). Alien subjectivity and the importance of consciousness. In A. Pautz & D. Stoljar (eds.), *Themes from Block*. Cambridge, MA: MIT Press.

Lewis, D. (1983). New work for a theory of universals. *Australasian Journal of Philosophy* 61: 343–377.

Mackie, J. L. (1977). *Ethics: Inventing Right and Wrong*. Harmondsworth; NY: Penguin.

McDowell, J. (1985). Functionalism and anomalous monism. In Brian P. McLaughlin & Ernest LePore (eds.), *Action and Events*. Oxford: Blackwell.

McLaughlin, B. P. (2003). A naturalist-phenomenal realist response to Block's harder problem. *Philosophical Issues* 13: 163–204.

Parfit, D. (2011). *On What Matters*. Vol 2. Oxford: Oxford University Press.

Peacocke, C. (1992). *A Study of Concepts*. Cambridge, MA: MIT Press.

Peacocke, C. (2004). *The Realm of Reason*. New York: Oxford University Press.

Prior, A. (1967). The runabout inference ticket. In Peter Strawson (ed.), *Philosophical Logic*. London: Oxford University Press.

Searle, J. (1989). Consciousness, unconsciousness, and intentionality. *Philosophical Topics* 17 (1): 193–209.

Sider, T. (2011). *Writing the Book of the World*. Oxford: New York : Oxford University Press.

Smithies, D. (2012a). The mental lives of zombies. *Philosophical Perspectives* 26: 343–372.

Smithies, D. (2012b). A simple theory of introspection. In D. Smithies & D. Stoljar (eds.), *Introspection and Consciousness*, 259–293. New York: Oxford University Press. p. 259.

Stoljar, D. (2006). *Ignorance and Imagination: The Epistemic Origin of the Problem of Consciousness*. Oxford: Oxford University Press.

Taylor, B. (1993). On natural properties in metaphysics. *Mind* 102: 81–100.

Wittgenstein, L. (1953). *Philosophical Investigations*. New York: Macmillan.

Suggestions for Further Reading

Horgan, Terry, and John Tienson. 2002. "The Intentionality of Phenomenology and the Phenom-
enology of Intentionality." In *Philosophy of Mind: Classical and Contemporary Readings*, ed.
D. J. Chalmers, 520-533. Oxford: Oxford University Press.
*This paper argues against the separation of the mind into a sensory, phenomenal domain and a
cognitive, intentional domain—and in favor of an "inseparatist" picture in which the sensory
is inherently intentional and the cognitive is inherently phenomenal.*
Ryle, Gilbert. 1949. *The Concept of Mind*. London: Routledge, 2009.
*This influential book systemically argues that our very grasp of the mental domain is founded on our
grasp of dispositions to behave in certain ways, not on anything like direct acquaintance with
inner consciousness.*
Siewert, Charles. 1998. *The Significance of Consciousness*. Princeton, NJ: Princeton University
Press.
*This book presents a thoroughly first-personal approach to consciousness and its centrality to mental
life, making influential arguments that such phenomena as intentionality, cognition, and self-
knowledge are shot through with phenomenality.*
Strawson, Galen. 1994. *Mental Reality*. Cambridge, MA: MIT Press.
*This book argues that the mental domain is essentially the domain of conscious experience, and any
connection to behavioral dispositions is limited, indirect, and accidental.*

Supplemental Guide to Further Controversies

The previous sections in this volume present five of the most central controversies in the philosophy of mind. Listed below are three additional important controversies for the curious reader, with lists to the essential readings for each controversy.

Perception and Perceptual Representation

Ayer, A. J. 1956. The Problem of Knowledge. London: Macmillan.
Byrne, Alex. 2001. "Intentionalism Defended." Philosophical Review 110: 199–240.
McDowell, John. 1994. "The Content of Perceptual Experience." Philosophical Quarterly 44: 190–205.
Siegel, Susanna. 2010. The Contents of Visual Experience. New York: Oxford University Press.

Cognitive Phenomenology

Carruthers, Peter, and Bénédicte Veillet. 2011. "The Case against Cognitive Phenomenology." In Cognitive Phenomenology, ed. T. Bayne and M. Montague, 35-56. Oxford: Oxford University Press.
Chudnoff, Elijah. 2011. "What Intuitions Are Like." Philosophy and Phenomenological Research 82: 625–654.
Moore, G. E. 1953. "Propositions." In Some Main Problems of Philosophy. London: Routledge.
Pitt, David. 2004. "The Phenomenology of Cognition—or What Is It Like to Believe That P." Philosophy and Phenomenological Research 69: 1–36.

Mental Causation

Block, Ned. 1990. "Can the Mind Change the World?" In Meaning and Method: Essays in Honor of Hilary Putnam, ed. G. Boolos. Cambridge: Cambridge University Press.
Kim, Jaegwon. 1989. "Mechanism, Purpose, and Explanatory Exclusion." Philosophical Perspectives 3: 77–108.
Stich, Steven. 1978. "Autonomous Psychology and the Belief-Desire Thesis." Monist 61: 573–591.
Yablo, Steven. 1992. "Mental Causation." Philosophical Review 101: 245–280.

Index